THE COEN BROTHERS

First published in Great Britain in 2024 by
Greenfinch
An imprint of Quercus Editions Ltd
Carmelite House
50 Victoria Embankment
London EC4Y 0DZ

An Hachette UK company

A CIP catalogue record for this book is available from the British Library

ISBN 978-1-52943-848-2
Ebook ISBN 978-1-52943-850-5

10 9 8 7 6 5 4 3 2 1

Cover design by Luke Bird
Interior design by Ginny Zeal

Printed and bound in Slovakia by TBB, a.s.

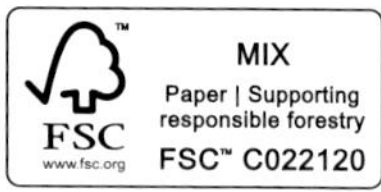

ICONIC DIRECTORS SERIES

THE COEN BROTHERS

THE COMPLETE UNOFFICIAL GUIDE

DAN JOLIN

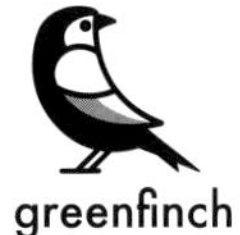

greenfinch

CONTENTS

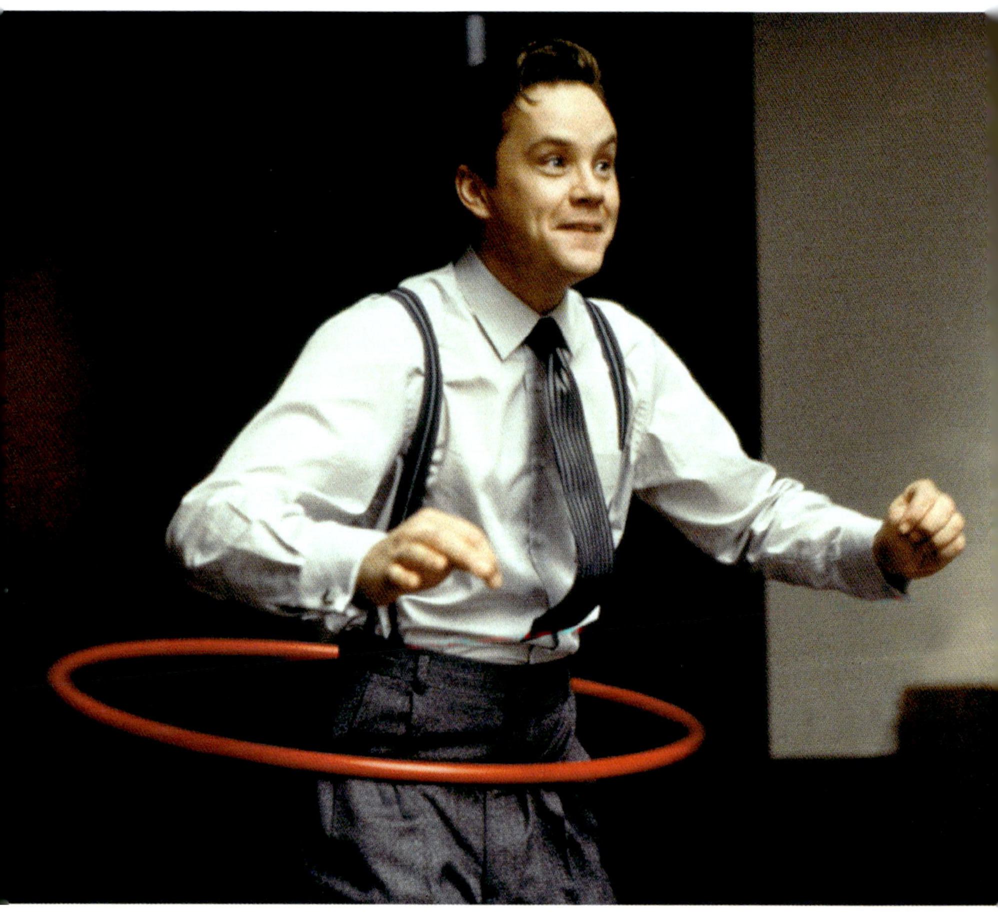

'All good art is entertainment.
Anyone who says different is a stuffed shirt
and juvenile at the art of living.'
RAYMOND CHANDLER

ABOVE: Tim Robbins as Norville Barnes in *The Hudsucker Proxy*,
presenting his 'extruded plastic dingus', also known as the Hula Hoop.

INTRODUCTION

It all began with a circle. A simple outline on a neatly folded piece of paper, kept in a shoe. A circle whose meaning was only evident to the goofball who drew it: 'Y'know. For kids!'

The Hudsucker Proxy is not the Coen brothers' first film. And it is by no means their best or most important. In fact, it's widely considered one of their weakest and was their biggest box-office flop. But, soon after I turned 20, it arrived on my TV screen via a VHS rental and introduced me to a whole new cinematic world.

If I'm honest, the film's references to Frank Capra, Howard Hawks and Preston Sturges did not specifically register. Thus far I'd grown up on a diet of Lucas, Spielberg, Cameron and Carpenter, with Tarantino as the hot new thing. Did I understand that Jennifer Jason Leigh was impersonating Rosalind Russell and Katharine Hepburn? No, I was too busy recognizing her from Paul Verhoeven's medieval trash-romp *Flesh+Blood*. My strongest point of connection with *Hudsucker*'s absurdly high-rise, retro-futuristic world was Terry Gilliam's *Brazil*. Did that matter? Not at all. I thought it was a hoot. Especially the gag about the circle.

It wasn't the movie's inspirations that drew me in, but the movie itself. It spoke for itself. With little hesitation, I dived into the Coens' output, honking at the tarmac-tearing comedy of *Raising Arizona*, puzzling over the oblique but compelling *Barton Fink*, falling head over heels for the sharply stylized gangsterism of *Miller's Crossing*. By the time their next film *Fargo* arrived, I was Arts Editor on my university newspaper, *Leeds Student*. So it's the first film of theirs I ever appraised, and praised, in print. Yes, I believed the whole 'true story' thing. And I don't mind one bit.

I got their offbeat humour. I became enraptured by their impeccable design and smooth, assured camera moves. I revelled in the joyous cadence of their precisely scripted dialogue. To me, their characters spoke like real people, while also sounding like nobody I knew or had ever met. I've never outgrown quoting them in everyday conversation: 'I was just speculatin' about a hypothesis'. . . 'I'm not gonna debate you'. . .'That's just, like, your opinion man.'

Without realizing it, I'd joined the cult. I began to identify members of the Coen company of actors, becoming excited whenever, say, Jon Polito popped up, or Steve Buscemi or Frances McDormand. And I grooved on the rhythm of their trademarks. In my mind, I'd play Coen Bingo: Small yappy dog? *Check.* Self-important man behind a desk? *Check.* Repeated line of dialogue? *Check.* Low-gliding tracking shot following a pair of feet down a corridor? *Check.* A circle? *Bingo!* These hallmarks gave the films an impressive sense of cohesion, despite all their differences in genre and setting.

Four decades after their debut, it remains impossible to be bored by the Coen brothers. Their 18 films together, from *Blood Simple* to *The Ballad of Buster Scruggs*, bear up beautifully under re-examination. Even their early Noughties missteps (*Intolerable Cruelty* and *The Ladykillers*) are quirkily watchable, if a little frustrating. Theirs is a body of work rarely matched for consistency of quality, cogency of vision, appealing idiosyncrasy, and quiet, confident independence. Where else could you find a brutal neo-Western rubbing shoulders with a domestic existential-crisis drama, a Homeric prison-break bluegrass musical, a Fifties Hollywood satire about religion and communism, and a no-frills, snow-covered tragicomedy?

My focus here is quite deliberately on the movies rather than the men. Joel and Ethan have never been great sharers when it comes to their private lives, and have been blessed by a lack of drama on that front. There simply isn't a huge amount to report. I met them together once, briefly, in 2001, at a Cannes Film Festival

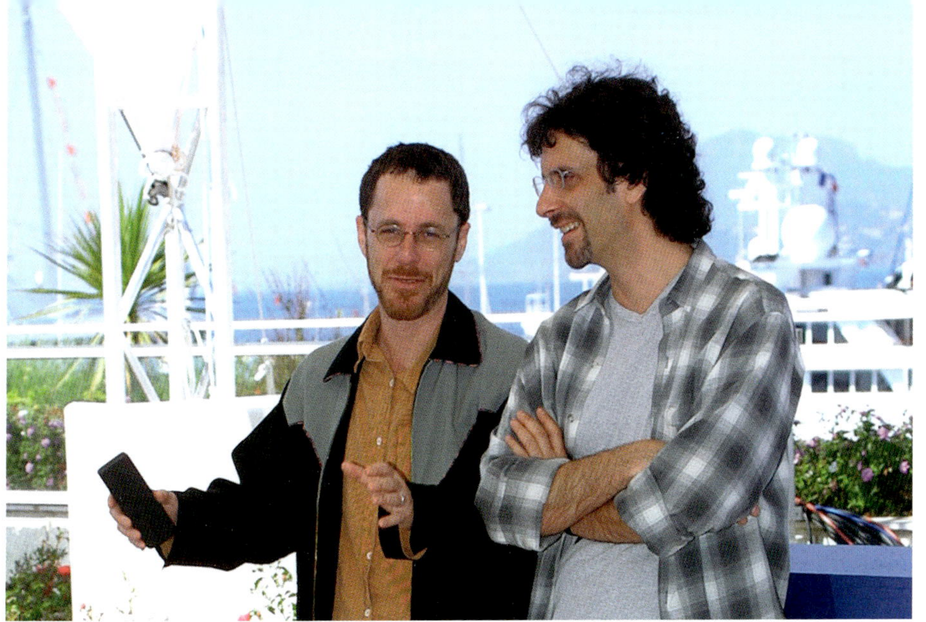

ABOVE: Ethan (left) and Joel Coen at the Cannes Film Festival, 2001, where they won Best Director for *The Man Who Wasn't There*, shared with David Lynch for *Mulholland Drive*.

press event for *The Man Who Wasn't There*, and I've met Ethan again more recently, with his *other* other half Tricia Cooke, to talk about *Drive-Away Dolls*. Despite warnings that they can be difficult interviewees, I found them to be friendly, if a little wary and weary, and happy to answer questions that weren't crushingly banal, or demanding that they explain the meanings of their films. They always seem happier talking about other peoples' movies that they grew up with, or have inspired them, or impressed them.

So it feels appropriate that the story of Joel and Ethan Coen should be the story of their films. Films that so many have now grown up with, and been inspired by, and impressed by. Films embraced by the Hollywood establishment, even though the resolutely New York-based Coens have never been a part of it. Films that enthral, and amuse, and perplex, and shock, and, above all else, beg to be rewatched.

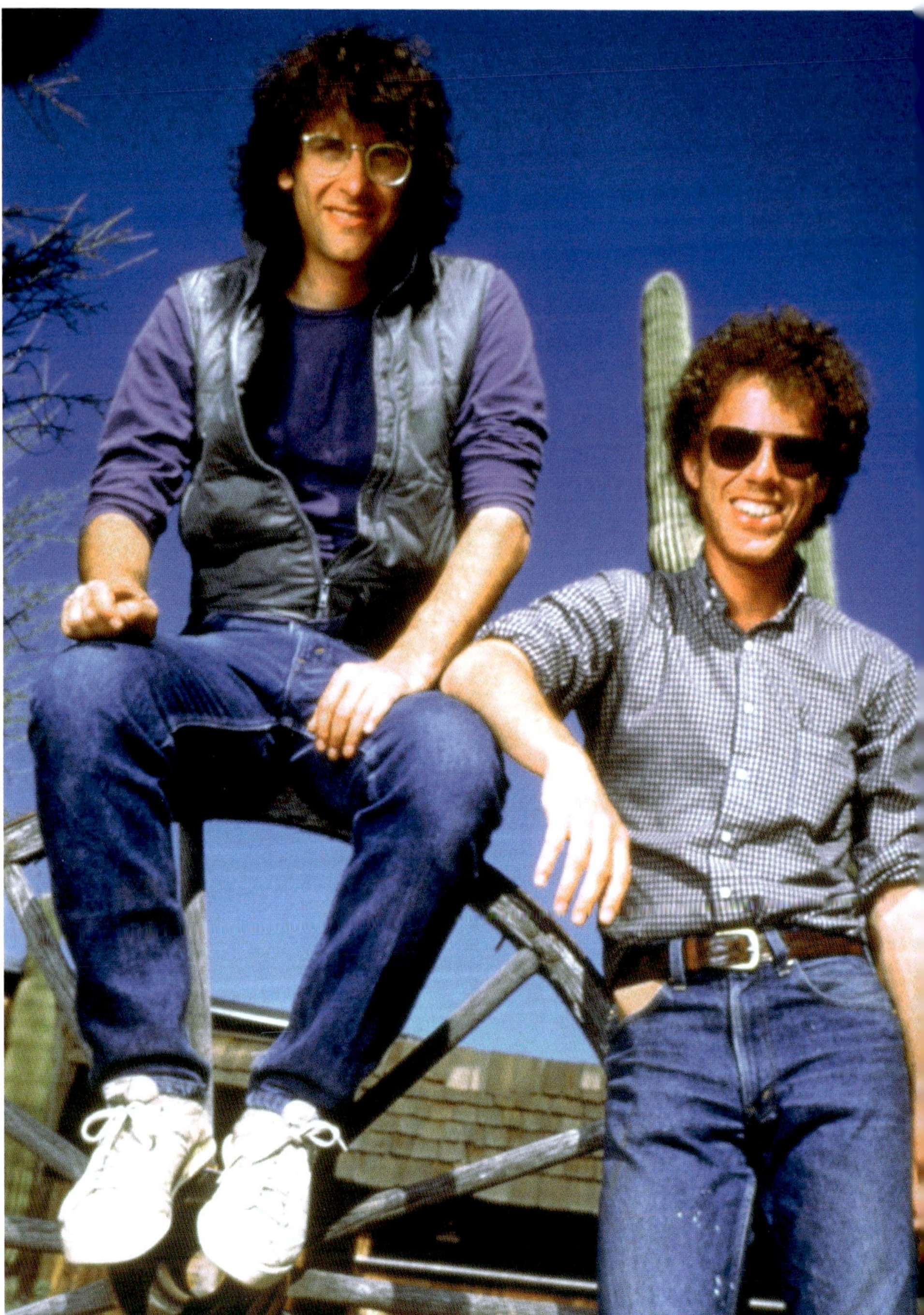

Raising Minnesota

THE EARLY YEARS

The mid-Sixties. In St Louis Park, a sleepy western suburb of Minneapolis, Minnesota, a pair of young brothers are shooting a remake of 1943's *Lassie Come Home*. Titled *Ed. . .A Dog*, this light-hearted, no-budget take on MGM's canine-themed weepy is just one of several homegrown productions the two have been working on – usually comedic re-makes of old movies they've just seen on TV. And they watch *a lot* of old movies on TV, from Tarzan adventures to Bob Hope comedies to Doris Day confections such as *Pillow Talk*.

The eldest, Joel, operates the Vivitar Super 8 camera he purchased with hard-earned lawn-mowing money. Younger brother Ethan has taken the role of the family matriarch, played in the original by Elsa Lanchester. To convince in the part, he's put on a tutu he borrowed from their sister Debbie. The short film climaxes with Ethan being thrown across a room by their pal Mark Zimmering, playing the dog-loving son, whose sudden show of force is his way of persuading his parents to let him keep the eponymous hound.

While their commitment cannot be questioned, neither sibling has much knowledge of even the most basic filmmaking techniques. They don't even know you can cut film after it's been shot, so they edit as they go, in-camera. They still have much to learn. But if they harbour dreams of a future in which they make it big, those dreams will come true. For in these home movies, we find the appropriately offbeat genesis of a creative collaboration that will endure for six decades (and counting). Although Ethan will move firmly behind the camera. And lose the tutu.

Born three years apart – Joel on 29 November 1954, Ethan on 21 September 1957 – to Edward, a professor of economics, and Rena, an art historian, the Coen brothers grew up in a relatively traditional Jewish household that supported creative expression and tolerated their high jinks. Edward Coen was a fan of Ealing comedies of the Forties and Fifties and passed on a love of the absurd to his two sons, while Rena indulged their escapades. The boys ran around making 'jungle movies' in the swamp behind their home, she recalled in 1992, also remembering the local newspaper they printed and sold, and the unfortunate chicken that Joel and a friend dissected on her ironing board. 'We thought, "Well, Joel might be interested in medicine."' Ethan, it should be said, was uninvolved in this poultry atrocity. He was off somewhere, 'in his own world'.

Such rambunctious behaviour was rooted, the Coens would say later, in an urge to compensate for their lives being so mundane; Ethan once described his homeland as 'like Siberia,

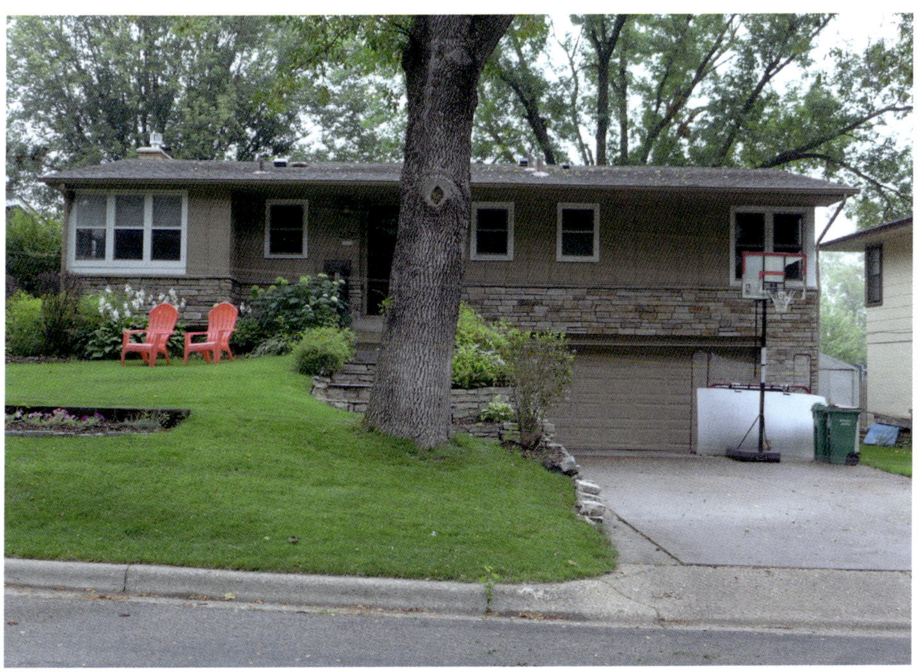

ABOVE: The childhood home of the Coen brothers in St Louis Park, Minnesota.

except you have family restaurants there'. At high school, they found some mental stimulus in Cinema Club, refining their tastes through the discovery of higher-brow fare, such as François Truffaut's *The 400 Blows*. But it's unsurprising that, once they were both done with college, they put St Louis Park in their rear-view as soon as possible.

In 1974, Joel, the more hands-on and technical of the pair, started studying film at the Tisch School of the Arts at New York University. Here, he spent four years 'sat at the back of the room with an insane grin on my face,' and submitted a 30-minute thesis film that was a world away from *Ed. . .A Dog* and its ilk. *Soundings* concerns a woman who has sex with her deaf boyfriend, while loudly fantasizing about making love to his best buddy, who is listening in the next room. On graduating, Joel decamped to the University of Texas film school in Austin. However, he only lasted a semester, before quitting and marrying a woman he'd fallen fast in love with, moving with her to New York. (They divorced soon after.)

Ethan, the more thoughtful one, headed to Princeton University to study philosophy, writing his senior thesis on Ludwig Wittgenstein. 'God knows why,' he later shrugged. 'I don't see too many connections with my work as a filmmaker.' At one point, he decided to take a term off and failed to inform the college that he intended to return. In an attempt to expedite his re-admittance, he faked a doctor's note explaining that he'd lost an arm in a hunting accident – in his brother-in-law's living room. It was cheeky, absurd and earned him a referral to a psychiatrist. Now *there's* a connection with his work as a filmmaker.

The brothers reunited in New York, where Ethan moved in with Joel and his wife at their apartment on 280 Riverside Drive, Upper Manhattan. To earn his keep, he found data-entry work via a temp agency. His first taste of the entertainment industry came with a modest gig contributing to scripts for popular TV cop show *Cagney & Lacey*. Meanwhile, Joel had gained employment as an assistant editor, mostly working on low-budget horror films under the mentorship of Edna Ruth Paul. These included 1981's *Fear No Evil*, in which a high-schooler turns out to be the Antichrist, and the psycho-slasher *Nightmare*, released the same year.

In early 1980, Joel worked on something much more significant. A young filmmaker named Sam Raimi arrived at Joel's cutting room with several canisters of footage in the trunk of his car. He'd

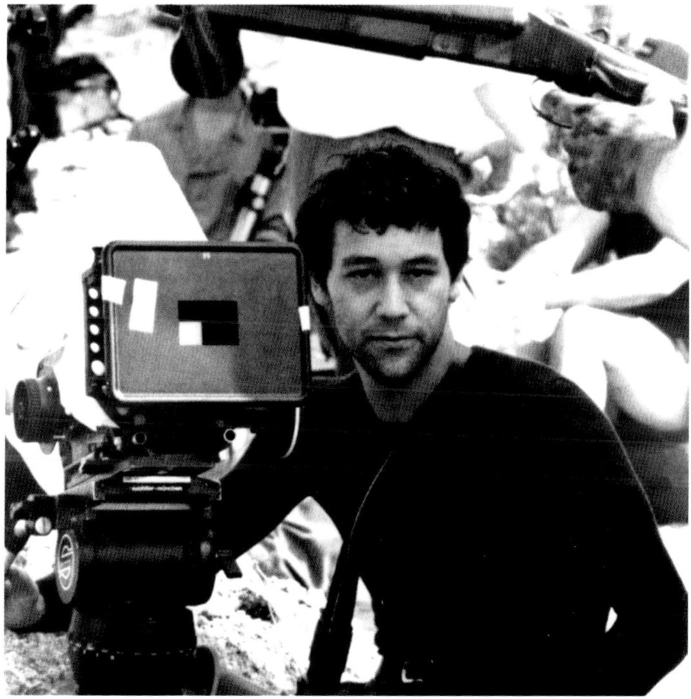

ABOVE: Director Sam Raimi, long-time friend and collaborator of the Coens.

driven there from his home city of Detroit, where he'd just finished shooting his debut feature, an insanely kinetic and outrageously gory horror film titled *The Evil Dead*, about a group of clean-cut kids who head to a remote cabin and accidentally unleash a demonic force. Joel was impressed with the movie, and would lift a few of its stylistic tricks for his own directorial debut, *Blood Simple*. 'A lot of the fun stuff, like the camera running upon the front lawn, is attributable to Raimi, who does a lot of shaky-cam stuff,' Joel admitted in 1985.

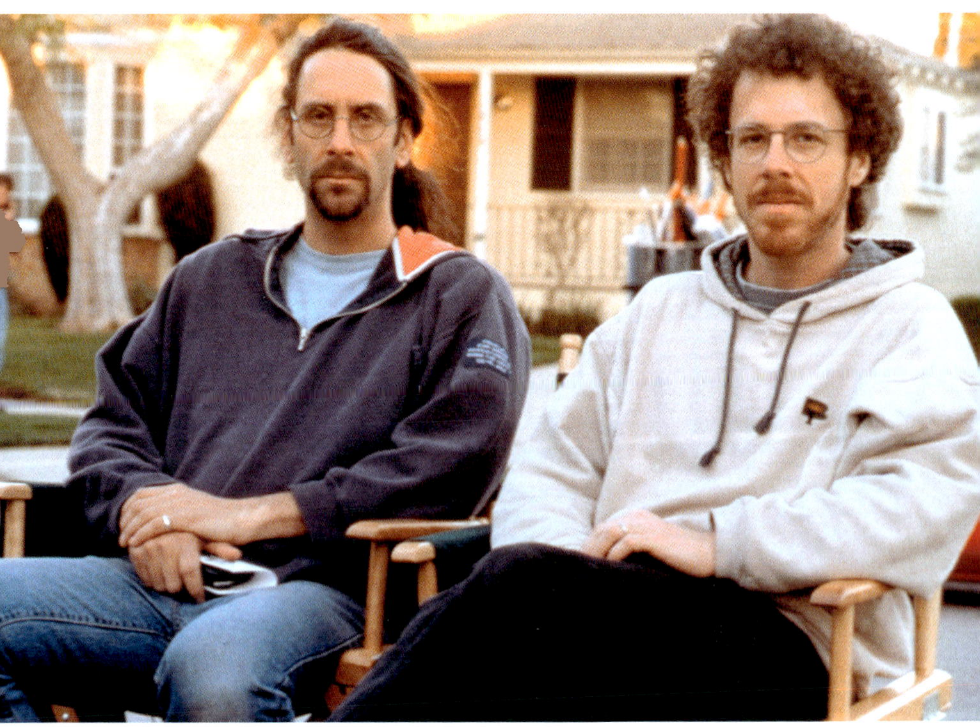

BELOW: Joel and Ethan relaxing (as much as they're able to) on the set of their debut film *Blood Simple*, in 1984.

He also clicked with Raimi personally, as did his brother. They shared childhood experiences of making daft home movies, and more importantly, a skewed sense of humour. It was a friendship that would result in two further collaborations: madcap crime-comedy *The XYZ Murders*, written by Joel, Ethan and Raimi and later directed by Raimi as 1985's *Crimewave*; and *The Hudsucker Proxy*, which was co-written with Raimi, and would take the best part of a decade to bring to the screen.

During this time, Joel also met cinematographer Barry Sonnenfeld at a party in Manhattan. 'We got talking about how great the cinematography was in Wim Wenders' *The American Friend*,' recalled Sonnenfeld. He later invited Joel to help out on a commercial film he was shooting. He was, according to Sonnenfeld, 'the world's worst PA. He got three parking tickets, came late, set fire to the smoke machine.'

He was a much better writer. Even at this early stage of their collaboration, he and Ethan gelled effortlessly, with little creative friction. Raimi compared their process to a game of badminton. 'Joel would mention a line of dialogue, and Ethan would finish the sentence, then Joel would say the punch line, and Ethan would type it up.' The first script the siblings ever wrote was a screwball comedy called *Coast to Coast*, in which a communist government clones Albert Einstein. 'It had 28 Einsteins in it,' Ethan boasted. They also, Joel once revealed, took a write-for-hire gig from a producer (whom they've never named), but that project never came to fruition.

It was probably just as well. To make their start as hired hacks might have set Joel and Ethan off on the wrong track, much like the misplaced Barton Fink in their 1991 film of the same name. As it was, they had their own plans. To make their own film, on their own terms.

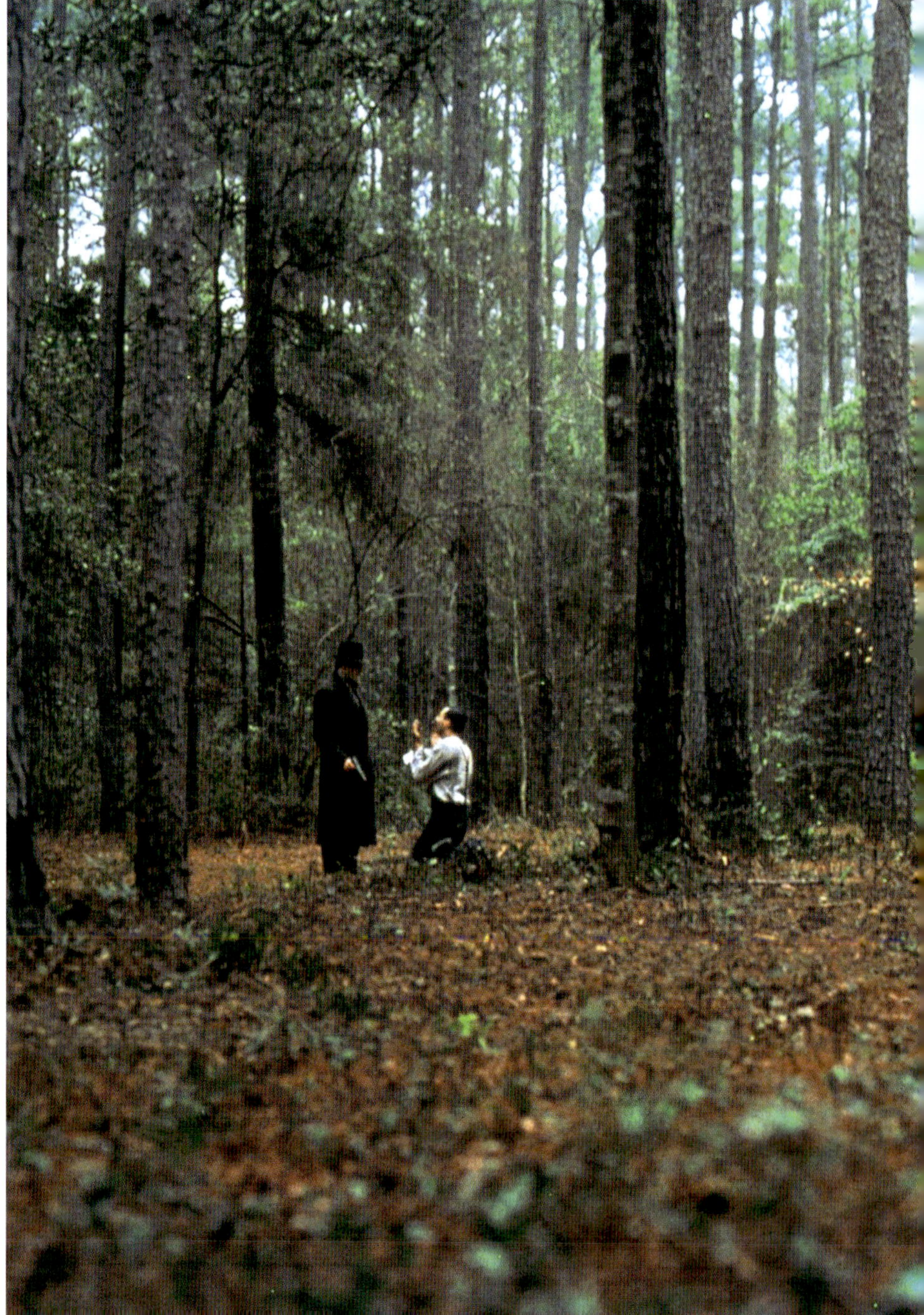

MAKING AN IMPRESSION

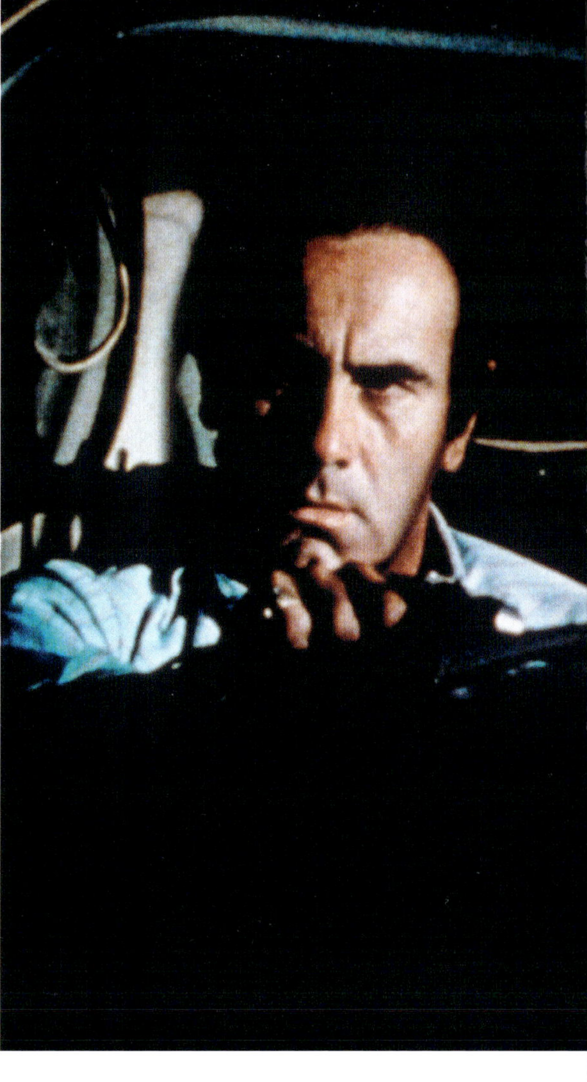

BLOOD
SIMPLE
1984

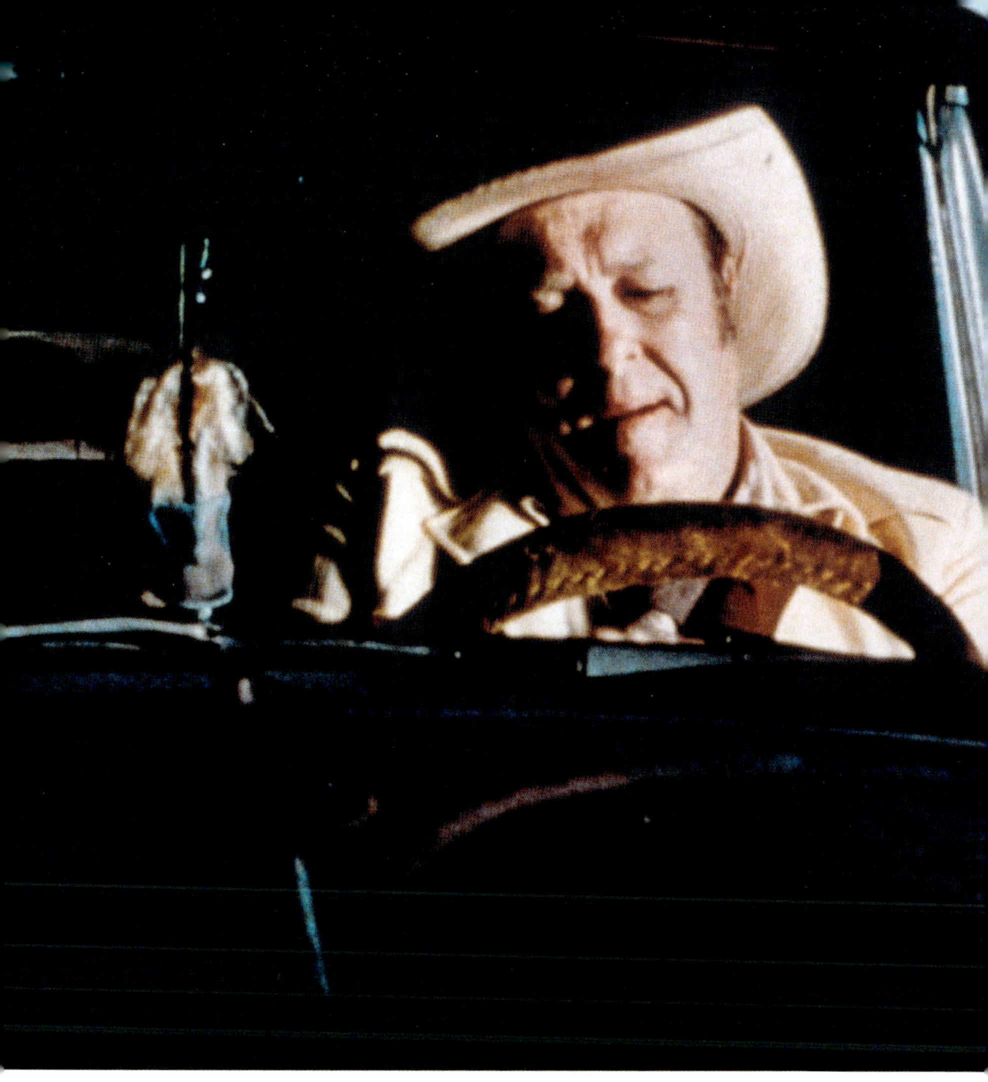

owboy boots crunch on broken glass. Gunshots blast through
the wall of a darkened room, creating shafts of smoky light. A
man in a fur coat drags a shovel along the asphalt of a night-
shrouded road, towards a bloody crawling figure played by *The Evil
Dead*'s Bruce Campbell. And a block of text reads, 'In Texas. . .You
get what you pay for.'

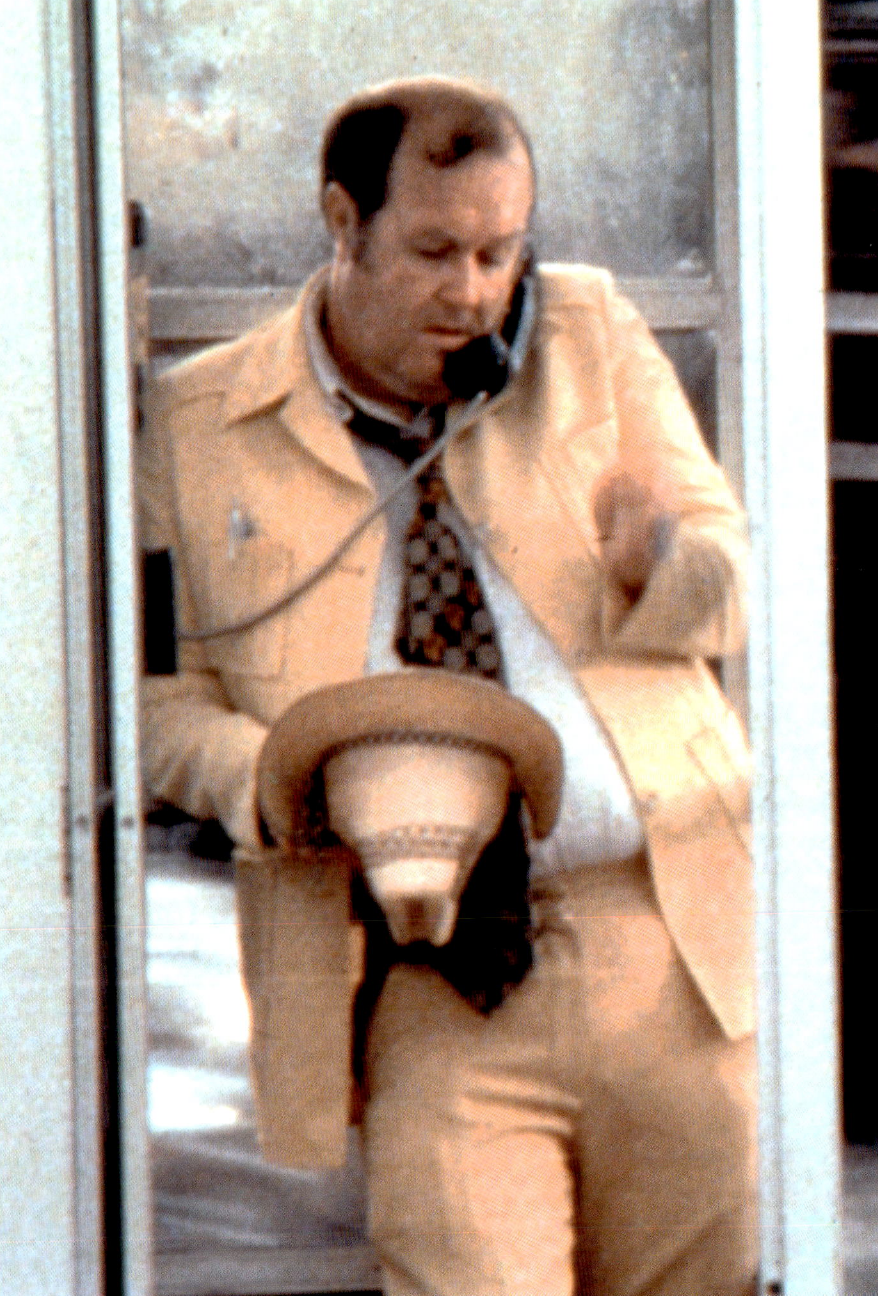

Over Presidents' Day weekend in 1982, just outside New York City, Joel, Ethan and Barry Sonnenfeld – with the help of Sam Raimi's actor buddy Bruce – cut together this two-minute trailer for what they hoped would be their debut movie, *Blood Simple*. They had to achieve maximum impact for minimal cost; hence, shooting it over the weekend to get three days with a rental camera for the price of one.

The brothers created the trailer to entice potential investors. 'We knew no one would buy [the script], particularly since we wanted to make it ourselves,' said Ethan. So they decided to raise the cash themselves, too. They needed just under a million dollars. With the trailer and a 16mm projector in the back of their car, they drove back to Minneapolis, where they could at least play the 'local boys trying to make something of themselves' card. And it worked. . .eventually. After the best part of a year lugging their taut teaser around homes, banks, junkyards, bowling alleys and urology clinics, they scraped the money together from around 60 investors. *Blood Simple* was greenlit – completely off the Hollywood radar.

The Coens' debut originated in their enthusiasm for the pulp noir novels of James M Cain, which they'd voraciously consumed a few years earlier, when all Cain's works – including *The Postman Always Rings Twice* and *Double Indemnity* – had been reissued in paperback. 'We liked his hard-boiled style, and we wanted to write a James M Cain story and put it in a modern context,' said Ethan.

Located in Joel's old stomping ground of Texas to offer 'something different' to noir's typically urban milieu, the film's tightly wound plot concerns humourless bar owner Marty (Dan Hedaya), who hires a private eye named Visser (M Emmet Walsh) to kill his wife Abby (Frances McDormand) and her lover, barman Ray (John Getz). One double-cross later, Visser murders Marty and frames Abby – only for Ray to discover the body and bury it, despite it turning out that Marty has survived the gunshot wound. While Ray and Abby start to wonder if they can trust each other, Visser realizes he's left evidence at the crime scene and sets his sights on Ray (who he kills) and Abby, who ultimately takes down Visser. At no point in the film does any character see the entire picture.

With the film set in the modern day to save the costs of period recreation, it was easy for critics to lump *Blood Simple* in with other neo-noirs in vogue at the time, not least David Mamet's adaptation of *The Postman Always Rings Twice* and Lawrence Kasdan's *Body Heat*, both released in 1981. However, the Coens insisted their take was different. '*Body Heat* was more of a mystery,' noted Ethan. 'We didn't want to write a whodunit. We wanted to do a movie where the audience knows what's going on every step of the way.' Though they must concentrate to follow it. For example, Visser never tells anybody he's trying to frame Abby; we must surmise this from his decision to use her gun and leave it at the scene. Furthermore, Joel and Ethan pointed out, they were mining the source material for film noir, rather than the noirs themselves. When it came to visual inspiration, they looked more to Bernardo Bertolucci's baroque political thriller *The Conformist* (1970) for its elegant styling, and, of course, *The Evil Dead*.

Blood Simple is a noir-horror hybrid. Apart from the rushing 'shaky cam' trick Joel learned from Raimi, there is Marty's apparent return from the dead, at first during the burial scene, and later in a dream sequence where he appears to Abby and vomits blood. There is also the eerie way that Marty's blood, smeared across the

OPPOSITE: In a memorably gruesome sequence, Ray (John Getz) is forced to bury Marty alive.

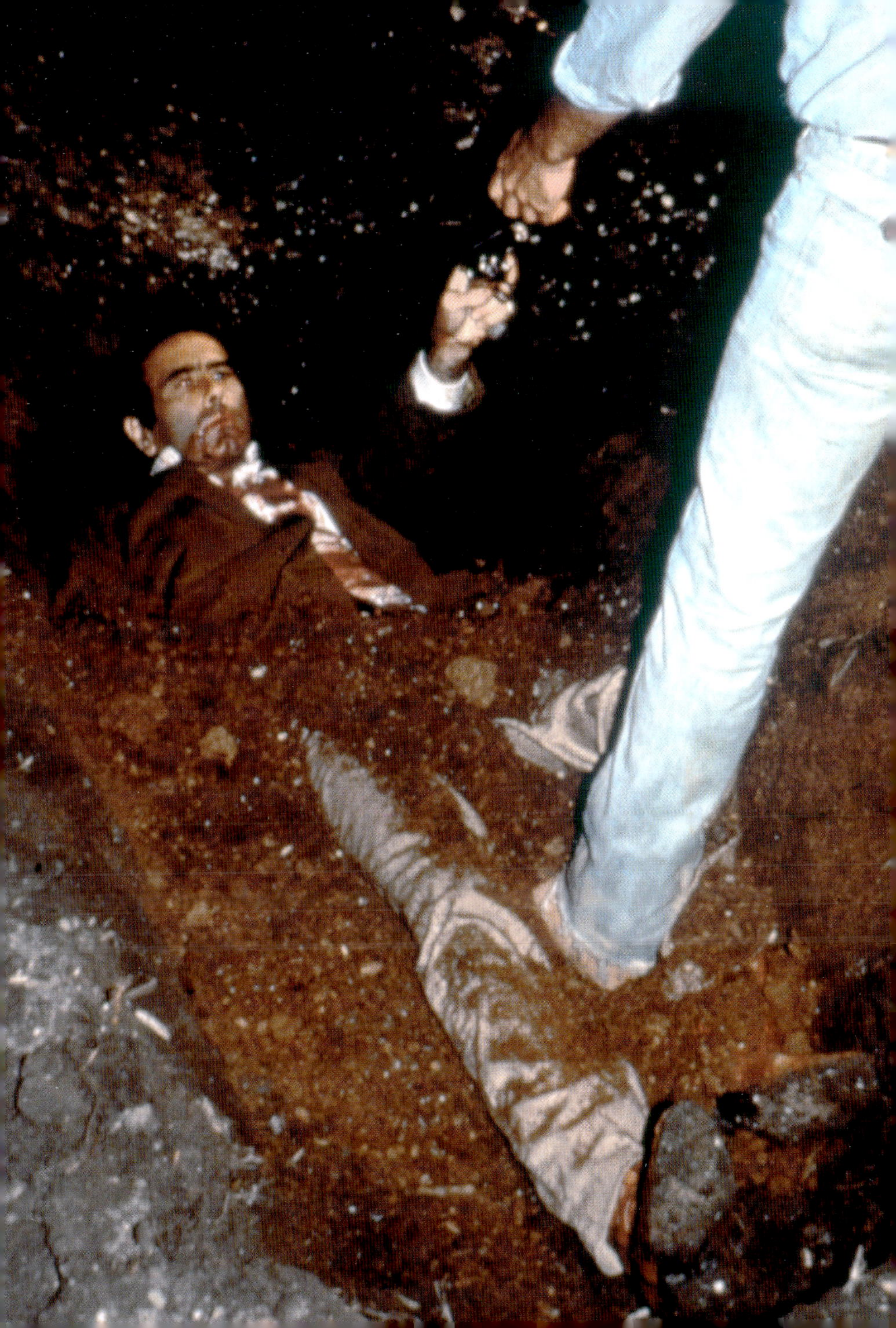

back seat of Ray's car, never seems to clot. It constantly seeps through the towels Ray throws over it, a bright crimson reminder of his crime. Carter Burwell's piano-led score, meanwhile, has shades of John Carpenter's work, particularly *Halloween*.

Blood Simple also has a grim sense of humour which, along with a joy of blending genre, would characterize almost every Coen movie that followed. There is a repeated gag where someone screeches away from Ray's home, not realizing he lives on a cul-de-sac, and must drive back past. And there's a winking knowingness to the way that Burwell's score strikes up as Ray starts to leave the burial scene, then pauses when his car refuses to start, and resumes once he's got the engine going and takes off.

Though it was shot on the cheap and lacks the sheen of their later work, *Blood Simple* is a fully formed Coen vision. It is packed with what would later be familiar trademarks: repeated lines that give the dialogue a distinctive rhythm ('I'm not a marriage counsellor'); their love of following characters at foot-level ('the lower the camera, the more dynamic it is,' said Sonnenfeld); and their ostentatious tracking shots. While planning an impressive camera glide along Marty's bar, which cheekily takes the audience up and over a slumped drunk, Joel asked Ethan if it might be too self-conscious. 'The whole movie is self-conscious,' said Ethan. 'Why pick on that shot?'

Such self-questioning is a reminder that, despite the finished product being so assured, the brothers were very much learning on the job. 'The first real movie set I was ever on was the first day of shooting,' recalled Joel. It was rather overwhelming for the introverted 28-year-old. 'If you look at photographs of me during

OPPOSITE: Frances McDormand made her feature film debut as *Blood Simple*'s unwitting 'final girl' Abby.

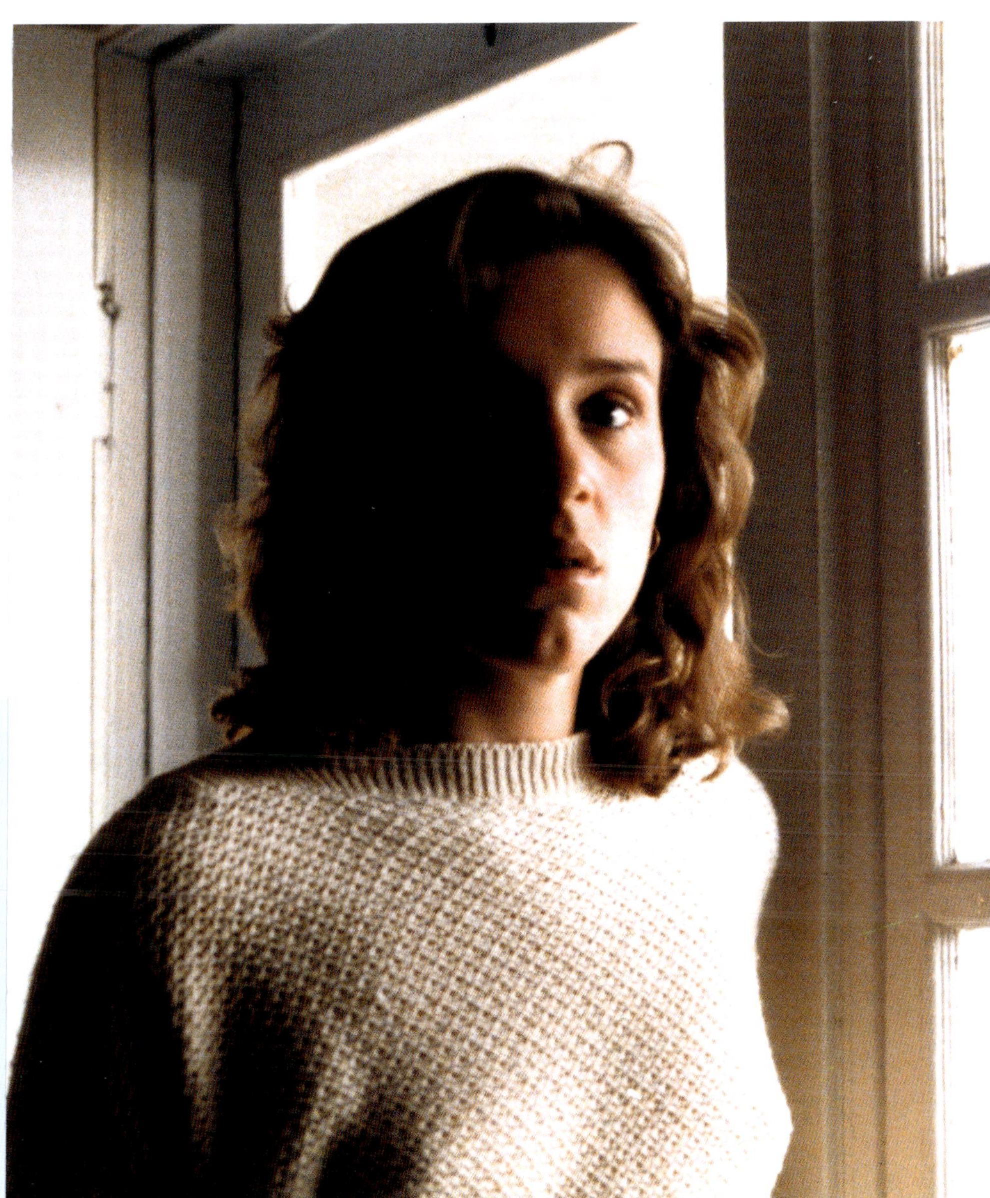

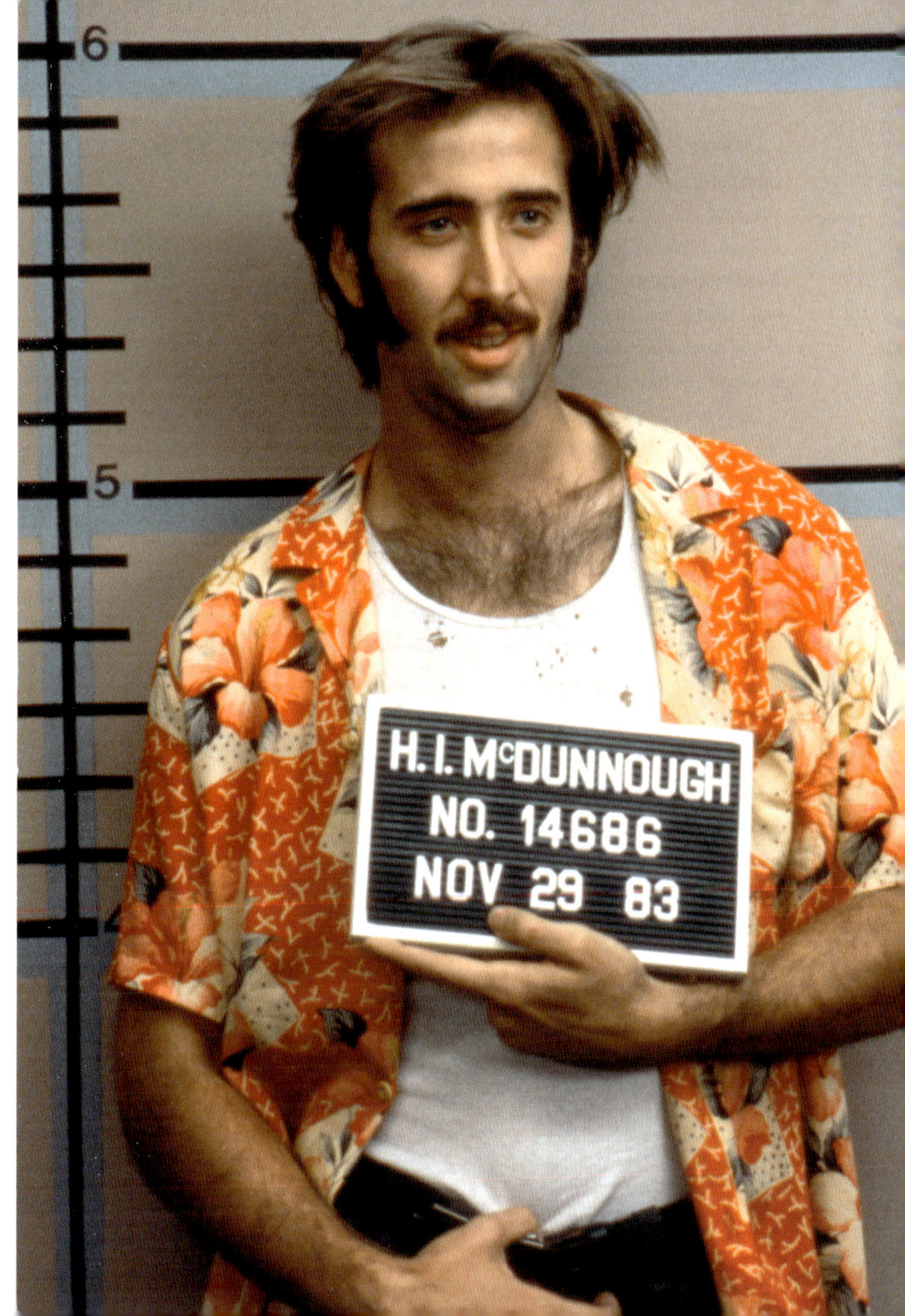
6
5
H.I. McDUNNOUGH
NO. 14686
NOV 29 83

RAISING ARIZONA
1987

One question Barry Sonnenfeld was asked a lot during the shoot for the Coen brothers' second picture was: 'Does it look wacky enough?' While constructing the film's madcap chase through a supermarket in north Phoenix, Arizona – which featured Nicolas Cage with tights on his head, gun-toting shop assistants and a pack of excited dogs – Sonnenfeld suggested raising his camera just a little, as its current low position was in danger of becoming too dazzled by the ceiling's fluorescent lights. However, to Joel and Ethan, placing it higher would make the action look less 'wacky'. So they established a golden rule: if in doubt, make it wackier.

The Coens' first priority with their *Blood Simple* follow-up was to 'make something completely different,' said Ethan. They did not want to be pegged as art-house filmmakers or neo-noirists. Their new movie couldn't be dark. It had to be something 'funny, with a quicker rhythm'. Originally they wanted to shoot the script they'd written with Sam Raimi immediately after *Blood Simple*: *The Hudsucker Proxy*. However, they soon realized the required budget was far beyond their reach. So instead they concocted a small-scale crime comedy about a frustrated childless trailer-park couple – ex-con H I 'Hi' McDunnough and ex-cop Ed – who kidnap a quintuplet born to unpainted-furniture magnate Nathan Arizona (Trey Wilson), to raise as their own.

The brothers had someone in mind for the female half of that couple: Holly Hunter, an old friend who they'd originally wanted for the part of Abby in *Blood Simple*, but hadn't been available. For soulful petty criminal Hi, meanwhile, the brothers cast their first star: Cage, the nephew of Francis Ford Coppola, who had impressed in the likes of *Rumble Fish*, *Birdy* and *Peggy Sue Got Married*.

In the film, Hunter's spiky determination and Cage's hangdog demeanour blend to make a comically potent mix, while their on-screen relationship has a touching innocence to it, despite Ed and Hi's morally questionable actions. However, Cage's methodology didn't gel well with that of his directors. Where the Coens had everything carefully storyboarded, planned and scripted, with every character's lines meticulously conceived, Cage liked to bring his own ideas to the table and became frustrated as the brothers kept brushing them off. For example, he suggested that Hi would always be checking his watch, as if he's forever pressed for time. The Coens reasoned this wouldn't be a great idea; it might get the audience checking their watches, too. (Although one little watch-check did make it into the film, to amusing effect during the crazed supermarket dash.)

An even trickier performer to handle was Randall 'Tex' Cobb, a heavyweight kickboxer hired to play the demonic 'Lone biker of the Apocalypse' Leonard Smalls, a *Mad Max*-type villain who enjoys exploding cute critters, has an oddly soft voice and may or

OPPOSITE: Randall 'Tex' Cobb as Leonard Smalls, described by Joel as 'less an actor than a force of nature'.

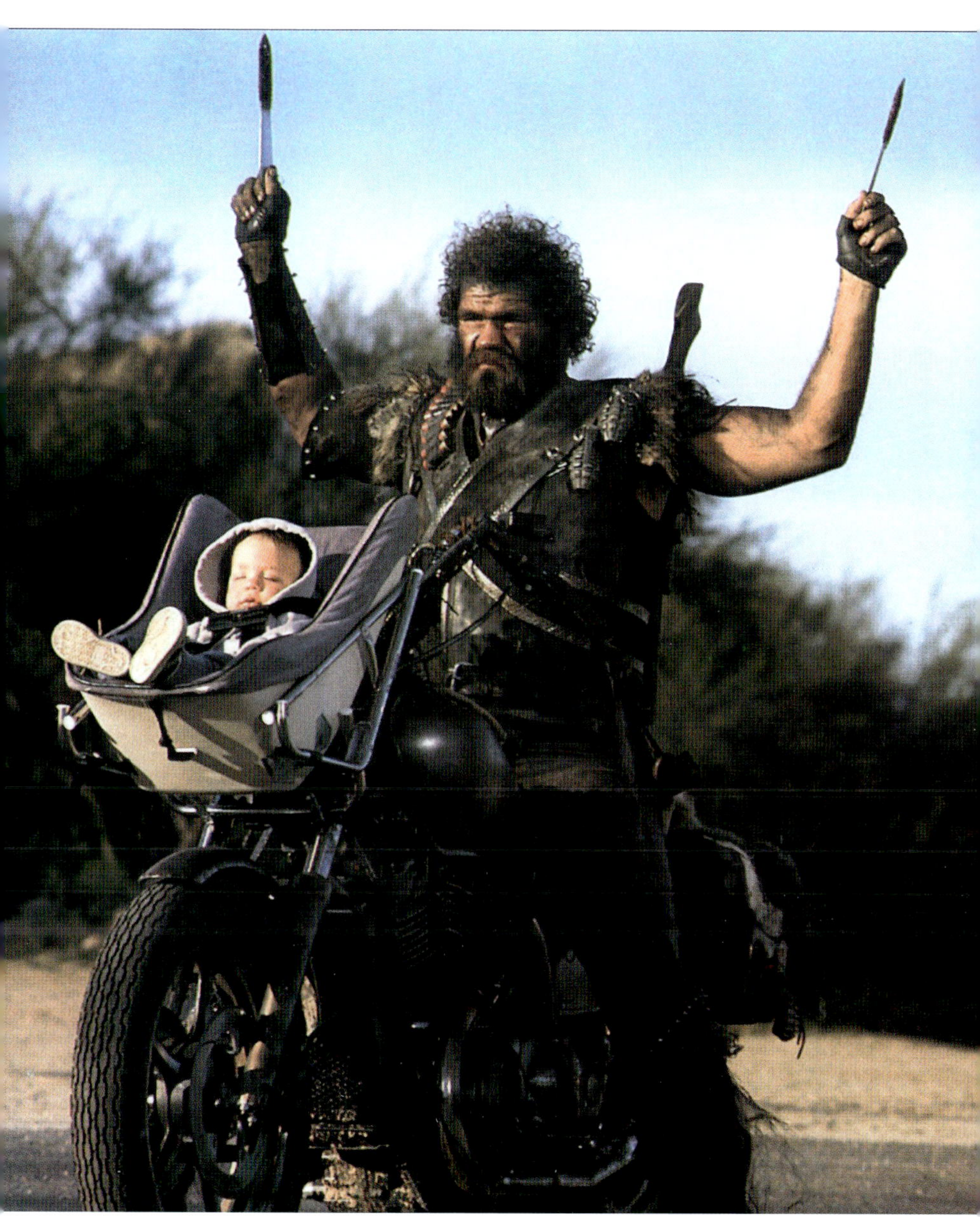

may not be a physical manifestation of Hi's fevered subconscious. 'He's not really someone it's easy to work with,' said Joel of Cobb, 'and I don't know if I'd rush headlong into employing him again.'

While Cobb had the requisite physique to play this fearsome biker, he turned out to be terrible at riding a bike, and kept stalling during takes. In one scene, he even rolled his Harley into a hole and was thrown to the ground. Then, according to editor Michael R Miller, Cobb's manager refused to let him return to shoot a few extra scenes after he'd wrapped, unless his fee was doubled, figuring he'd be impossible to replace.

But Cage and Cobb weren't the only challenging performers in the movie. There were also the babies.

'Joel and Ethan were trying to prove that they could do anything,' said composer Carter Burwell who stuck with the brothers for their second outing. 'They were shooting with dogs. They have scenes with babies. These are all the things that filmmakers are told not to work with.'

The main baby performer was eight-month-old T J Kuhn, who took the role of the heart-melting Nathan Jr. But, in addition to the infants who played his brothers (Harry, Barry, Larry and Garry), there were various baby doubles for long shots. 'We kept firing babies when they wouldn't behave,' said Joel. 'They didn't even know they were being fired, that's what was so pathetic about it.' The main sacking offence, he explained, was learning to walk. The Arizona quints were strictly crawlers, not toddlers. 'The parents were horrified. One mother actually put her baby's shoes on backward so he wouldn't walk.'

The Coens had a far better time with the remainder of their adult cast, including John Goodman, to whom they gave the role of burly jailbreaker Gail Snoats. Goodman would return for four more of their films, repeatedly undercutting the jolly, friendly persona

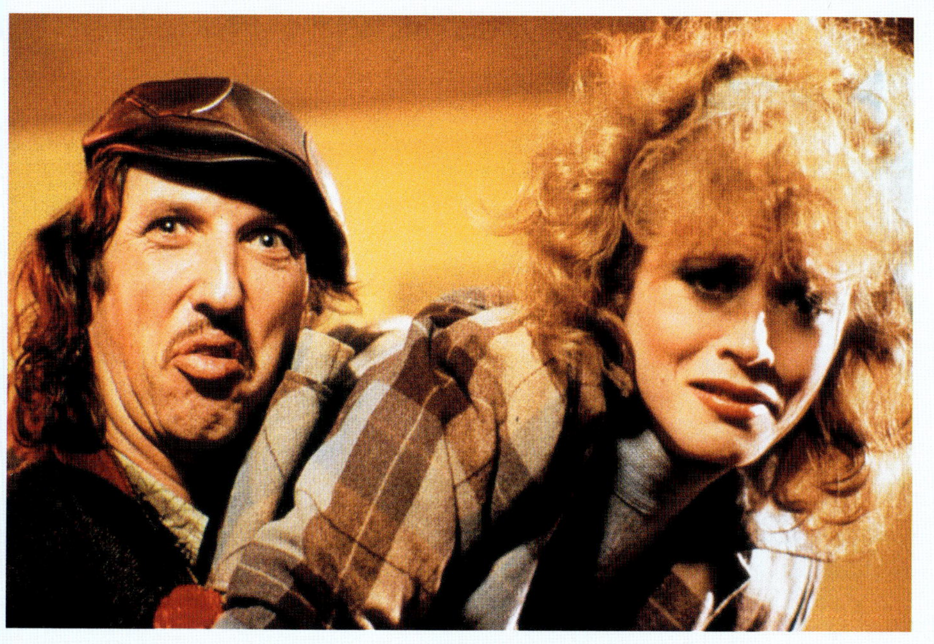

Coens on script: *Crimewave* (1985)

Perhaps Joel and Ethan's switch up from noir to slapstick might have
seemed less surprising if *Crimewave* had not failed so dismally. Written
by the brothers as *The XYZ Murders* for Sam Raimi to direct, it's a
B-movie about security technician Victor Ajax (Reed Birney), who
becomes wrapped up in a disagreement between his two bosses, one
of whom hires a pair of exterminators to murder the other. The duo
take things too far and wind up on a killing spree, for which Victor is
blamed and sent to the chair. There are defenestrations, electrocutions
and violent gags involving forks, bowling balls and a giant rat model.
(Pictured are one of the killers, Arthur Coddish, played by Brion
James, and Sheree J Wilson as one of their targets, Nancy). The film
is a confusing and clamorous mess, the result of a nightmarish
production, but also a studio (Embassy) that wrested control of the
edit from Raimi, supposedly to make the film more commercial. The
reviews were dire, the movie bombed and Raimi was scarred. The
Coens, at least, drew from it a lesson in why it's so important to secure
the final cut – something they have never failed to do.

most audiences associated with him from TV show *Roseanne*. And, of course, there was McDormand, who has a marvellous cameo as the awfully overbearing 'Mommier-than-thou' friend Dot, who harangues Hi about Nathan Jr's vaccines ('You gotta get 'em dip-tet boosters yearly or else they'll develop lockjaw and night vision') while her own children brattishly trash his home. This was just the second of eight appearances she'd make in Coen movies, and it's a humdinger.

The inclusion of McDormand isn't the only call back to *Blood Simple*. If that film provided a restrained hint of Joel and Ethan's camera-spinning verve, *Raising Arizona* showed what they could do unleashed. The phrase 'live-action cartoon' has been used more than once to describe the movie, and for good reason. The Coens send their audience whizzing and whirling around the larger-than-life and brightly coloured action, whether it's from a dog's-eye perspective during a chase, or from the view of Smalls' malevolent Harley. One astonishing tracking shot, used to reveal Florence Arizona's (Lynne Kitei) discovery of Nathan Jr's abduction, tears along the family driveway, over their car, up a ladder, through the window and right into the mother's screaming mouth. Most of this was achieved in a single take by a pair of sprinting crewmen who had to lift the camera over the car. But, Miller recalled, the ladder segment was shot separately, by Joel. 'He actually injured himself. He slashed his arm on the window or something.'

The injury, the egos of martial artists, the eager toddlers and the stars with big ideas – they were all worth it, in the sense that *Raising Arizona* proved the Coens were resoundingly capable of doing 'something completely different'. And while it bemused many critics, while irritating others, it was a modest box-office hit. Taking almost $30 million on release against a $5 million budget, it was the biggest commercial success of the brothers' early career.

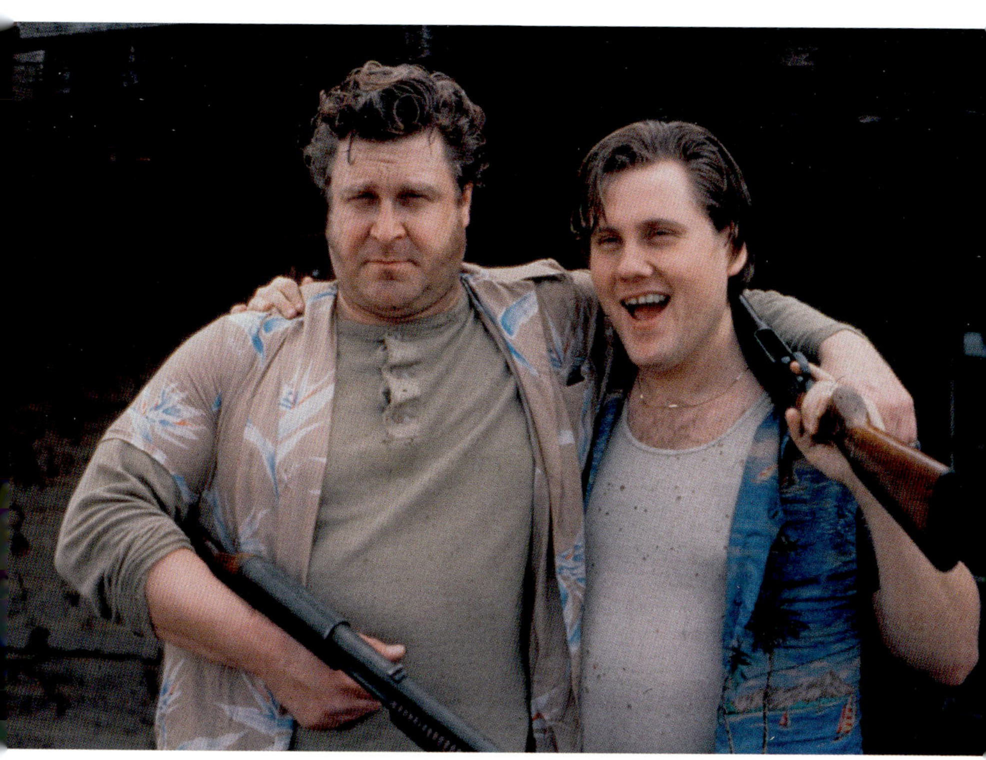

ABOVE: John Goodman and William Forsythe as jailbreak
siblings Gale and Evelle Snoats.

The film's humour has endured the passage of time, too,
unlike the other baby-themed comedies of the era, such as
Charles Shyer's *Baby Boom* or Frank Oz's *Three Men and a Baby*,
released the same year. It is certainly far more visually impressive,
anarchic and subversive. A 2023 poll of the 'funniest movies of
all time' on Reddit even ranked *Raising Arizona* at number one,
just ahead of *Airplane!*

Comedy, it was clear, wasn't just something the Coens were
trying out to avoid accusations of producing 'more of the same'.
It was very much their heartland.

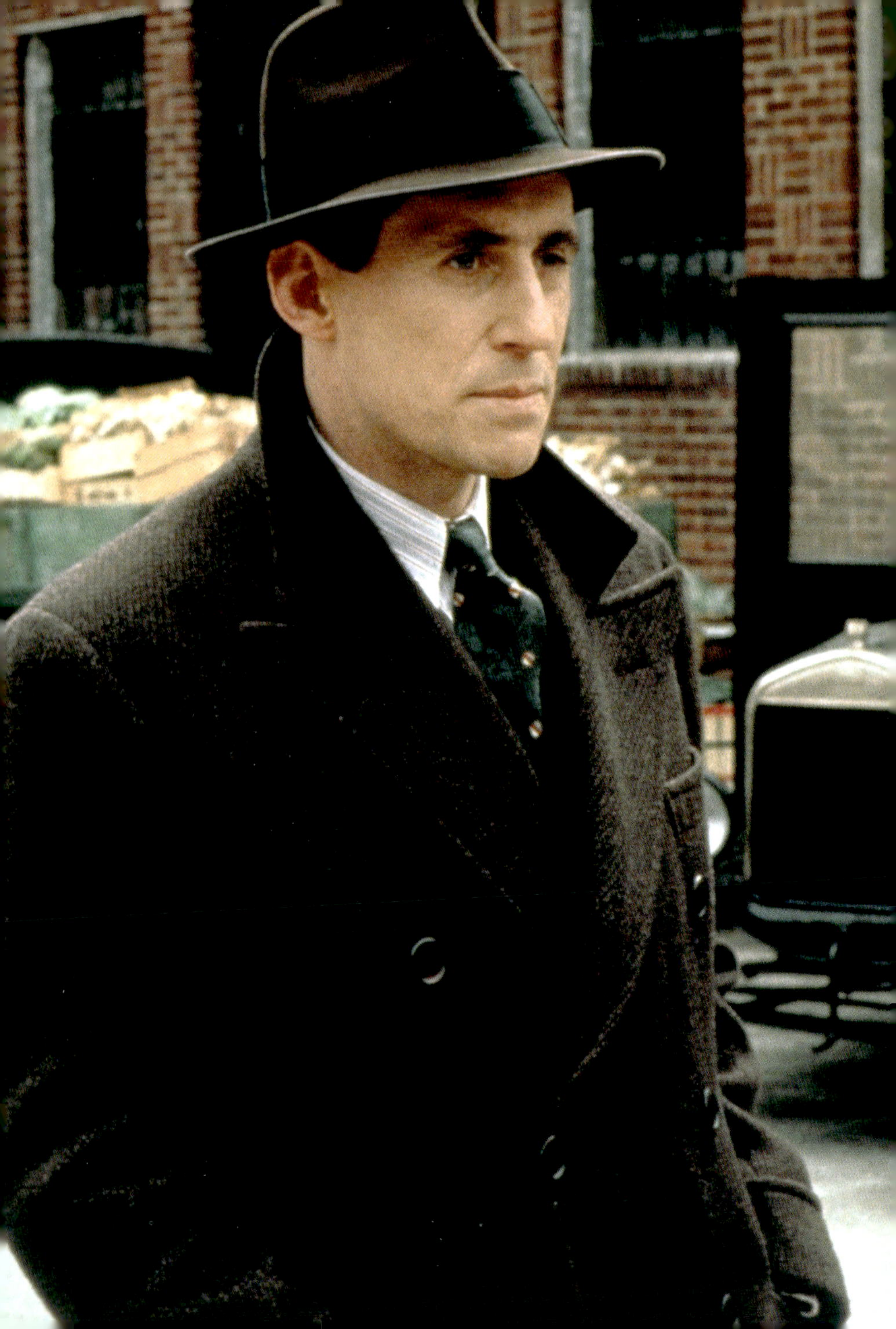

MILLER'S CROSSING
1990

The year 1990 brought a spate of gangster movies. Francis Ford Coppola delivered the final chapter of his epic underworld trilogy with *The Godfather Part III*, Martin Scorsese dug into the grimy world of Mafia middle-management in *GoodFellas*, and Warren Beatty took audiences back to the genre's comic-strip excesses with *Dick Tracy*. But these films had little bearing on the Coens' own spin on the well-worn genre.

The brothers had long loved gangster films. But their primary inspiration for *Miller's Crossing* was the clipped, hard-boiled writing of Dashiell Hammett, particularly his novels *The Glass Key* and *Red Harvest*. 'He took the genre and used it to tell a story that was interesting about people and other things besides just the plot,' Joel said. 'In Hammett, the plot is like a big jigsaw puzzle that can be seen in the background. It may make some internal sense, but the momentum of the characters is more important.'

While writing *Miller's Crossing* – their toughest-to-nail script yet – they took inspiration from Hammett's rich characterization. Like *The Glass Key*'s Ned Beaumont, they made their shady protagonist Tom Reagan (Gabriel Byrne) an advisor and close friend to a crime boss (Albert Finney's Leo), plaguing him with gambling debts, inflicting on him regular beatings and giving him a romance with his boss's girlfriend (Verna, played by newcomer Marcia Gay Harden). Meanwhile, they borrowed the fictional Prohibition-era city setting from *Red Harvest,* though Hammett's Personville/Poisonville became an unnamed late Twenties East Coast conurbation, which the brothers created in New Orleans, the closest modern-day match they could find.

However, Joel and Ethan's primary aim was not to reheat Hammett for an early Nineties audience. First and foremost, the film was 'a conscious effort not to repeat ourselves,' the brothers insisted, returning to the theme of pigeon-hole avoidance. They could have done this by accepting a post-*Raising Arizona* offer from Warner Bros to direct the new *Batman* movie, but that would have meant sacrificing their much-valued independence, and they characteristically turned it down. It also would have meant ignoring a compelling image they'd conjured together and wanted to develop into a feature: 'Big guys in overcoats in the woods – the incongruity of urban gangsters in a forest setting.'

That forest setting gave the movie its title, and its signature scene, in which a kneeling John Turturro, as weaselly bookie Bernie Bernbaum, memorably begs a pistol-clutching Tom to spare his life: 'Look in your heart!' But more significant is the intention behind its inclusion: to bring the aforementioned incongruity to a very familiar and beloved genre. This tendency towards subversion and surprise has always peppered the Coens' films, from dipping a stoner bowler into a Chandler-esque mystery in *The Big Lebowski,* to inserting UFO references in their existential noir *The Man Who Wasn't There.* 'You want to keep surprising the audience,' said Ethan in 1990.

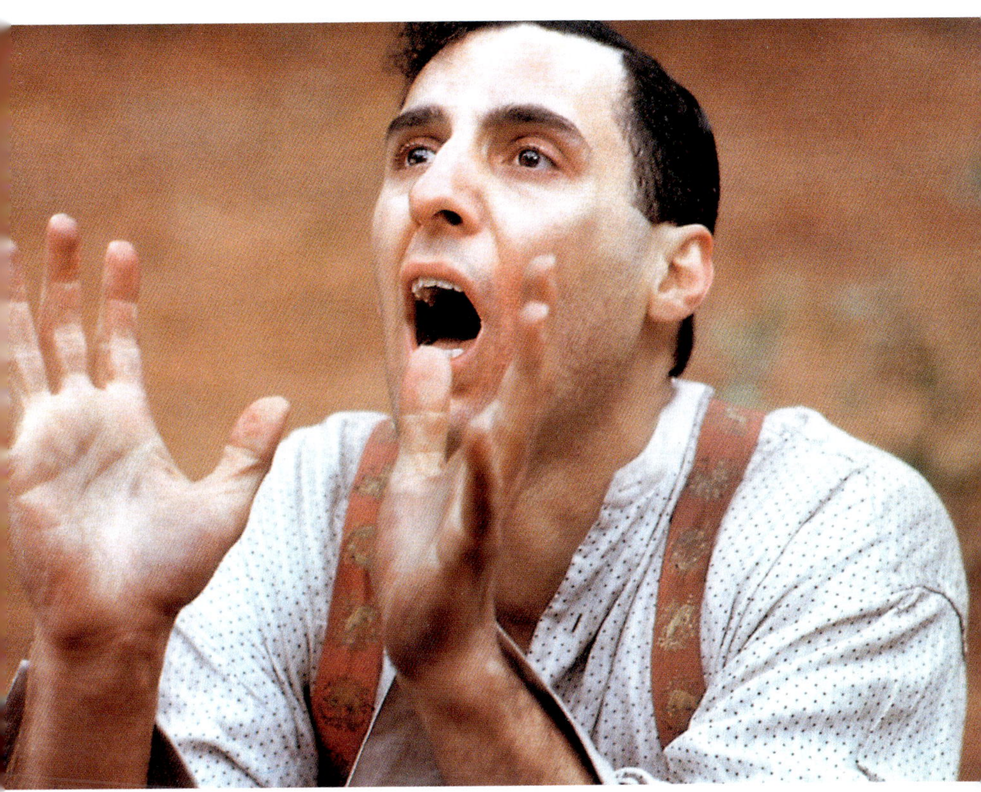

ABOVE: 'Look in your heart!' Duplicitous bookie Bernie Bernbaum (John Turturro) pleads for his life.

It's also found in *Miller's Crossing*'s absurdist sense of humour, such as the moment when rival Mob boss Johnny Caspar (Jon Polito) is interrupted during a tense scene by his overexcited son, who Caspar then slaps, causing the kid to bawl his eyes out. 'Awww,' says the mobster, suddenly sympathetic and hugging his child, 'did somebody hit you?'

'It's not that obvious type of gangster film,' observed Byrne. 'It's much deeper than that. When I read the script, first of all I thought it was a comedy.' The Irish actor also compared it to a play, describing it as 'a movie you listen to as much as look at.'

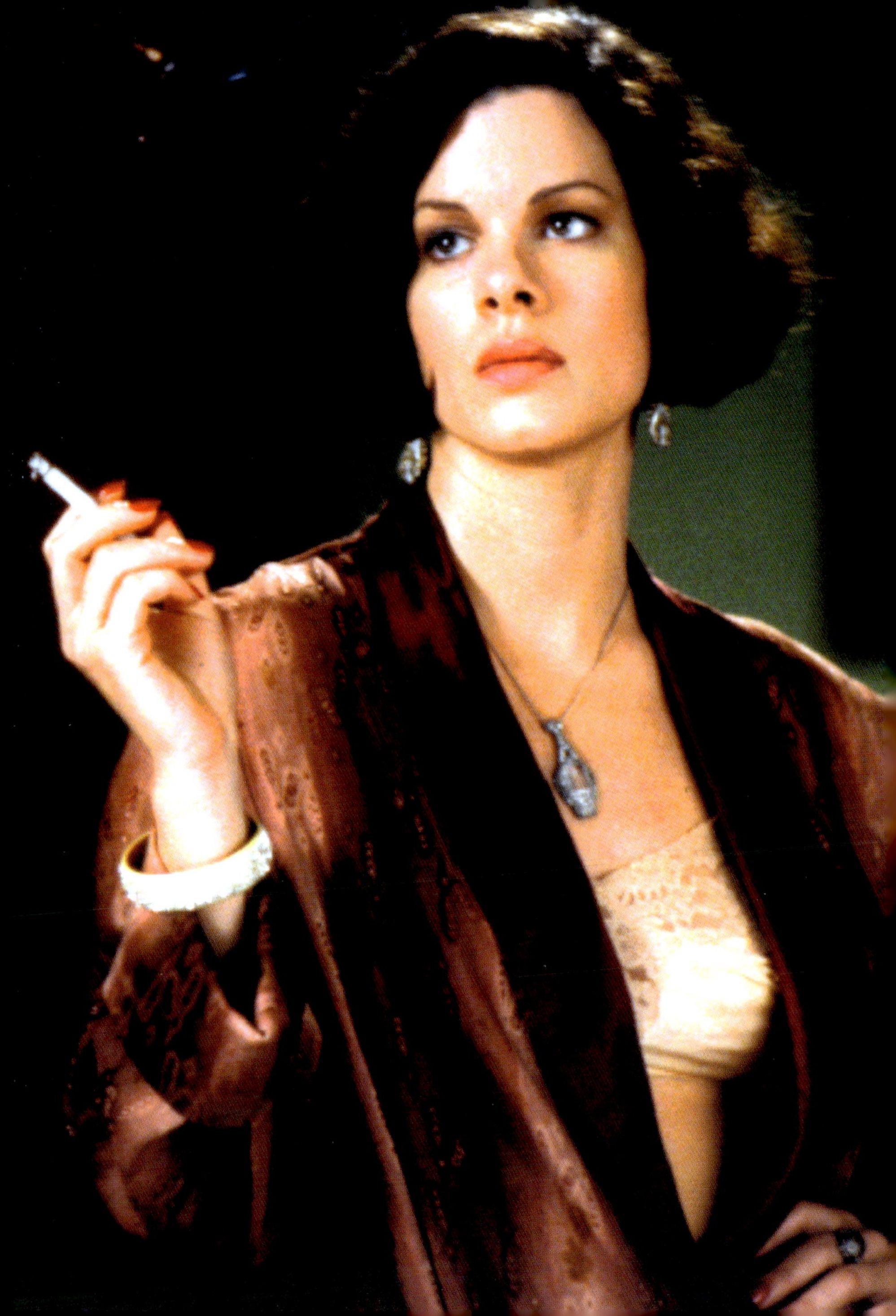

Miller's Crossing is an incredibly verbose movie – more so than *Raising Arizona* – opening with a dense, relentless, irony-swathed monologue about ethics, delivered by Caspar, while the Coens' camera slowly pulls out from a close-up of a whiskey tumbler. Interestingly, Tom is the last character present in the scene to speak. A listener rather than a talker.

And there is much for him – and the audience – to listen to. Not just in terms of volume (the script is a weighty 142 pages), but also its brilliantly colourful period-slang argot ('twist', 'schnook', 'what's the rumpus?', 'I'm sick of the high hat!') which gives the film a uniquely pleasing cadence. It certainly made *Miller's Crossing* a challenge for foreign distributors, whose subtitle and dub-script writers had to be given a Joel-and-Ethan-penned glossary of its pre-war (and sometimes just straight-up made-up) terminology.

But Joel and Ethan were well aware that the gangster movie is an action-driven genre, and knew when to shut their characters up. Indeed, when the film does finally cut to the action, it is all the more effective for marking the first point where the talking stops. Leo relaxes in his bed with a drink, a cigar and 'Danny Boy' playing on his Victrola, when Tommy-gun-wielding assassins break into his home. Barely breaking a sweat while his house burns, the seasoned boss dispatches them all, picking up one of the iconic submachine guns as he does so, jumping out of a window and blasting a fleeing car until it crunches into a tree and explodes in his street.

It was one of the Coens' most challenging sequences yet, taking weeks to mount and requiring the use of several locations around New Orleans, plus a soundstage where production

OPPOSITE: Newcomer Marcia Gay Harden as hard-nosed moll, Verna.

designer Dennis Gassner had to oversee the construction of an elevated bedroom set, to more easily shoot the moment where Finney rolls under his bed.

The action doesn't have the unhinged Looney Tunes quality of the fights and chases in *Raising Arizona*, but it comes close. Particularly at the moment where one assailant is riddled with so many bullets he becomes a dancing puppet, firing off his own Tommy gun in all directions. 'What sells the hit is the dance,' said Ethan. 'We always knew we wanted to do that.'

'You keep thinking of things you want to add to the scene,' continued Joel. 'He shoots up the chandelier, the paintings, his toes. All kinds of fun things. The only regret is it goes by so fast, you almost kind of miss it. Without the sequence, Joel joked, 'the movie's in danger of becoming tasteful.'

In truth, *Miller's Crossing* was by far the Coens' most tasteful production yet, with Gassner wisely limiting its colour palette and echoing the titular forest in the grand columns of the city's architecture. Sonnenfeld kept the camerawork sober and stately, following Joel and Ethan's brief to make it 'handsome and muted and not wacky. And also beautiful and manly.' And Carter Burwell had to learn how to score orchestral music for the first time, giving the film its lush string-led theme, based on the traditional Irish song 'Come Back to Erin Carter', which was suggested by Byrne.

The movie is a Coen milestone in a number of ways. Most obviously, it is their first period film. They would stay in the past for the majority of their features to come; only *Intolerable Cruelty, The Ladykillers* and *Burn After Reading* would have contemporary settings. They're not grand world-builders like, say, Ridley Scott, but they revel in the opportunity to recreate bygone fashions, locations, manners of speaking, cultural references and even shooting styles. And as *Miller's Crossing* proved, they're good at it.

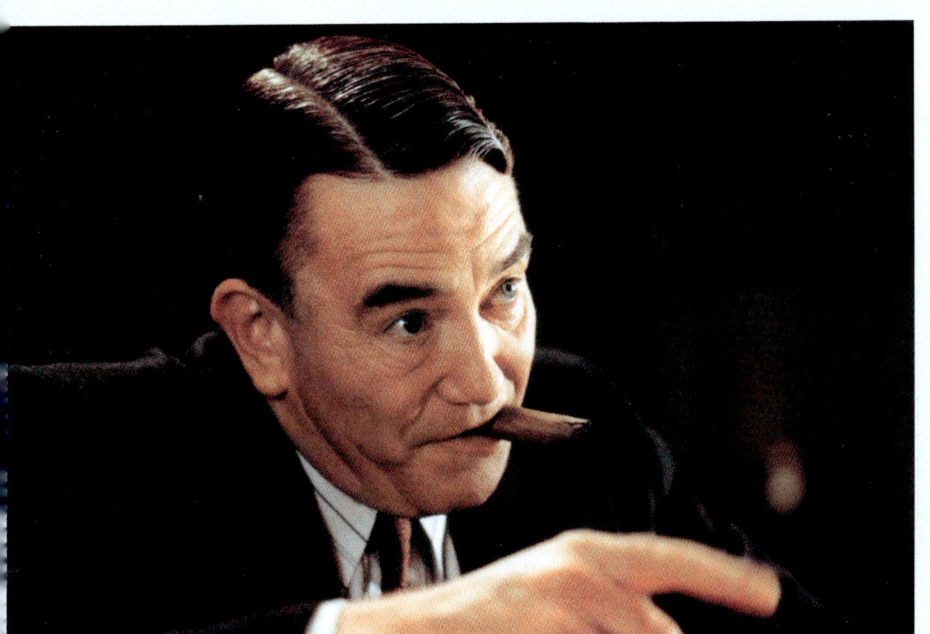

The Finney factor

Leo O'Bannion is a rare example of a Coen brothers' character played by an actor whom they never imagined in the role. Originally, they had earmarked Leo for *Raising Arizona*'s Trey Wilson. However, two days before shooting began, Wilson tragically died of a cerebral haemorrhage. Albert Finney (pictured above), available at short notice, made the role his own. 'What's strange is that the part would never have been written without Trey in mind,' said Ethan, 'whereas now it's impossible for us to imagine any other actor than Finney in the role.'

The film also, in retrospect, sealed the sense of a 'Coen company' – a set of reliable character actors who would crop up again and again in their works. While only McDormand returned from *Raising Arizona* in a brief appearance as the mayor's flirty secretary, Turturro and Polito would become Coen regulars over the next few decades. As

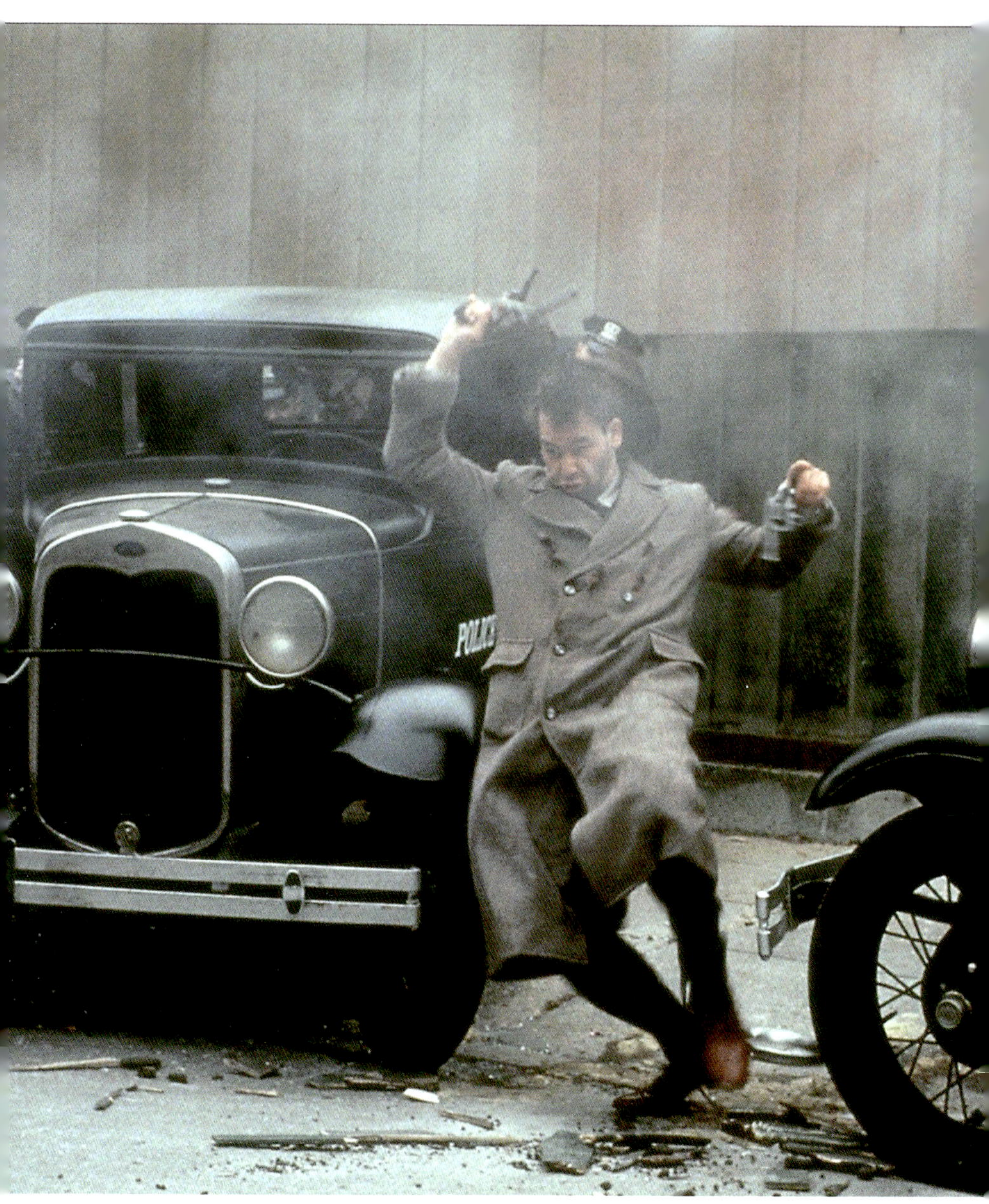

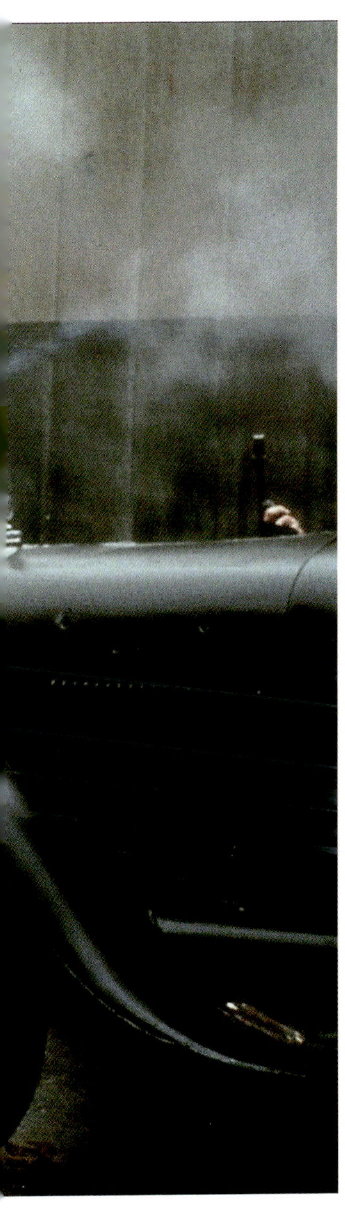

would Michael Badalucco (Caspar's driver) and Steve Buscemi, who takes the small but pivotal role of Mink, one of the corners in the film's two overlapping love triangles that combine to tear Tom's city apart.

Finally, the film settled the Coens into their role of bemused creators batting away attempts to interpret their works. It opens with a hat blowing through a forest, an image later referred to by Tom while describing a dream to Verna. Throughout the movie he is constantly losing his hat, then retrieving it. What is its significance? Does it represent his wits? His strength? His dilemma? His *soul*?

'There isn't any answer,' said Joel. 'It's an image that came to us, that we liked, and it just implanted itself. It's a kind of practical guiding thread, but there's no need to look for deep meanings.'

They say as much in the film itself, through Tom's surly reaction to Verna's guess that he chased the hat in his dream and when he caught it, 'it changed into something else, something wonderful.'

'Nah, it stayed a hat and no, I didn't chase it. Nothing more foolish than a man chasin' his hat.'

LEFT: Coen buddy Sam Raimi makes a cameo as Snickering Gunman, whose smile is wiped off his face when he's riddled with Tommy-gun bullets.

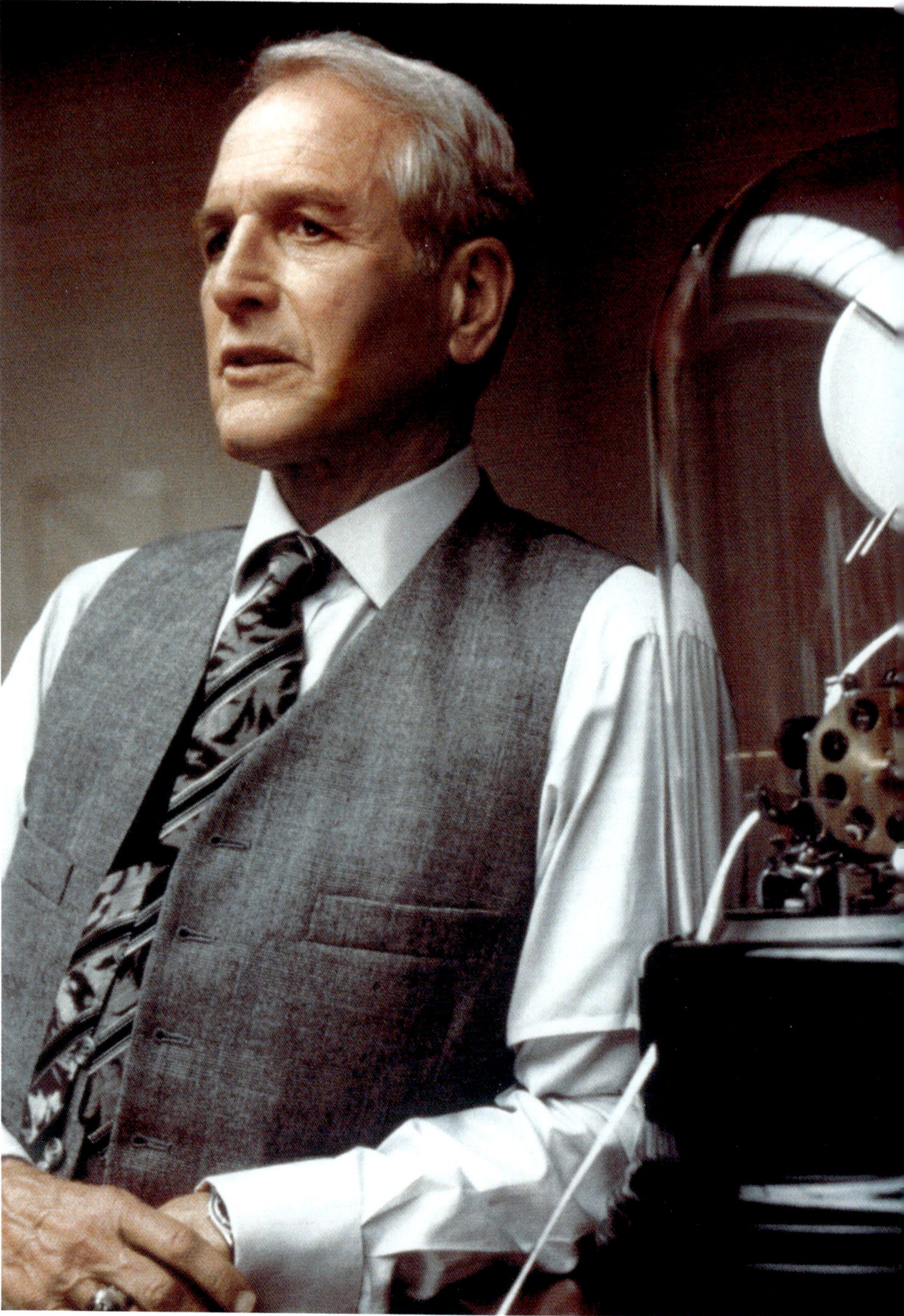

*'How'd he get so high?
And why's he feeling so low?'*

WIN SOME,
LOSE SOME

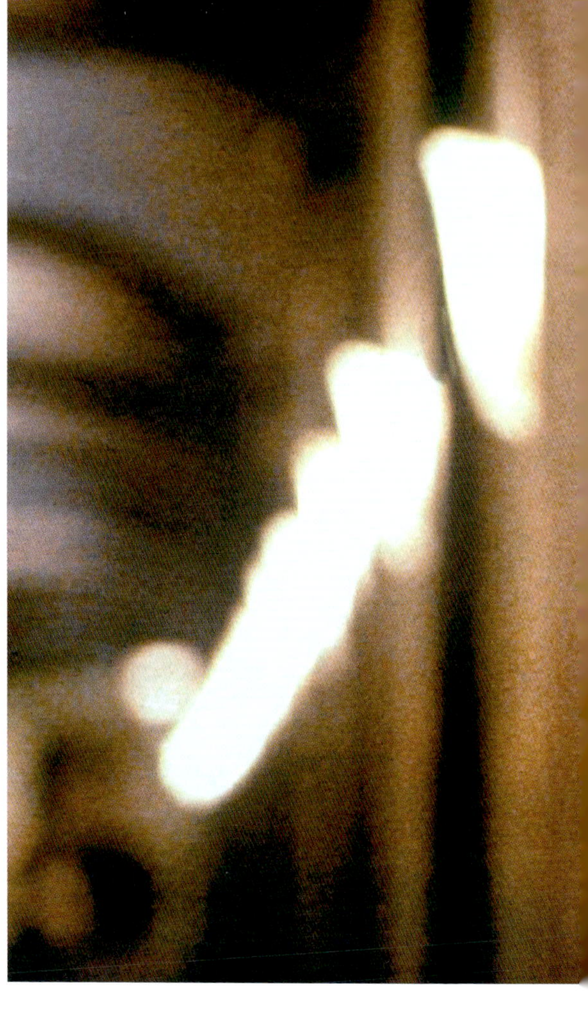

BARTON FINK
1991

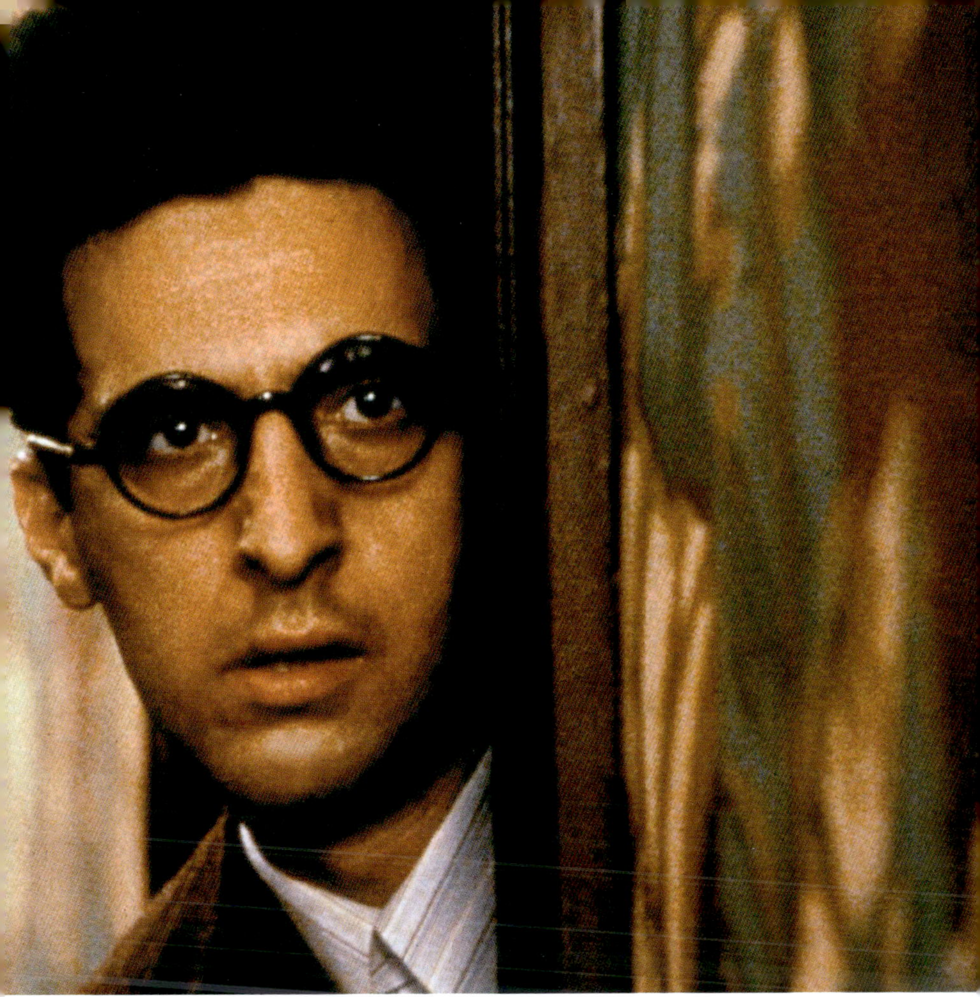

The Coens' fourth film was, to some degree, a happy accident. 'We just sort of burped out *Barton Fink*,' said Ethan. 'Yeah, we belched and there it was,' added Joel.

The brothers were in the midst of writing *Miller's Crossing*, when its intricate and tangled plotting got the better of them. It wasn't writer's block, the brothers insisted (a fair assumption, since that's exactly what Barton Fink suffers). They just needed a break from Tom Reagan's shenanigans. A mental palate cleanser.

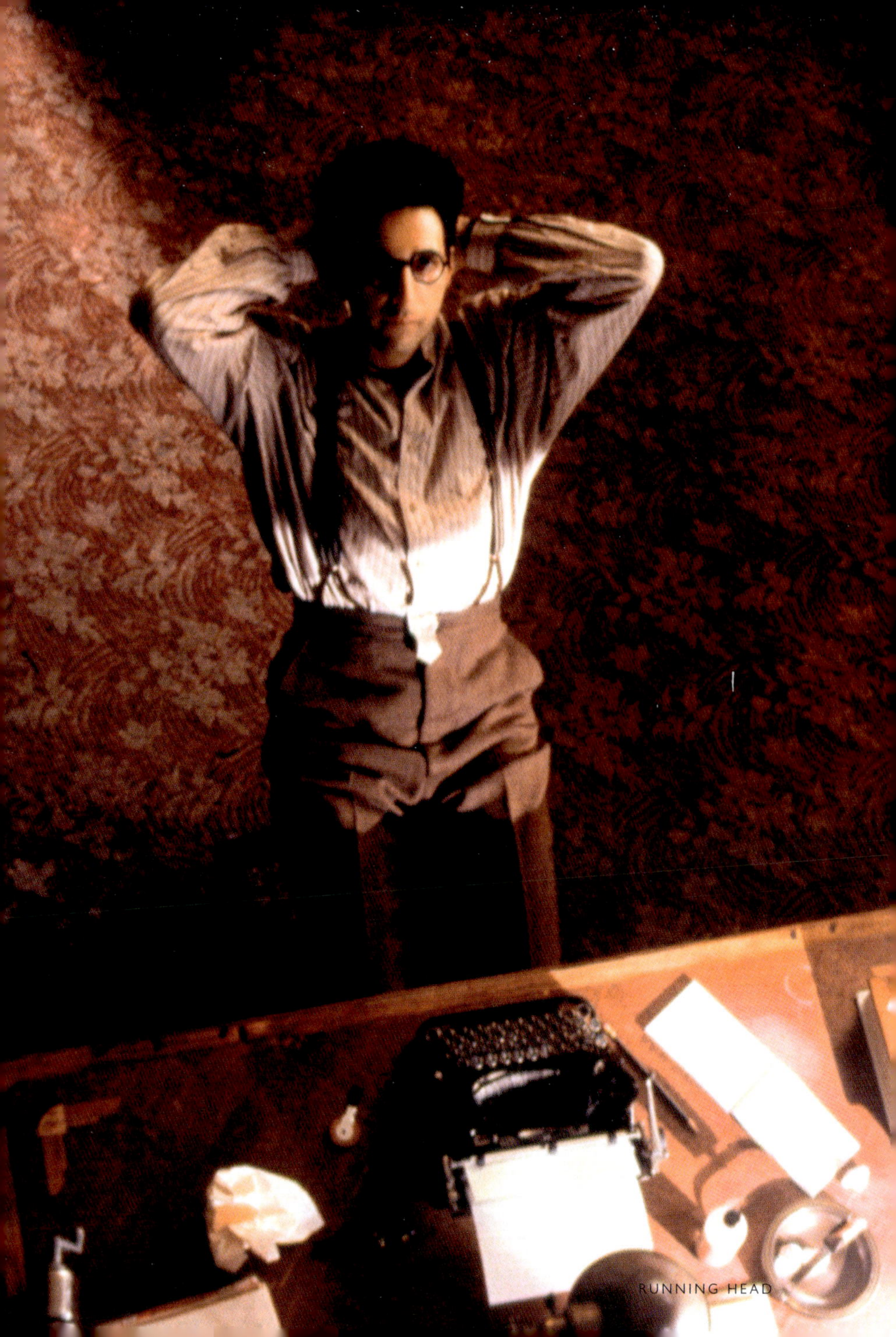
RUNNING HEAD

'Our rhythm was slowed up and we wanted to put ourselves at a certain distance,' said Joel. 'In order to get out of the problems we had with that story, we had begun to think about another one.'

This new story – set only a decade or so later, on the eve of the US entering World War II – was of a much smaller scale than *Miller's Crossing*. It had two origin points. Like *Raising Arizona*, it arose in part out of a desire to create a character for an actor they loved – in this case John Turturro, the 33-year-old Italian American performer who'd recently stood out in Spike Lee's *Do The Right Thing* (1989), and who they would also cast as Bernie Birnbaum. And, like *Miller's Crossing*, it flowered from a single, dominating mind's-eye image: in this case 'a huge neglected old hotel'. A vast 'ghost ship' of a place that you'd guess was empty if it weren't for the all shoes left outside the doors, with thin walls, a mosquito infestation, and sweating, peeling, pus-yellow wallpaper. 'You can imagine it peopled with travelling salesmen who've had no success, with their sad sex lives, crying alone in their rooms,' said Joel.

From there the script flowed as smoothly as spilled blood. It was done in three weeks, before Joel and Ethan returned, refreshed, to the machine-gun patter of their gangsters. This speedy process suggests *Barton Fink* must have been brewing somewhere in the back of their shared mind for some time, especially as its influences are so glaringly obvious. Not merely in terms of its creepy, psychological-horror vibe, where this disturbing location echoes a disquieted mind-state; much like Roman Polanski's *Repulsion* (1965) and *The Tenant* (1976), with shades of Stanley Kubrick's *The Shining* (1980). But mainly in the way they, for the first time in their career, drew on real people for their characters.

OPPOSITE: Barton fails to find inspiration in the oppressive environs of his hotel room.

Barton Fink is an egotistical Jewish New Yorker playwright who, after being lauded for his socially conscious theatre work, is transplanted to Los Angeles, where he is tasked with bashing out a banal wrestling picture for beefy B-lister Wallace Beery. Barton is a clear analogue for left-wing dramatist Clifford Odets, a member of the influential Group Theatre collective. Though the Coens pointed out that Odets was successful in Hollywood and had a very different personality to Fink – far more extroverted – the script's debts to Odets' work only emphasize the connection. His 1949 play *The Big Knife* was about an actor being chewed up by the Hollywood machine, and was inspired by Odets' own frustration writing scripts for the studios during the Forties.

Unmade Coens: *Old Fink*

Perhaps it was a joke. Maybe they were genuine. But in 2009, while promoting *A Serious Man*, Joel and Ethan told MTV that they would one day like to make a sequel to *Barton Fink*, titled *Old Fink*. The film, they explained, would be set during 1967's Summer of Love, and pick up with Barton, now in his late fifties, as teacher at the University of California in Berkeley. 'He ratted on a lot of his friends to the House Un-American Activities committee,' said Joel. 'He's got the George Kaufman hair but he's going grey,' added Ethan. 'He wears a medallion.' The idea was to wait for John Turturro to be old enough to return to the part. 'He's getting there,' said Ethan. Given Turturro is now in his sixties, it's fair to say he's gone past there, unless the Coens relocate the movie to the late Seventies or early Eighties.

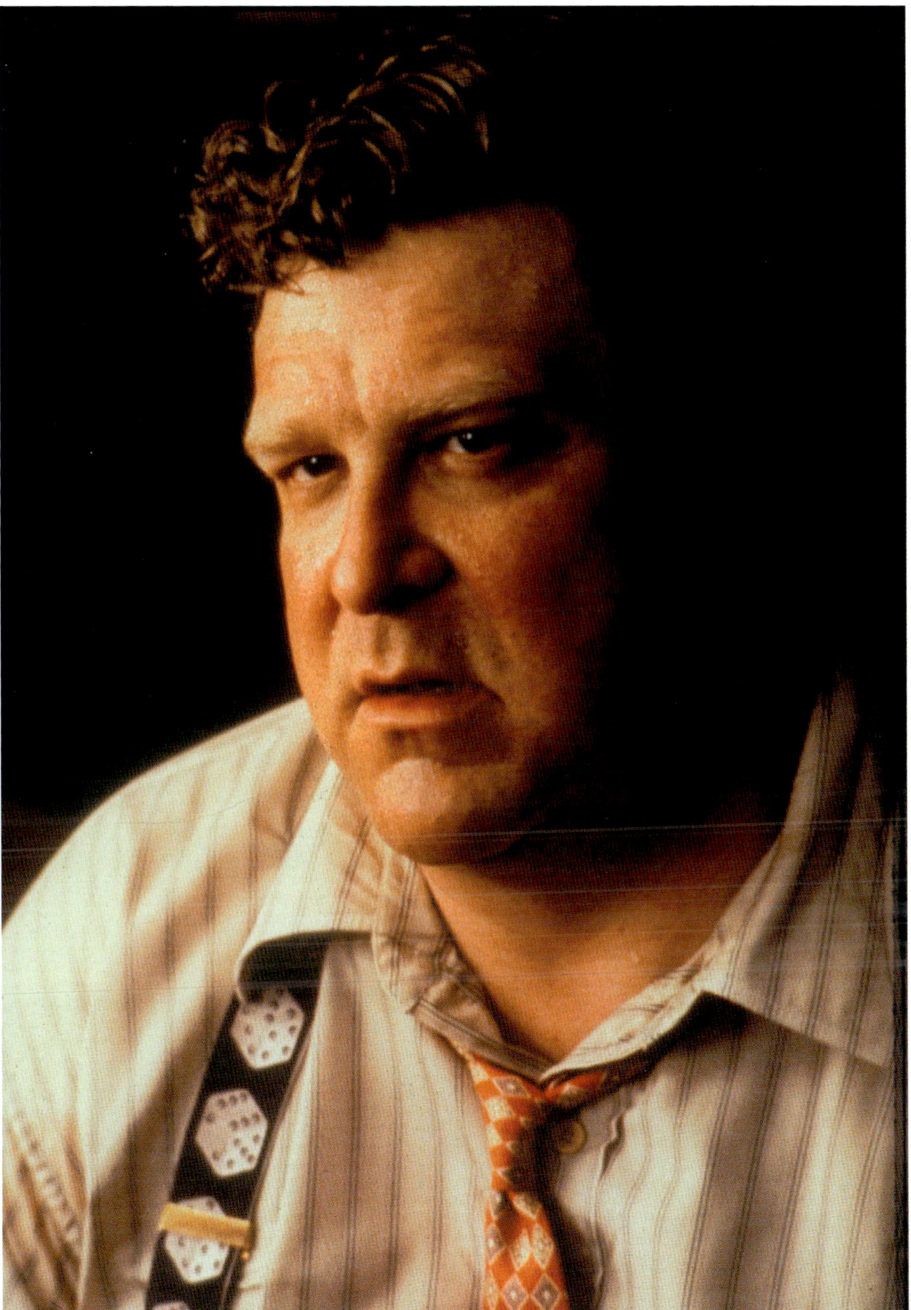

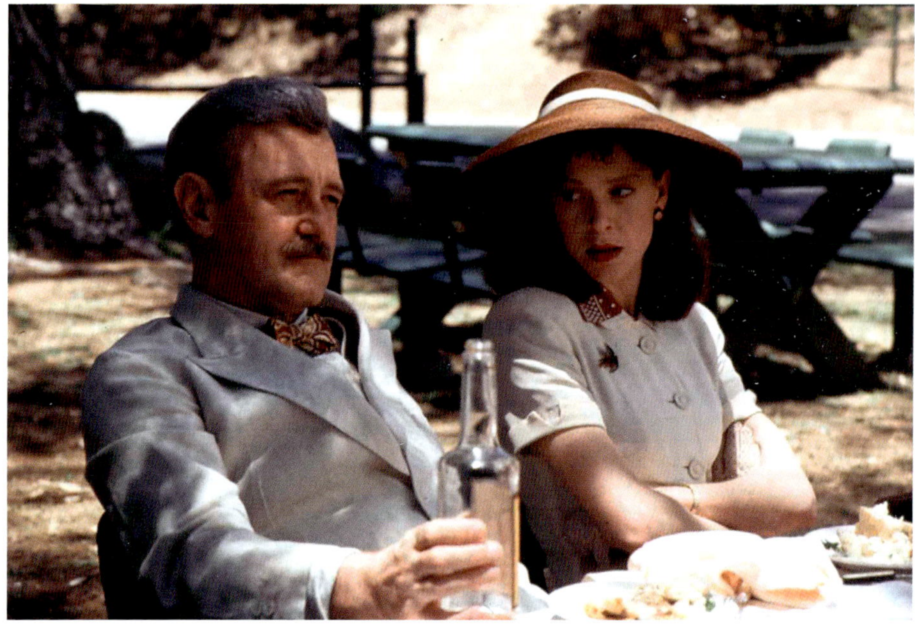

ABOVE: Novelist Bill Mayhew (John Mahoney), an obvious analogue for William Faulkner, with his muse Audrey (Judy Davis).

Meanwhile, his 1946 noir *Deadline at Dawn* involves someone who discovers that the woman he just spent the night with has been murdered – as happens to Barton in the film's horrifying second-act twist.

Elsewhere, the Coens found inspiration for the character of alcoholic writer Bill Mayhew (John Mahoney) in Mississippi-born novelist William Faulkner, a Nobel laureate who really did write a Wallace Beery wrestling movie (1932's *Flesh*). And overbearing studio boss Jack Lipnick (Michael Lerner) was a gestalt of Hollywood legends Harry Cohn, Louis B Mayer and Jack Warner.

The character of Charlie Meadows, however, is a pure fabrication, and another role crafted with a specific actor in mind: John Goodman. In contrast to Gale in *Raising Arizona*, Charlie enters the frame as an apparently benevolent figure, very much in line with Goodman's prevalent on-screen persona. He is an amiable insurance salesman whose assertion that 'fire, theft and casualty are not things that only happen to other people,' only sounds sinister in hindsight.

The Barton/Charlie double act is central to the plot. Charlie is 'the common man' whom Barton is so keen to represent in his work, yet the writer cuts across all Charlie's attempts to share his stories and barely listens to him, instead pontificating about his own commitment to revealing 'the life of the mind'. Later, Charlie will be revealed as Karl 'Madman' Mundt, a serial killer, who will punish Barton for his arrogance by murdering his muse Audrey (Judy Davis) – along with, it is insinuated, her lover Mayhew and Barton's parents and uncle back in New York – before shooting dead two cops and burning down the hotel. This climactic sequence presents an indelibly horrific image: Goodman charging down a flame-wreathed corridor with a shotgun, bellowing, 'I'll show you the life of the mind!'

It's tempting to see *Barton Fink* as an ironic statement by the Coens on their own position in Hollywood. Fink is the first lead character who has their faith and shares their vocation. Turturro spent a month with the brothers before shooting, during which he may have picked up some of their tics and mannerisms. But, unsurprisingly, they quickly shot that theory down. 'It isn't a personal comment in any way,' insisted Joel. 'Our professional life in Hollywood has been particularly easy, which I'm sure is very unusual and very unfair.'

Thanks to their simultaneous creation, production began on *Barton Fink* very soon after *Miller's Crossing* wrapped, but not so quickly that Joel and Ethan could keep hold of Barry Sonnenfeld as their cinematographer. He departed camp Coen to pursue his own career as a director. To replace him, the brothers settled on British director of photography Roger Deakins, whose work they'd admired on *Sid and Nancy* (1986) and *Stormy Monday* (1988). On the strength of the script, Deakins ignored his agent's advice to turn down their offer, joined them in Los Angeles and synced with Joel and Ethan immediately; he's since shot the majority of their films. But, right from the beginning of their fruitful working relationship, the Coens liked to keep Deakins on his toes.

'There were some very particular shots [in *Barton Fink*] that were difficult,' he recalled in 2015. 'One was the camera starting underneath the bed, tracking across the room, into the bathroom and down the plughole. You read it on the page and you go, "Oh shit, how are we going to do that?" I figured out how to recalibrate a lens to focus up a plughole; we figured out how to get focus with a string and knots in it. . .All this sort of stuff.'

To execute the burning hallway sequence, production designer Dennis Gassner rigged the set with gas piping, with each flame jet activated by a crew member on a catwalk as Goodman ran past it. This use of practical flame required Deakins, his dolly grip and the actors to be coated in a flame-retardant gel. It was a complicated, challenging setup.

Barton Fink was a less expensive movie than *Miller's Crossing*, with a budget of only $9 million compared to $14 million. While neither were studio films, both received significant funding and distribution from 20th Century Fox (in the US only for *Fink*), but neither would make a profit.

However, *Barton Fink* was still a significant achievement for the Coens. Having been their first film selected for competition at the prestigious Cannes Film Festival in 1991, it won the Palme d'Or (beating out Krzysztof Kieslowski's *The Double Life of Véronique* and Spike Lee's *Jungle Fever*, among others), with Joel also accepting an award for Best Director and Turturro winning Best Actor. Slightly awkwardly, the president of the jury that year was

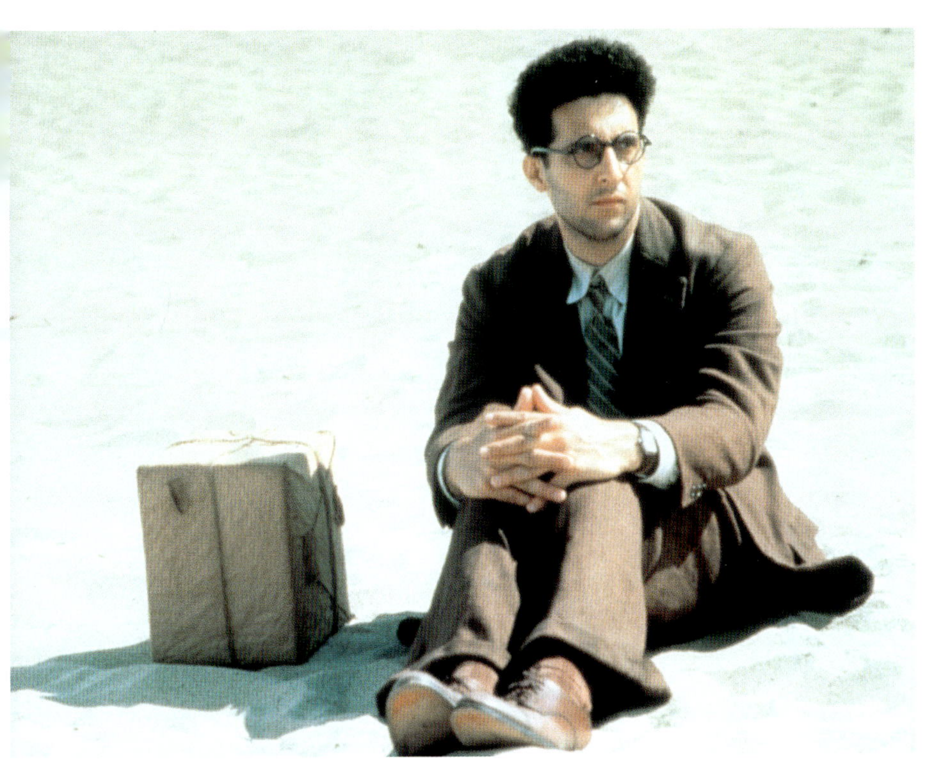

ABOVE: What's in the box? Thanks to the film's appealingly oblique ending, we never find out, though most have assumed it contained the unfortunate Audrey's head.

Polanski, who'd been such an influence on the film. Joel confessed during the festival that he and Ethan had avoided the French Polish director, for fear of giving the impression that 'we kissed his ass'.

Still, the brothers received further validation when, in 1992, the film garnered three Oscar nominations: for Lerner as Best Supporting Actor, for Gassner and set decorator Nancy Haigh's art direction, and for Richard Hornung's costume design. The Academy do love a movie set in Hollywood, even one so dark and twisted as *Barton Fink*. The establishment, it seemed, had finally accepted the Coen brothers. Surely now, the only way was up.

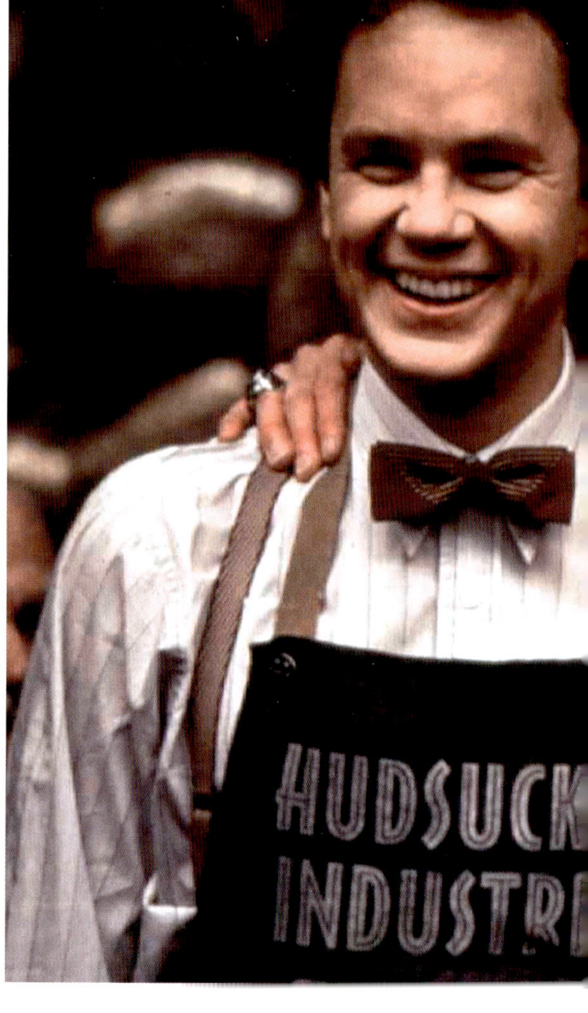

THE HUDSUCKER PROXY
1994

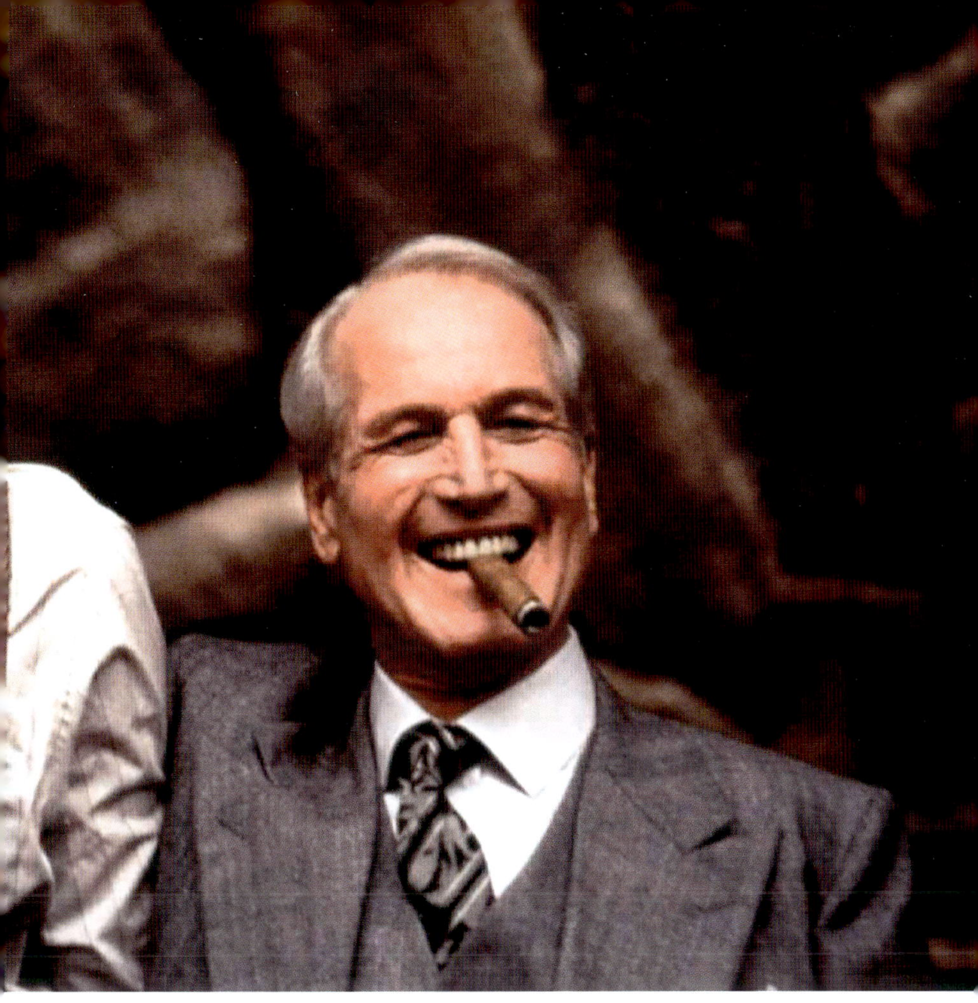

When the Coen brothers started production on *The Hudsucker Proxy*, Circle Films' Jim Jacks remarked that 'Joel always thought they could do a commercial movie pretty much whenever they wanted to, so it'll be interesting to see if there's something in their personality-slash-style that prevents their movies from being all-out commercial movies.'

If you look at the stats, *The Hudsucker Proxy* was very much a commercial movie. The brothers had completed their four-picture

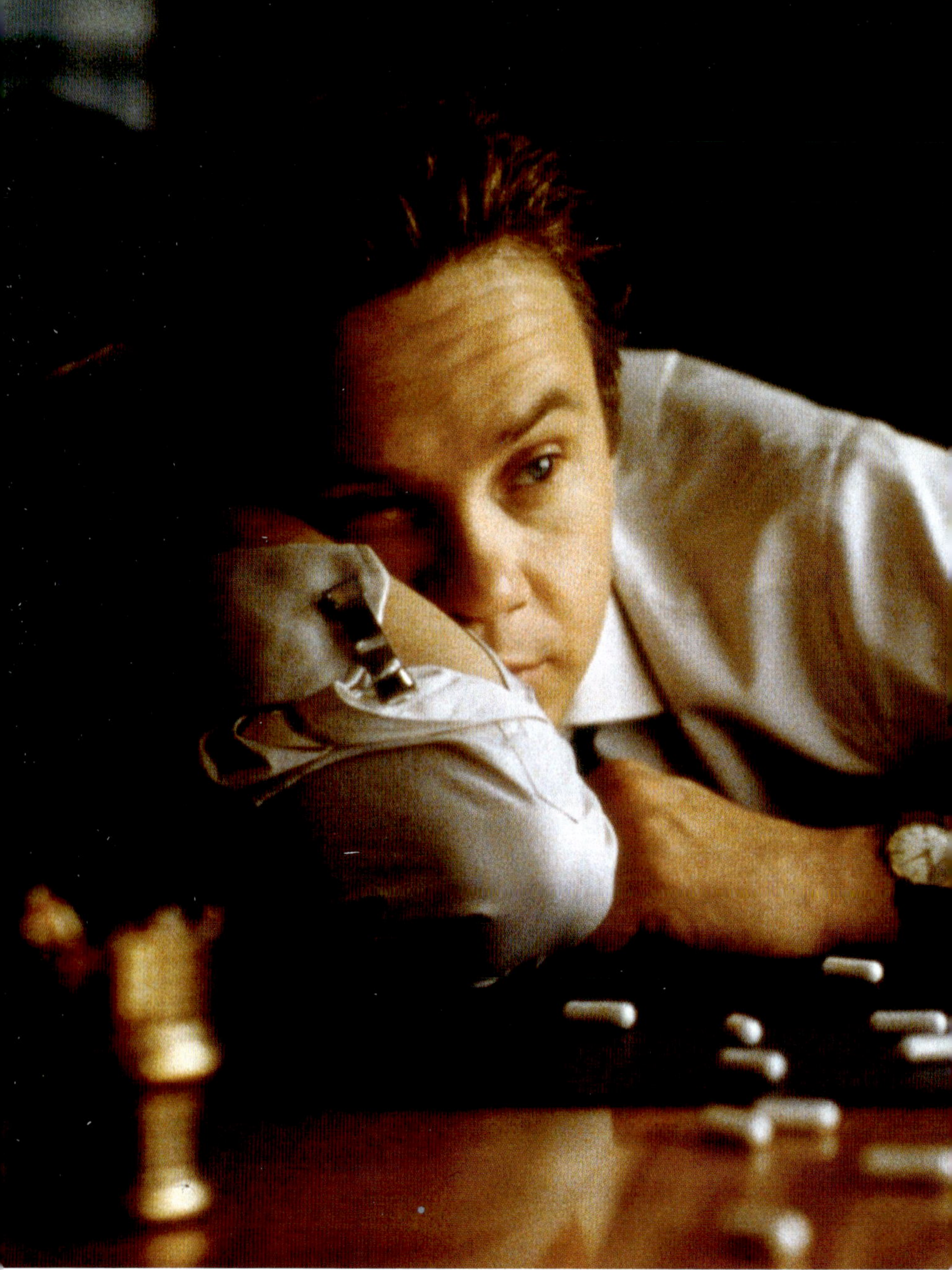

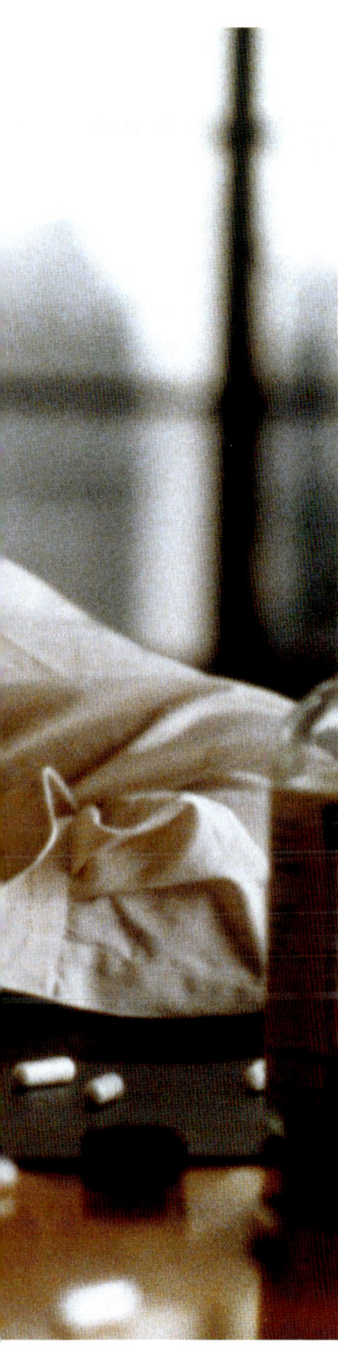

deal with Circle and were now in business with Warner Bros – who remarkably allowed them to retain final cut – with backing from British production company Working Title. *Hudsucker's* $25 million budget far outweighed anything the Coens had done before; it was more than double that of their previous biggest film, *Miller's Crossing*. The production sprawled across eight sound stages at Carolco Studios in Wilmington, North Carolina, with a full-on visual effects department headed by Michael J McAlister, who'd worked on *Willow* (1988) and the most recent Indiana Jones movie, *The Last Crusade* (1989). And it required a collaboration with possibly the most unlikely producing partner anyone could have imagined at the time: Joel Silver, the slick operator behind some of Hollywood's biggest wham-bam action movies, including *Lethal Weapon* (1987), *Predator* (1987) and *Die Hard* (1988).

Silver had been suggested to Joel and Ethan by their agent Jim Berkus. He claimed to be a long-time fan, and was sufficiently impressed with the script to collaborate with them. 'I felt it was the most accessible of any of the pictures

LEFT: Life is tough at the top – especially when you're required to fail, Norville discovers.

they had done,' he said. 'I really thought it potentially could be a very big hit movie. And I happen to like very big hit movies.' The Coens wondered if there would be a catch. But no catch materialized. It seemed they had ascended to a whole new level.

Joel and Ethan denied that *The Hudsucker Proxy* was a conscious attempt to go mainstream. They pointed out they'd been hankering to make the film for almost a decade, but had to wait until they found the requisite funding. After the critical success and industry attention they'd attracted from *Barton Fink*, and with the timely patronage of Silver, they were just finally in that position.

Indeed, the film's concept isn't exactly mainstream. It's late 1958 and goofy Norville Barnes (Tim Robbins) suddenly finds himself running a Manhattan-based company as part of a nefarious plan by its board, headed by the cigar-chewing Sidney Mussburger (Paul Newman, cast brilliantly against type), to manipulate the stock. It was inspired by Preston Sturges, the filmmaker who in the Thirties had invested the screwball comedy genre with a never-before-seen naturalism and sophistication. He had long been a favourite of the Coens, and his influence can also be felt on *Raising Arizona*, *Barton Fink* and, later, in *O Brother, Where Art Thou?* whose very title was lifted from Sturges' *Sullivan's Travels* (1941). The setting and tone, meanwhile, owed more to Frank Capra, including *Mr Deeds Goes to Town* (1936), *Meet John Doe* (1941) and, with its fantastical elements (including an angel played by Charles Durning), *It's a Wonderful Life* (1946). Plus its fast-talking dialogue channels Howard Hawks' *His Girl Friday* (1940), as underlined by Jennifer Jason Leigh's cracking

OPPOSITE: Jennifer Jason Leigh took on a lighter role than usual as the Rosalind Russell-like Amy Archer.

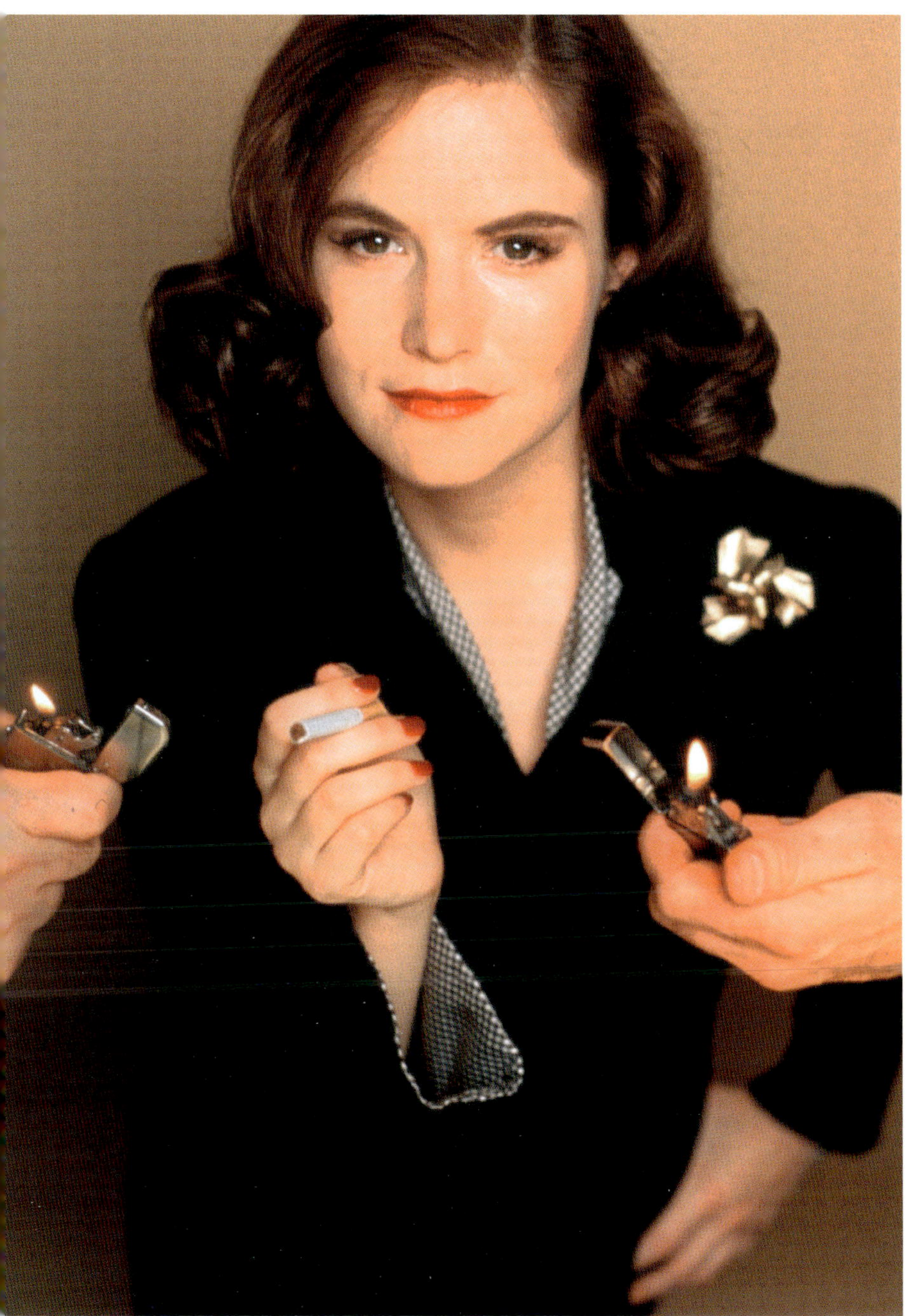

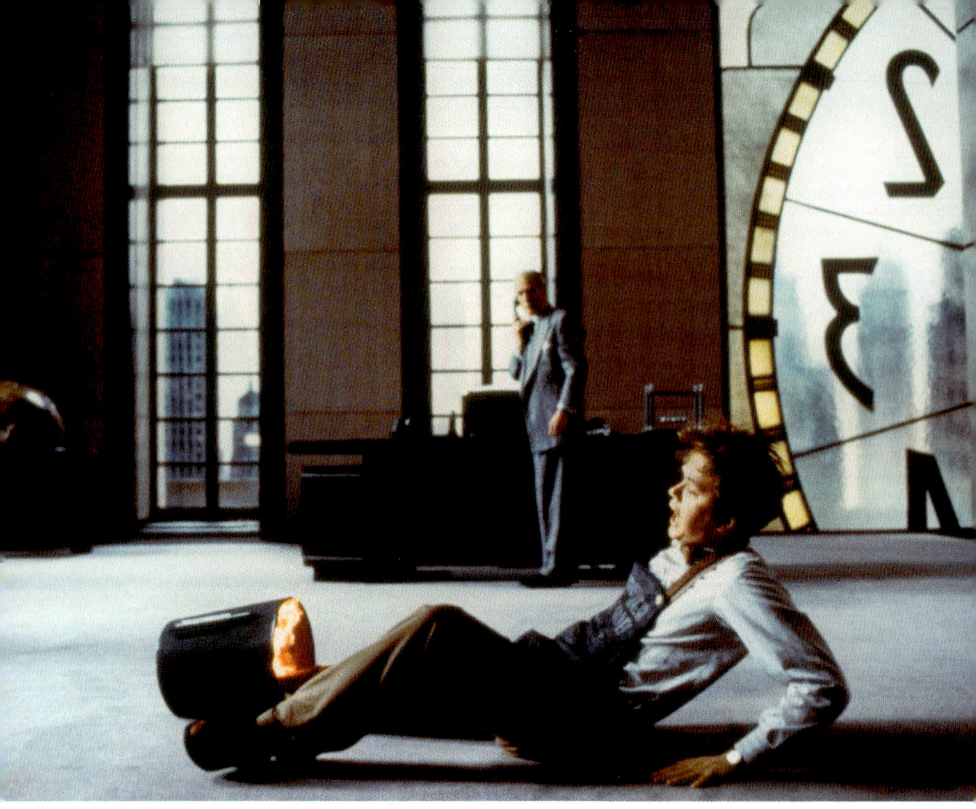

ABOVE: Robbins pulls off some great slapstick amid the vast grandeur of Mussburger's office.

Rosalind Russell impression as news reporter-turned-love interest Amy Archer. All these reference points belonged to an era so long-since departed that they'd be beyond the frame of reference of most mainstream audience members.

Not that Joel and Ethan saw this as a problem. After the film's US release, they noted this criticism. It was 'definitely not the case' that people who hadn't seen *Meet John Doe* et al wouldn't 'get' the film, said Ethan. 'It does sort of use the conventions of those movies, but it's not like anything could possibly be over anyone's head. When you get down to it, it's a very simple story with a rather banal moral to it. In that respect, it's sort of anally constructed, because it's structured around principles of design.'

Whether or not you connect with *The Hudsucker Proxy*'s knowing pre-war-era references, there's no denying the scale and elegance of its design, which contrasts the sharp straight lines of its skyscraper architecture with circular images – Norville's invention ('Y'know, for kids!'), the clock, the angel's halo – which are echoed by the story's circular structure. Production designer Dennis Gassner makes the Hudsucker building a towering Art Deco monolith, with elements drawn from Nazi architect Albert Speer and Terry Gilliam's Forties-influenced dystopian satire *Brazil* (1985). Mussburger's office is a stand-out example of the film's bold style: a long, spartan space set behind the building's huge clock, whose second hand forms a long dark shadow that stretches down the wall every time it passes.

The film also features a virtuoso montage, shot by Sam Raimi, who acted as second-unit director as well as co-writer. This traces the manufacture, failure and eventual success of Norville's apparently inane creation, initially dubbed the 'extruded plastic dingus', but later given the more familiar name 'Hula Hoop'. Beautifully scored by Carter Burwell, who makes great use of Aram Khachaturian's invigorating 'Sabre Dance', it follows a single red hoop which rolls down a street and 'finds' a young boy with a wonderfully serious face. He picks it up and proves to be an instant Hula Hoop savant, inspiring a crowd of gawping pre-teens to run off and buy their own dinguses.

Unfortunately, this ingenious segment, along with Gassner's majestic design and Roger Deakins' gleaming cinematography, was not as widely appreciated as it should have been. When *The Hudsucker Proxy* was released, it spectacularly flopped, grossing less than $3 million in the United States, with its eventual worldwide take not even covering half of its budget.

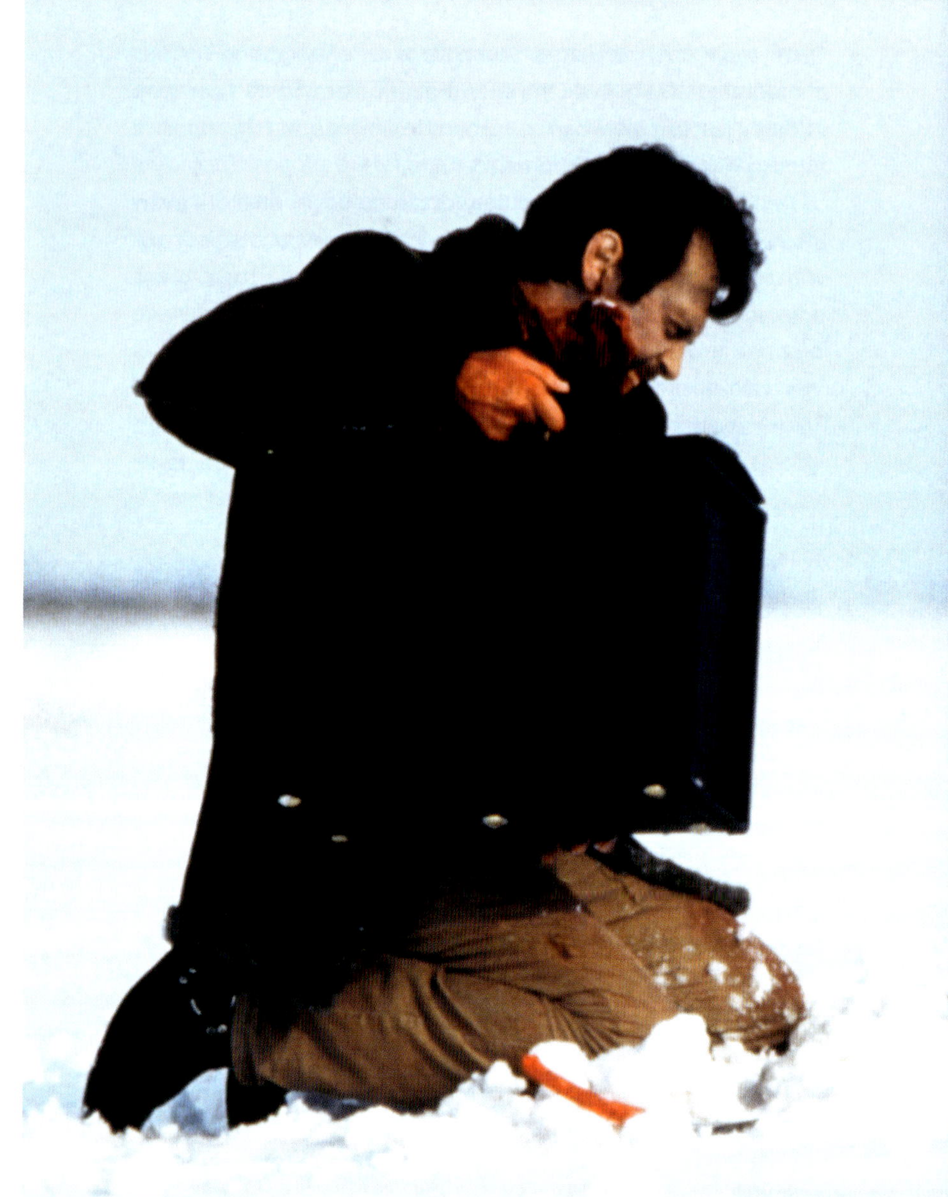

'Kinda funny lookin'

THE FEELGOOD PHASE

RIGHT: The Coen brothers
created their first true,
unalloyed hero in heavily
pregnant police officer
Marge Gunderson – a
role that won Frances
McDormand her first Oscar.

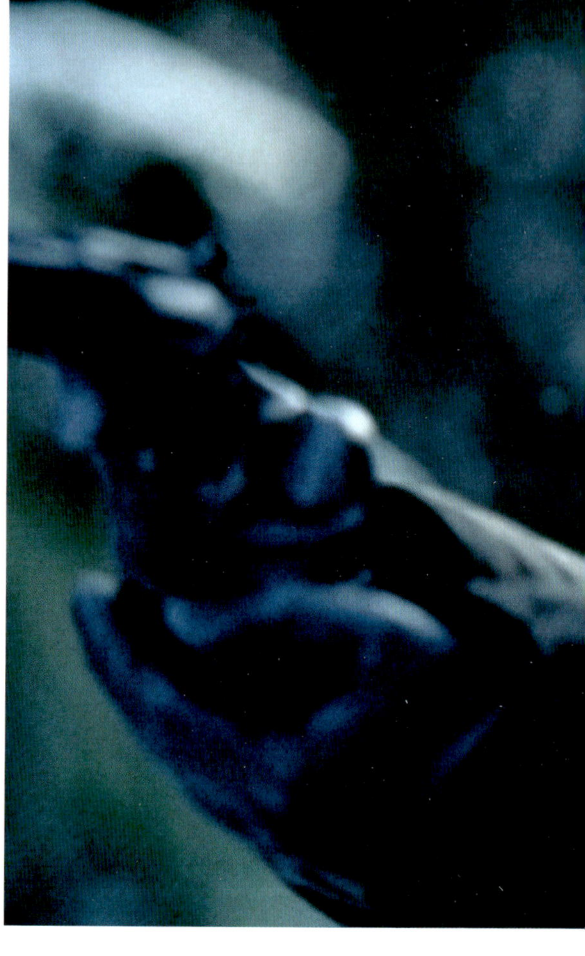

FARGO
1996

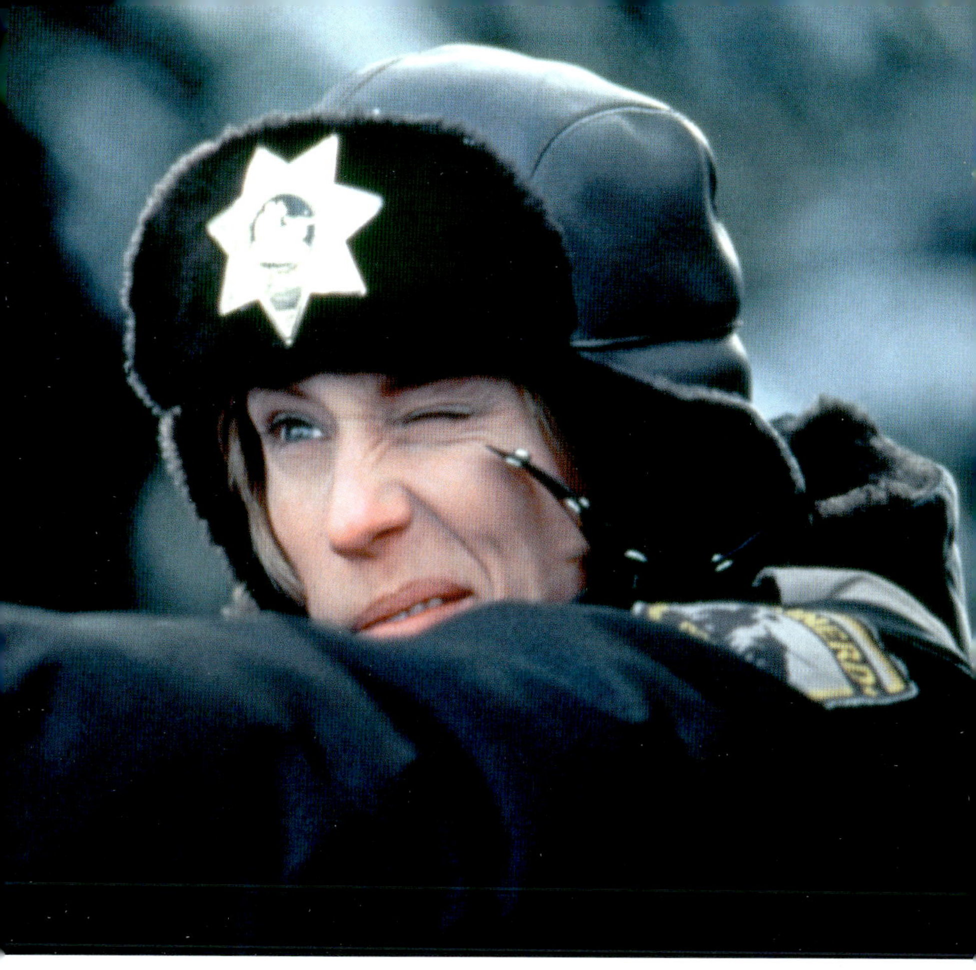

It is tempting to see *Fargo* as the Coens trying to reset the scales after the disastrous excess and VFX-driven zaniness of *The Hudsucker Proxy*. To strip everything down to low-budget basics and hark back to their *Blood Simple* roots with a relatively straightforward thriller. And with Quentin Tarantino sparking a fresh fad for quirky, violent crime flicks in the Nineties, it would have been the smart move commercially, too; better than all this Sturges/Capra-nostalgia daffiness. But Joel and Ethan were never ones for the easy narrative.

They had wanted to follow up *Hudsucker* with *The Big Lebowski,* but lead actors Jeff Bridges and John Goodman were tied up with other commitments. Also, *Fargo* was a script they'd been working on since before the *Hudsucker* shoot, so it could not have been conceived as a reaction to that film's reception.

That said, Joel did see *Fargo* as 'a new start from a stylistic point of view,' driven by a desire to 'make something radically different from our previous movies.' He and Ethan wanted to step away from the 'self-consciously artificial' style they were known for, and tell this story in a pared-down manner, with far less camera movement and narrative trickery. There would be no flashbacks, flashy montages or dream sequences. The intention was to present the film's events in 'a dry manner', with the camera telling the story as 'an observer'. This was especially important and appropriate, the brothers said, seeing as *Fargo* was based on true events. . .

Or was it? The film is prefaced with the following statement: 'This is a true story. The events depicted in this film took place in Minnesota in 1987. At the request of the survivors, the names have been changed. Out of respect for the dead, the rest has been told exactly as it occurred.'

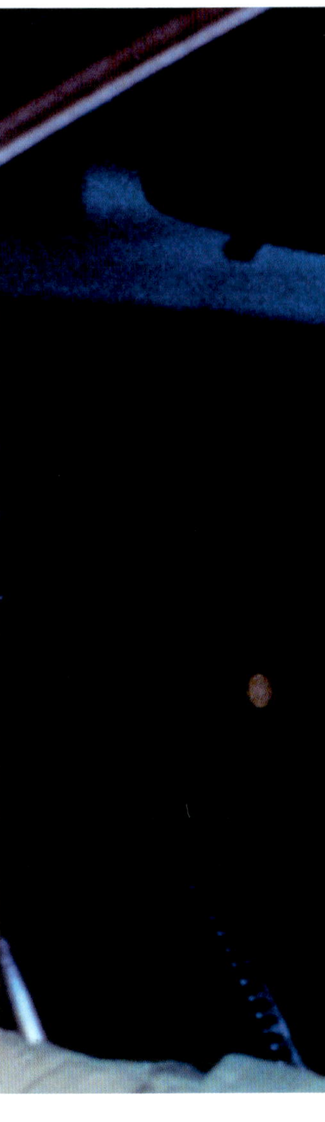

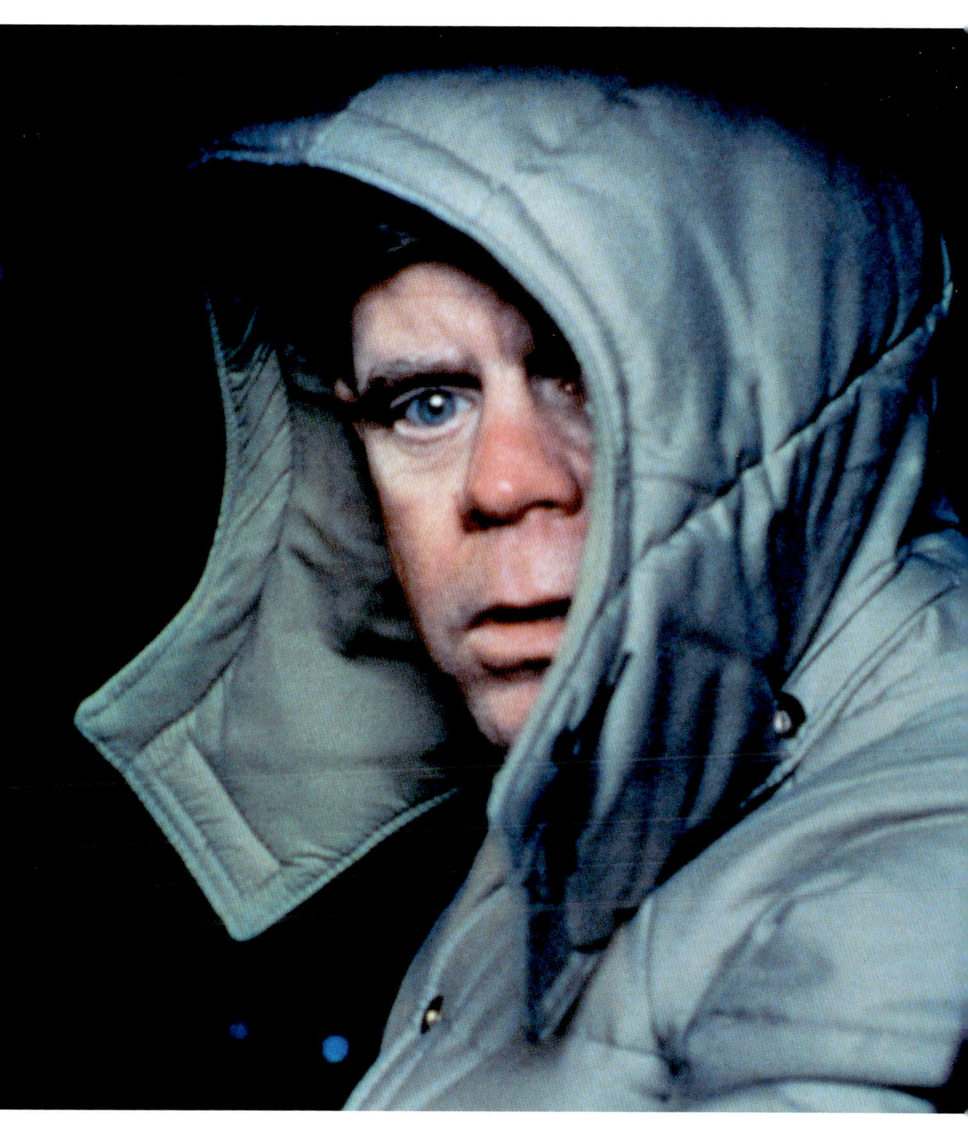

ABOVE: William H Macy as Jerry Lundegaard, whose badly conceived kidnap plot sparks a snowy murder spree.

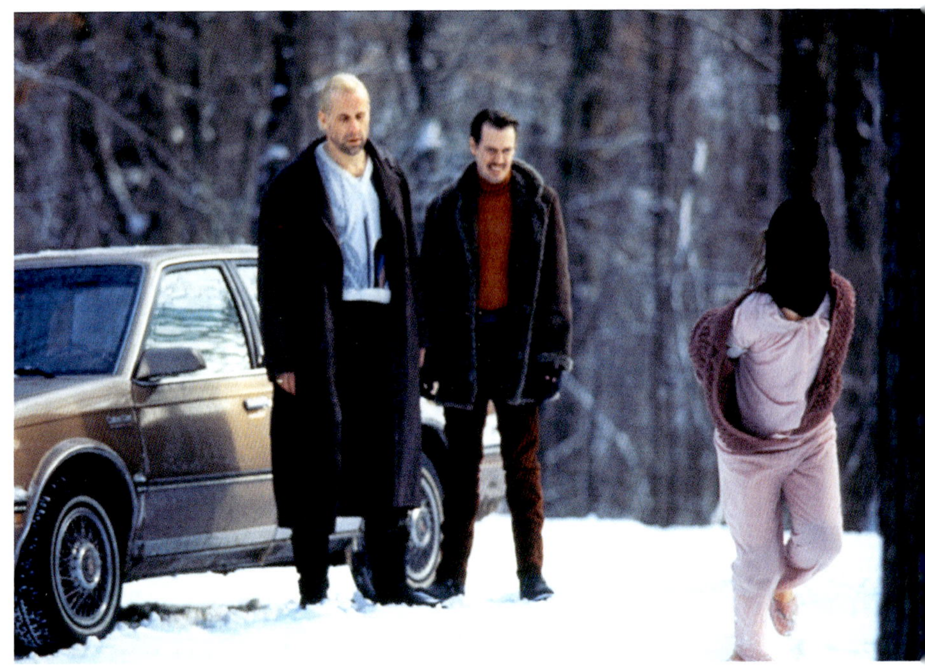

ABOVE: Kidnap victim Jean Lundegaard (Kristin Rudrüd) spends most of the movie with a bag over her head (and played by Rudrüd's double, Kelly Nathe).

Those events involve a Minneapolis car salesman named Jerry Lundegaard (William H Macy) arranging for his wife to be kidnapped by a pair of crooks (Steve Buscemi and Peter Stormare). His intention is to keep most of the money – paid out by his hard-ass father-in-law (Harve Presnell) – to back a business venture. However, things turn messy and the bodies start piling up, sparking a homicide investigation headed by pregnant Brainerd police chief Marge Gunderson (Frances McDormand). Eventually, Marge tracks down the felons to find one of them feeding the other's body into a woodchipper, and brings him to justice. The money given to pay the ransom is never found.

While the Coens were promoting the film, talk show host Charlie Rose asked them to confirm if the story was indeed based on real events. Joel replied, 'Yeah the story is. The characters…You know, we weren't interested in making a documentary, and the characters are really inventions, based on the sort of outline of events.' Yet during the shoot, they told a different story. Three weeks into production, Macy took the Coens aside and asked them for some details about this true case that inspired the script. 'It's not based on any story,' they told him. 'We just made it up.'

'You can't do that!' he protested.

'Why not?' was their answer.

'It was so calculated,' said McDormand. 'It was calculated to say, "Okay, if an audience thinks this is true, will they go with it longer? Will they make more leaps of faith?"'

Usually, the Coens employ devices that create a distance between audience and characters, establishing a well-defined frame through which they view the events on screen, such as the omniscient narrators of *The Hudsucker Proxy*, or the literal storybook format of *The Ballad of Buster Scruggs*, or simply the use of a stylized period setting. Here, between the observational camera style and the sneaky, cheeky invitation to treat everything as a depiction of true events, they are doing the opposite: inviting the audience to come in closer to what's happening, and 'buy in' to it to a degree that surpasses anything they'd done before.

This might also explain why the brothers elected to set *Fargo* on their home turf. (Most of the events take place in and around Brainerd, Minnesota.) 'We thought it was an interesting opportunity to make a movie about the Upper Midwest,' said Joel. 'Going back there again, that was a little bit odd.' It gave them the chance to portray on screen a swathe of the United States that was rarely seen in cinema, giving it an almost exotic feel, even for North

Americans – the landscape of slate skies and flat snowscapes that the siblings had been so keen to flee in their youth. 'Everything is white, just an empty field of vision,' said Joel.

However, the Minnesotan weather did not comply. 'We just happened to be shooting in Minnesota in the second warmest year in the last hundred years, and probably the driest,' said Ethan. So they had to use fake snow for some scenes, and truck in real snow from further north for others, while the scene where Buscemi buries the ransom (idiotically using an ice scraper as a marker) was relocated entirely to North Dakota where there was at least *some* snow for him to dig into.

There was another kind of flatness that attracted the Coens to the region, too: 'That flat, Midwestern effect,' as Ethan put it, to the way Minnesotans talk. The Scandinavian-rooted sing-songy accent of the region becomes a kind of unexpected music to the audience's ears, with its 'Yahs' and its 'You bet'chas', and all that intense politeness that exudes from the locals in their every interaction. 'Given Joel and Ethan's temperament and eccentricities, it must have seemed like a looming threat to them as children in Minneapolis – that feeling of people being nice to them,' joked McDormand. In the film it certainly creates an interesting tension between the friendly manner of many of the characters and the horrific violence that punctuates the narrative.

Though the film is truly an ensemble piece, with McDormand, Macy and the Buscemi–Stormare double act (blabbermouth and the 'mute') sharing screen time, it was McDormand's Marge Gunderson who won the greatest share of audience affection – despite not appearing until 34 minutes into the movie.

In McDormand's capable hands, Marge is arguably the warmest, most likeable character in the Coens' sprawling dramatis personae: friendly, resourceful and relatable. Her scenes with her husband Norm (John Carroll Lynch) provided what McDormand saw as a 'safe haven' for the audience – 'and often Joel and Ethan don't give audiences that for their movies'. Marge proved so popular, there was even an attempt to give her further adventures in a *Fargo* TV show (not to be confused with Noah Hawley's), but it never progressed beyond the pilot.

Yet despite Marge's appealing warmth and perkiness, and the film's success at the box office (taking over $60 million worldwide), the Coens' treatment of their characters continued to draw the criticism of condescension. After all, schmucky Jerry Lundegaard has no redeeming qualities and his wife is treated appallingly. The excitement of Minnesotans at a movie finally being made in their state was tempered somewhat by the film's violence, and the suspicion that the Coens might be laughing at them.

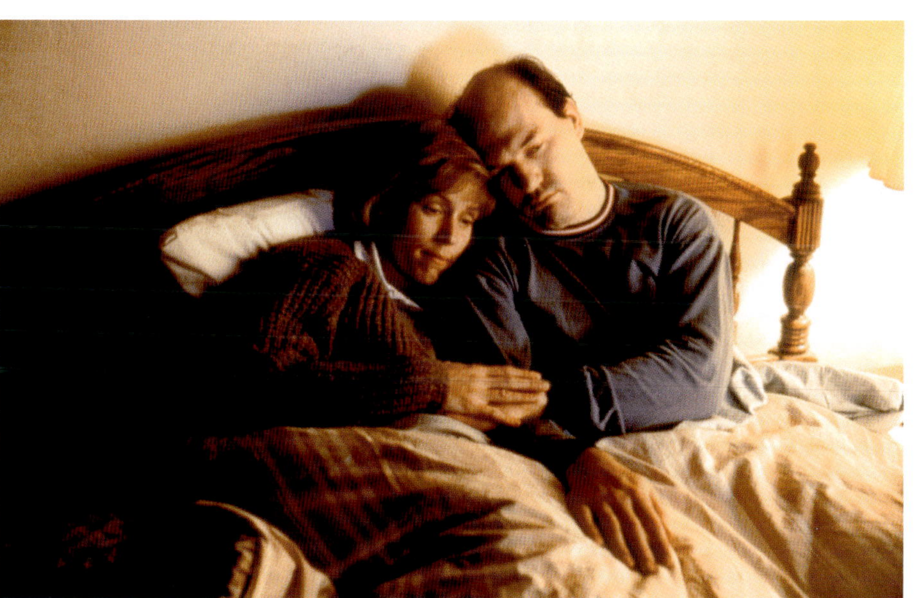

ABOVE: Marge Gunderson's scenes with her husband Norm (John Carroll Lynch) are unfiltered, unpretentious domestic bliss.

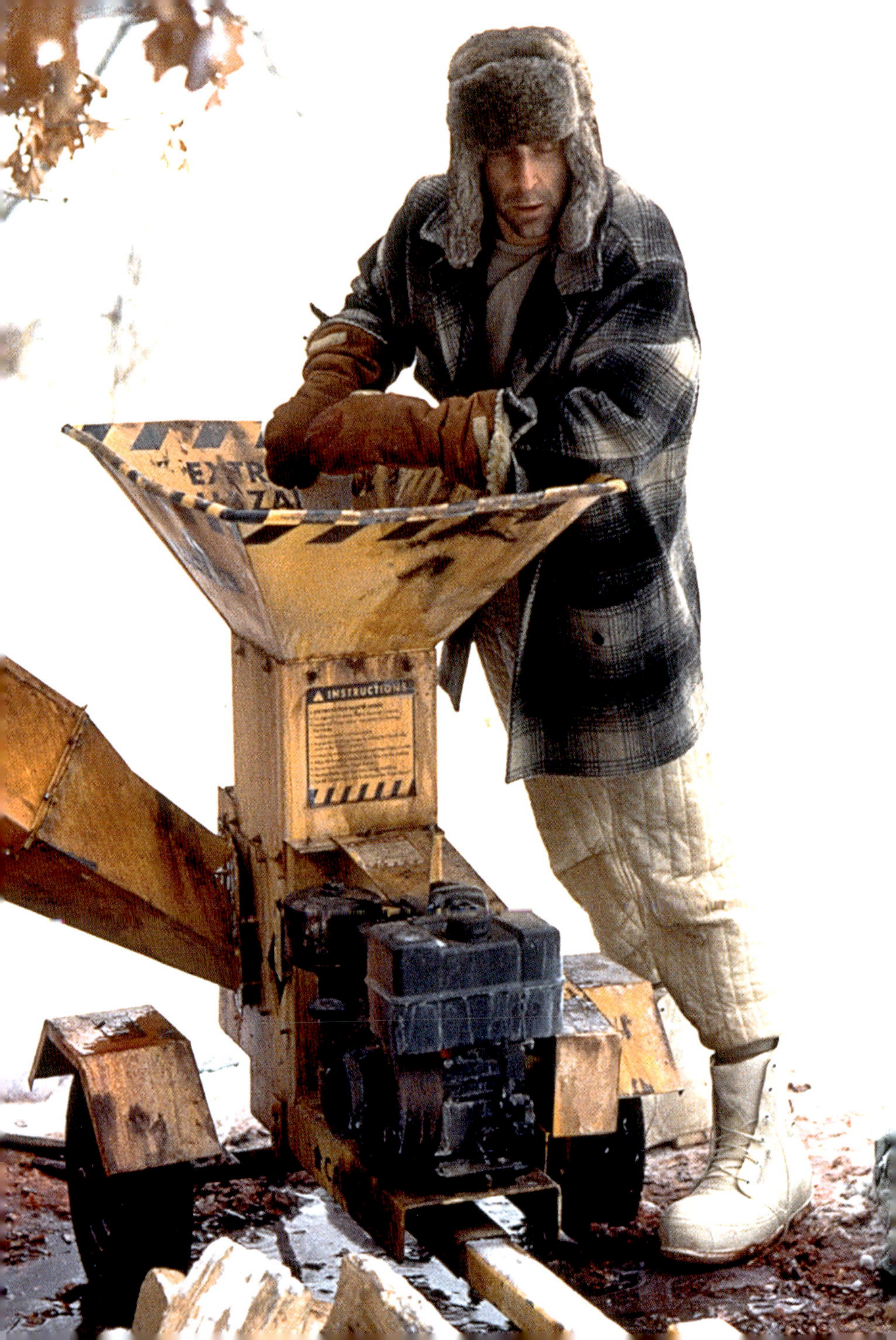
INSTRUCTIONS

'We hear that a lot – that we're poking fun at people in the Midwest or in Texas or in the Southwest or wherever the hell it is,' said Joel. 'It's a fundamental misperception.' Ethan put it down to their blend of comedy and violence (though they claim not to have considered *Fargo* a comedy when writing it). 'A lot of people feel uncomfortable with laughing at horrible situations. They think if you're laughing at a character, somehow you're condescending to them. We don't give cues about how you're supposed to react. That's just boring Hollywood filmmaking.'

However, Hollywood itself embraced *Fargo*. After just over a decade of making movies their own way, with scant interference and only modest support from studios, the Coens were finally rewarded for their efforts, winning Best Original Screenplay for *Fargo* at the 1997 Academy Awards, with McDormand winning best actress. (Macy received a nomination for Best Supporting Actor, alongside nominations for editing, cinematography, directing and Best Picture – all won by Anthony Minghella's *The English Patient*.) McDormand made sure to highlight *Fargo*'s independent spirit in her acceptance speech, thanking production companies Working Title and Polygram 'for allowing directors to make autonomous casting decisions based on qualifications and not just market value.'

Joel and Ethan were as bemused by *Fargo*'s success as they were by the failure of *The Hudsucker Proxy*. 'Most people don't like *Hudsucker*, and I don't know the reason,' said Joel. 'It's as much of a mystery to me that people went to see *Fargo*, which was something we did thinking, "Ah, y'know, about three people will end up seeing it, but it'll be fun for us."' But, as their next film would confirm, they were now on an audience-pleasing roll.

OPPOSITE: Kidnapper Gaear Grimsrud (Peter Stormare) finds a novel way to dispose of the body of his partner Carl Showalter (Steve Buscemi).

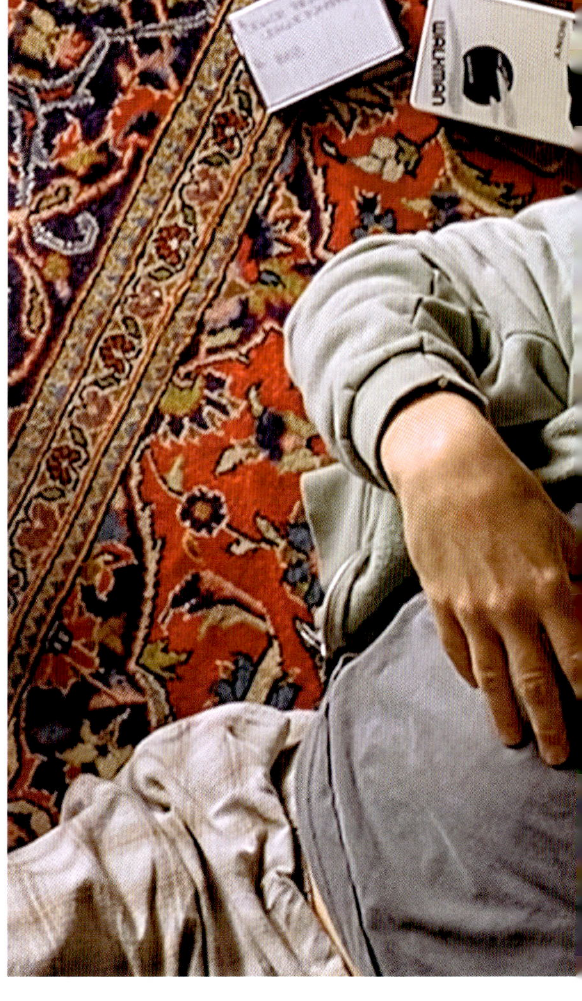

THE BIG LEBOWSKI
1998

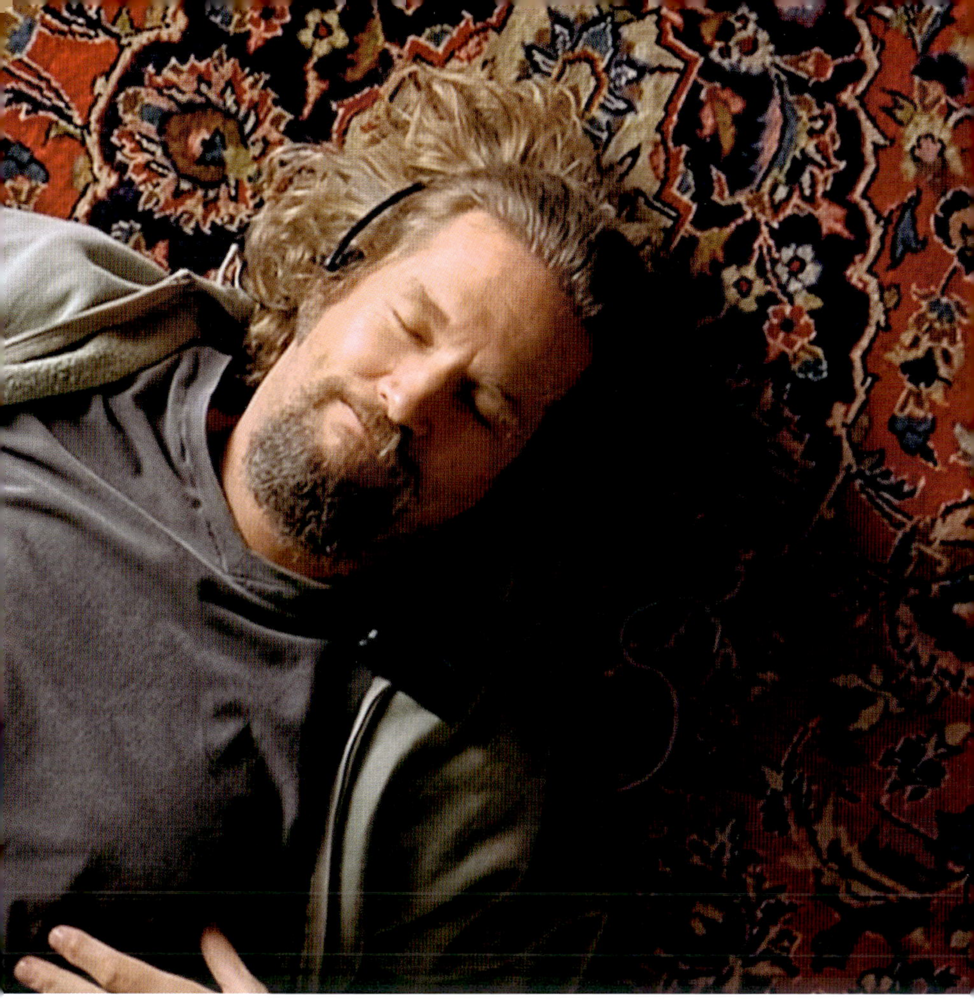

If the Coens were influenced by the way audiences received their movies, their *Fargo* follow-up would have been styled in a similarly naturalistic and observational fashion. But *The Big Lebowski* more closely resembles *The Hudsucker Proxy*, with its eccentric characters, unconventional narration and dream sequences. And where the events in *Fargo* took place on their doorstep, *The Big Lebowski* involved a journey to a place where the Coens felt very far from home.

'We're still tourists in LA,' said Joel. 'Happily, it is possible to make movies and not live there.' Though *Barton Fink* was set in Hollywood, it is of a different, more distant era. This would be the brothers' first portrayal of modern Los Angeles, even though they rewind a little to 1991, in the midst of the First Gulf War, and underline their outsider perspective by introducing the story through an unnamed folksy Western narrator, played by Sam Elliott, himself just a tourist.

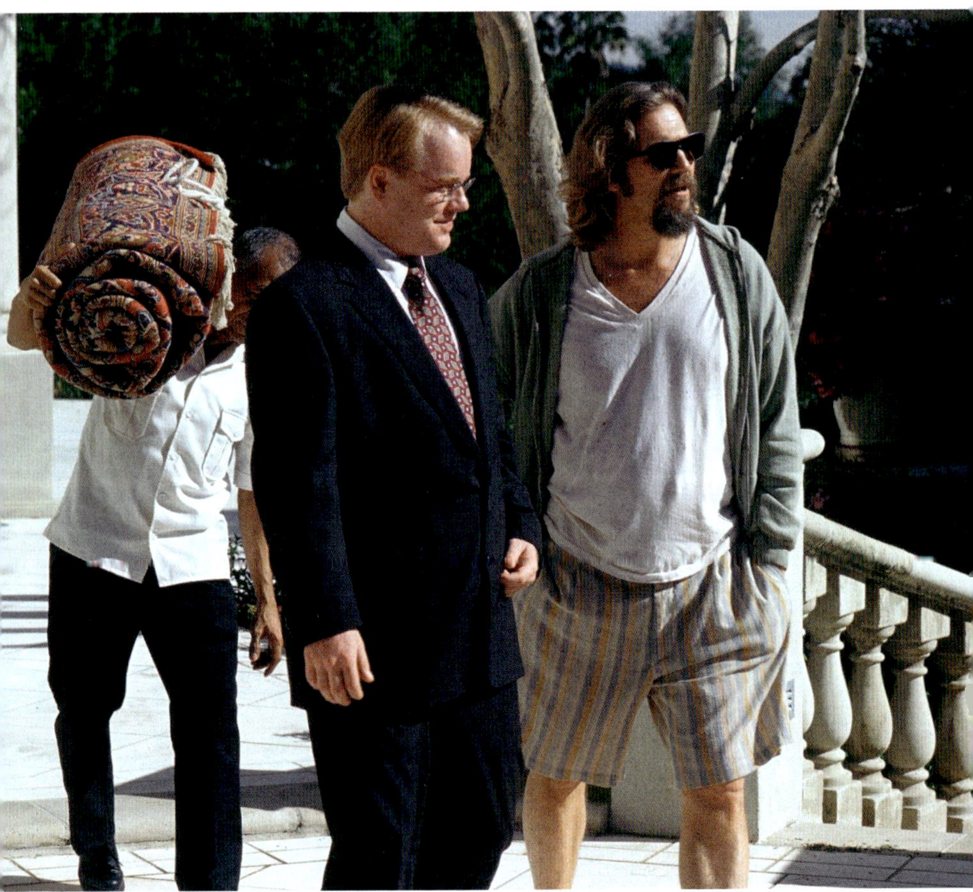

The location primarily arose out of a desire to construct a mystery in the style of Raymond Chandler's detective novels, and the Coens were particularly inspired by Robert Altman's loose Seventies-set take on *The Long Goodbye*, in which Elliot Gould plays a schlubby version of detective Philip Marlowe. They loved how Chandler's stories move episodically through LA, 'as well as having a hopelessly complex plot that's ultimately unimportant.'

Coens on script: *The Naked Man* (1998)

The same year The Dude ambled into our lives, *The Naked Man* also arrived. This odd little movie was co-written by Ethan Coen with the brothers' long-time storyboard artist J Todd Anderson, making his directorial debut.

It is the closest either of the Coen brothers has come to a superhero movie, concerning a chiropractor played by Michael Rapaport, who moonlights as a wrestler in a unitard that depicts muscle and bone, like an anatomical drawing. When his parents are killed by a drug dealer with spina bifida (Michael Jeter, sporting crutches that double as machine-guns) and an Elvis-impersonating henchman (*Fargo*'s John Carroll Lynch), he uses his in-the-ring persona to become a vigilante and 'fight against malefaction'.

Awkward and uneven, *The Naked Man* failed to reach cinemas, and all but vanished as a straight-to-video curio. Ethan understood why. 'It's nobody's idea of a big audience mainstream movie,' he said. 'I thought it was very funny.' Still, there is something cute about one of the creators of *Barton Fink* writing his own wrestling B-pic, and failing.

OPPOSITE: The Dude, with his wealthy namesake's personal assistant Brandt, played by Philip Seymour Hoffman.

They were also led to the City of Angels by the characters they'd constructed around the time they made *Barton Fink*, most of whom were based on real people; there is a pleasing irony in *The Big Lebowski* being more rooted in reality than *Fargo*. Their pot-smoking protagonist, Jeffrey 'The Dude' Lebowski (Jeff Bridges), was partly inspired by an LA-based producer named Jeff Dowd, who drank White Russian cocktails, had been part of the Seattle Seven anti-Vietnam War group in the Sixties, and liked to be called 'The Dude' (a play on his surname).

His short-tempered buddy Walter Sobchak (John Goodman) was a hybrid of an old friend of the brothers' named Peter Exline, a veteran defined by his experience in Vietnam, and the gun-loving filmmaker John Milius, who they met during the shoot for *Barton*

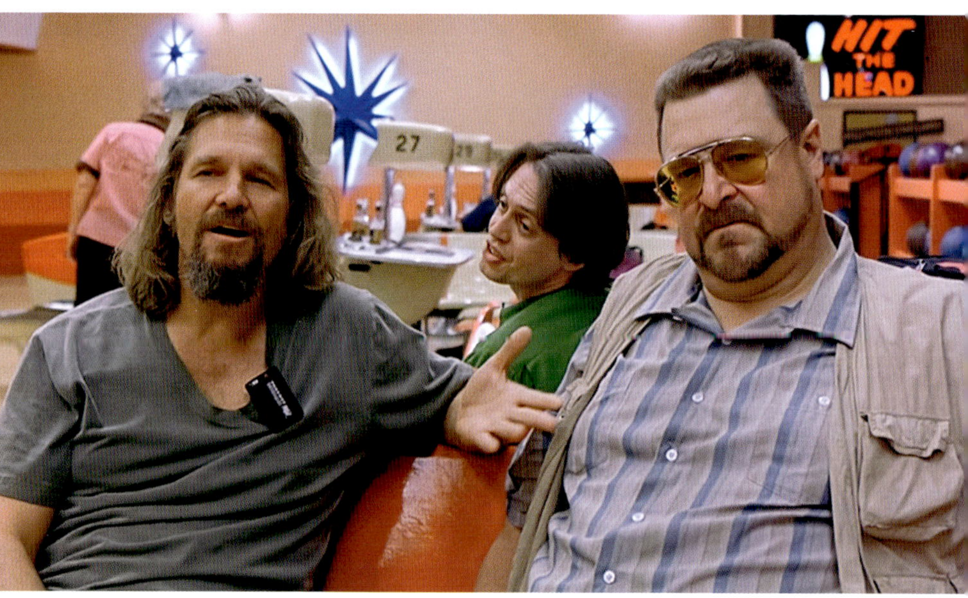

ABOVE: Odd couple The Dude and Walter with their sadly doomed bowling buddy Donny (Steve Buscemi).

Fink. Walter's fervent commitment to Orthodox Judaism, meanwhile, was inspired by the Coens' own grandfather. 'He didn't drive his car on the Sabbath,' recalled Joel. 'I remember, as a child, that I found it weird he didn't want to light the cooker. That didn't seem such a big job to me!'

Exline was obsessed with playing softball, but the brothers substituted that sport with ten-pin bowling, which they felt provided a more novel backdrop, holding more visual potential: 'The architecture, the machines, it's all sort of retro to the Fifties and Sixties,' said Ethan. 'You see it all over LA.' The film's bright, crisp look and saturated colours were all informed by bowling alley chic.

The Dude and Walter embark on a quest to replace The Dude's rug (which 'really tied the room together'), after it is soiled by a thug who confuses him with another Jeffrey Lebowski (David Huddleston), who apparently owes porn-magnate Jackie Treehorn (Ben Gazzara) money. This then drags them into a kidnapping case, after the other Lebowski's wife, Bunny (Tara Reid), is apparently abducted by a trio of German nihilists (one of whom is played by *Fargo*'s Stormare). Along the way, The Dude also encounters Lebowski's no-nonsense daughter, Maude (Julianne Moore), who was modelled on experimental artists Carolee Schneemann and Yoko Ono. 'All the characters are pretty much emblematic of Los Angeles,' said Ethan. 'They're all types who seem like people you would meet there.'

As the Coens noted, the film's plot is designed to be both convoluted and irrelevant. The joy of *The Big Lebowski* is character-driven, both in watching this slobby, ageing pothead try to fill the role of a private eye, and in its colourful cast of supporting characters, from creepy, purple-clad bowling rival Jesus Quintana (John Turturro), to the shrill giggling video artist Knox Harrington (David Thewlis), to the ill-fated Donny

(Steve Buscemi) who can't say anything without Walter telling him to 'shut the fuck up'.

But the movie's heart is Bridges, who has rarely been better, calling on his own youthful experiences to flesh out The Dude, and requiring very little direction from the Coens. You never sense him reaching for laughs, he just attracts them naturally via a kind of comedy osmosis, immersing himself completely in Dudeness. Note the scene where he first meets Huddleston's Lebowski and is subjected to a loud blast of derision for being a 'bum'. During the rant, he quietly pulls out his sunglasses and puts them on, as if to dim the harsh glare of Lebowski's negative vibes.

The Big Lebowski also signalled the Coens' needle-drop savviness, with their best use of songs since 'Danny Boy' in *Miller's Crossing*. While there's a propulsive thrill to the Gipsy Kings' cover of 'Hotel California' introducing Jesus, the highlight has to be the Busby Berkeley-inspired dream sequence involving Saddam Hussein, Maude as a Valkyrie and The Dude becoming a human bowling ball – all set to Kenny Rogers' magnificently catchy 'Just Dropped In (To See What Condition My Condition Was In)'.

The music was as character-driven as the film itself, with the brothers seeking a 'signature song' for each character. This is why, Ethan said, there is nothing contemporary on the soundtrack. 'They're all from previous eras, consistent with the characters, who had attitudes shaped by the Sixties, Seventies or earlier.'

While certain tunes, like 'Just Dropped In', were baked into the script, the Coens also sought advice. This was their first collaboration with T Bone Burnett, a renowned and prolific producer and musician who'd started out playing guitar for Bob Dylan, and received a credit on *Lebowski* as 'musical archivist'. 'He has such a wide and deep knowledge of music,' said Joel. 'He brought in a lot of the less obvious stuff, like Yma Sumac, Meredith Monk and this track from an Italian soft-core porn music album.'

The Big Lebowski went on to become the Coens' cultiest of cult hits. It didn't perform especially well at the box office, but found a longer life via home entertainment and word of mouth, as more and more viewers got into its idiosyncratic groove, and fell for its 'congress of misfits', as Ethan described its characters. It helped that it was one of the Coens' most quotable films. Goodman – who said he enjoyed shooting this movie more than any other – receives the lion's share of great lines, both profane ('This is what happens when you fuck a stranger in the ass!') and eloquently odd ('I mean, say what you like about the tenets of National Socialism, Dude, at least it's an ethos.')

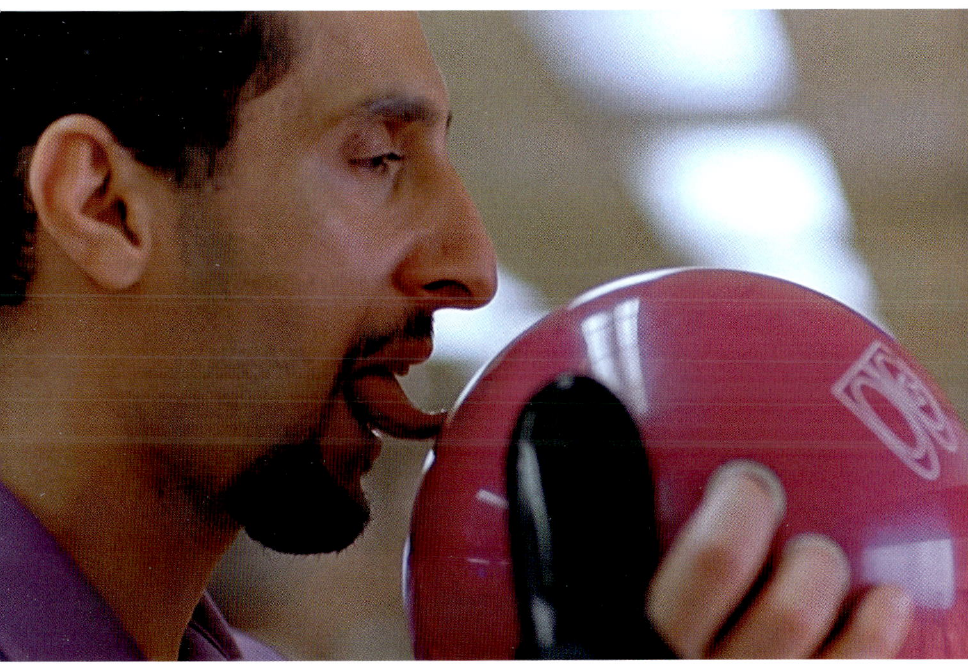

ABOVE: John Turturro as Jesus Quintana, who oddly returned in 2019 spin-off movie *The Jesus Rolls*, directed by Turturro.

Fans of the movie (who called themselves 'Achievers', after 'The Little Lebowski Urban Achievers') started gathering to share their love, leading to the establishment of Lebowski Fest in Louisville, Kentucky, in 2002. Its attendance swelled from 150 in its first year to 2,200 at a New York event in 2011, which hosted an on-stage reunion for Bridges, Goodman, Moore, Buscemi and Turturro. (The Coens themselves have yet to show up.)

For some Achievers, the film has taken on a philosophical significance that has flummoxed Joel and Ethan. It has even spawned a religion in Dudeism, or the Church of the Latter-day Dude, founded in 2005 by Thailand-based journalist Oliver Benjamin. He described it as 'a modern form of Taoism' based on the film which, he contended, 'is really a story about how to live your life, how to deal with conflict and how to maintain a peace of mind in a world gone crazy.'

It was, a perplexed Joel said, 'certainly one of the more bizarre afterlives to any of the things that we've done.' But The Dude himself believes there is something in the phenomenon. He recalled a friend of his, Zen Buddhist roshi Bernie Glassman, telling him over dinner that 'in many circles The Dude is considered a zen master.' *The Big Lebowski*, Glassman revealed, is full of koans – 'Zen questions that you can't really answer intrinsically, you just kinda be with them,' as Bridges put it. The pair collated all these koans into a book, titled *The Dude and The Zen Master*, published in 2014.

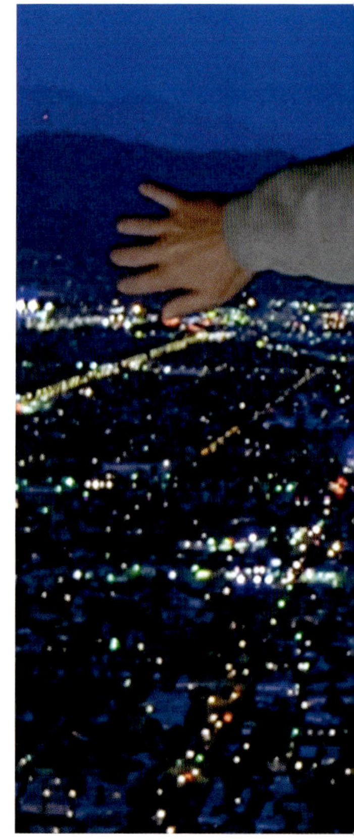

One of Bridges' favourites is "'That's just, like, your opinion, man" – that's not only good to say to somebody else, but to say to yourself!'

The Coen brothers have had bigger box-office hits, and films that have been more widely praised, but nothing they've made has enjoyed the pop-culture proliferation of *The Big Lebowski*. To quote another Coen koan: 'The Dude abides.'

BELOW: The Dude literally gets high in one of the film's dream sequences.

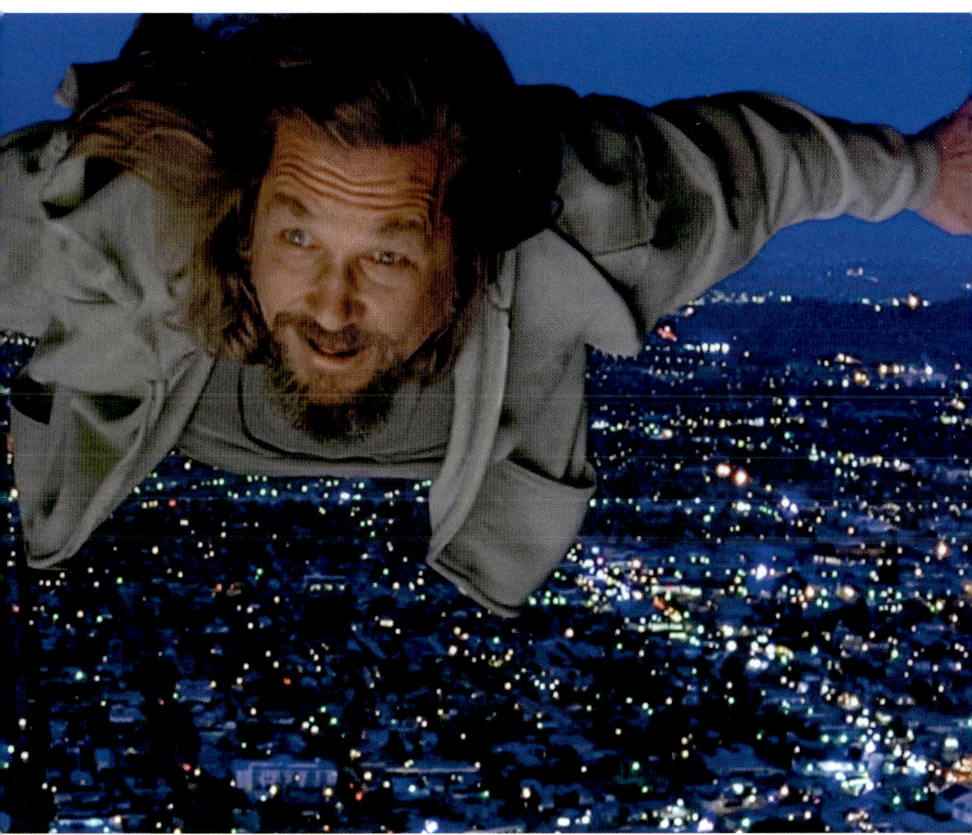

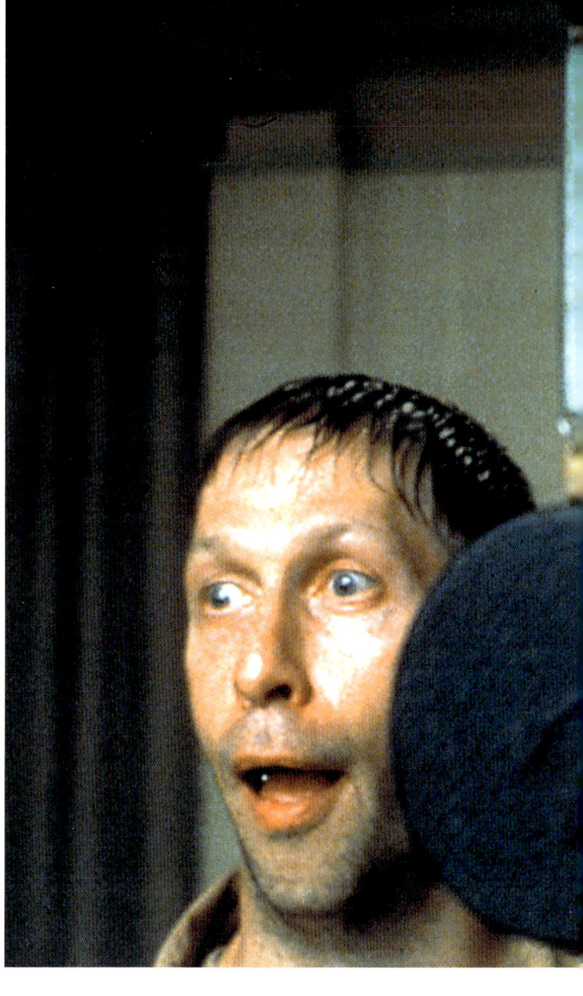

O BROTHER, WHERE ART THOU?

2000

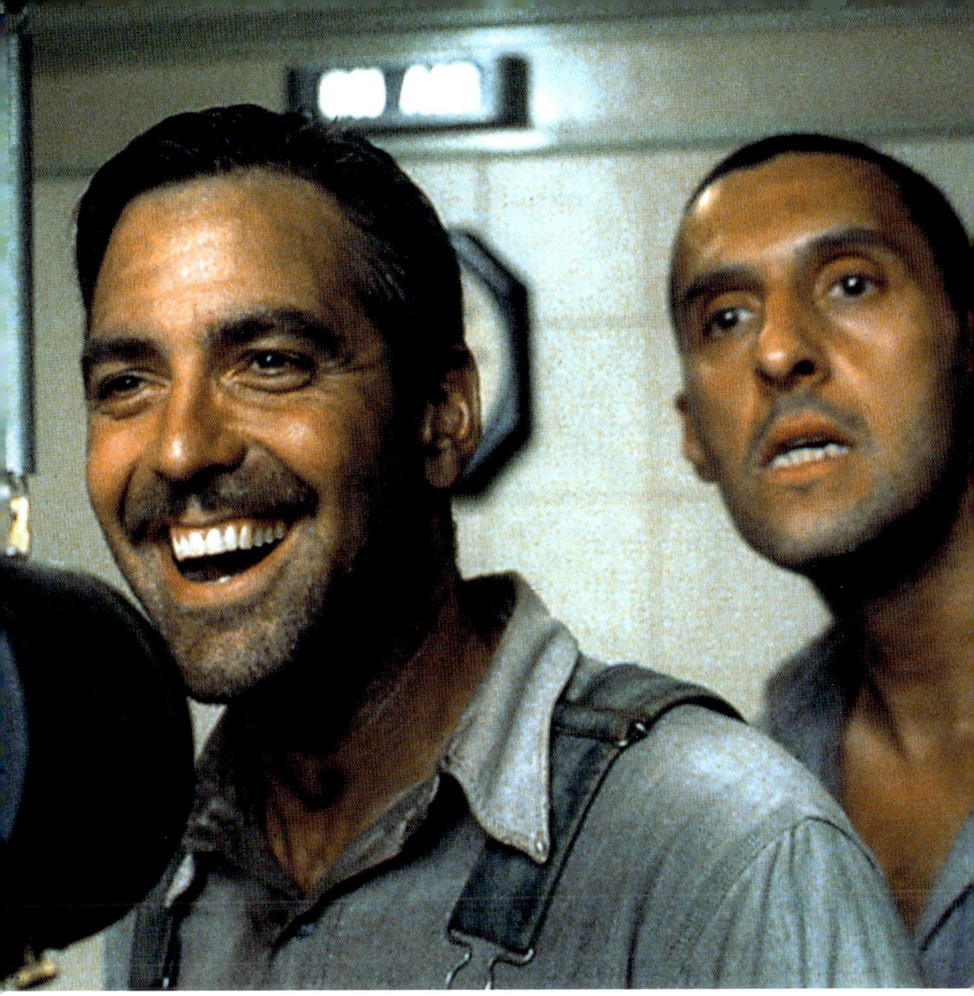

Tim Blake Nelson, an actor, director and playwright originally from Tulsa, Oklahoma, had known the Coen brothers for a few years by the time they made *O Brother, Where Art Thou?* together. They'd crossed paths as fellow members of the New York film and theatre scene and, over time, became friendly. One day, Nelson visited Joel's house and, having majored in classics, spotted on a bookshelf a copy of Homer's *The Odyssey* – the epic Greek poem that follows the fraught 10-year journey of warrior-king Odysseus

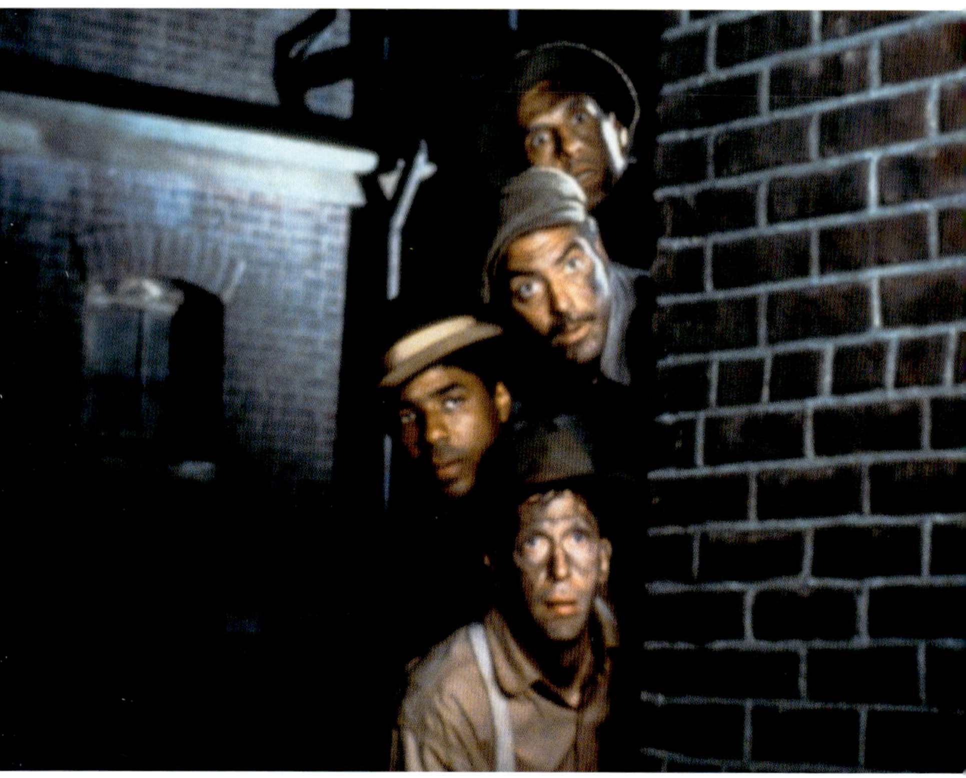

from Troy to his homeland, Ithaca. A note attached to the book read: 'Soon to be a motion picture by Joel and Ethan Coen'.

O Brother is an unlikely gumbo of ingredients that began with Joel and Ethan's notion to make a 'Three Stooges movie, sort of epic in scale,' which they connected to *The Odyssey* via the simple fact that their 'saps on the run' were taking a long and dangerous homeward journey. Despite Joel owning the book, neither he nor Ethan claimed to have read it. 'Between the cast and us, Tim Nelson is the only one who's actually read *The Odyssey*,' said Ethan.

Knowing the bare bones of the poem was enough, it seems, to pepper their story with appropriate references. Its hero (George Clooney) is a con man rather than a king, but he is named Ulysses

Everett McGill, taking the Romanized version of Odysseus' name and combining it, for some reason, with one of David Lynch's regular actors. His wife, played by Holly Hunter, is named Penny, after Odysseus' wife Penelope, and is preparing to remarry, just like her Homeric equivalent. There's a blind seer (Lee Weaver), who represents Homer himself. Though there's also a character with the poet's name: Homer Stokes (Wayne Duvall), a 'ree-form' political candidate who turns out to be a Klansman. And, on Everett's chain-gang-escaping, picaresque journey through 1920s Mississippi with the dim Delmar (Nelson) and the abrasive Pete (John Turturro), there are equivalents for the dangerously enchanting Sirens and the brutal cyclops, who takes the form of John Goodman's eye-patched Bible salesman Big Dan Teague (also a Klansman).

The Deep South setting and title, meanwhile, are yet another Coen debt to Preston Sturges. In his 1941 film *Sullivan's Travels*, Sturges' film-director protagonist (played by Joel McCrea) has grown tired of comedies, and is so committed to making a big important film about the plight of the common people – titled *O Brother, Where Art Thou?* – he heads out on the road as a vagrant, and is eventually arrested and made part of a chain gang.

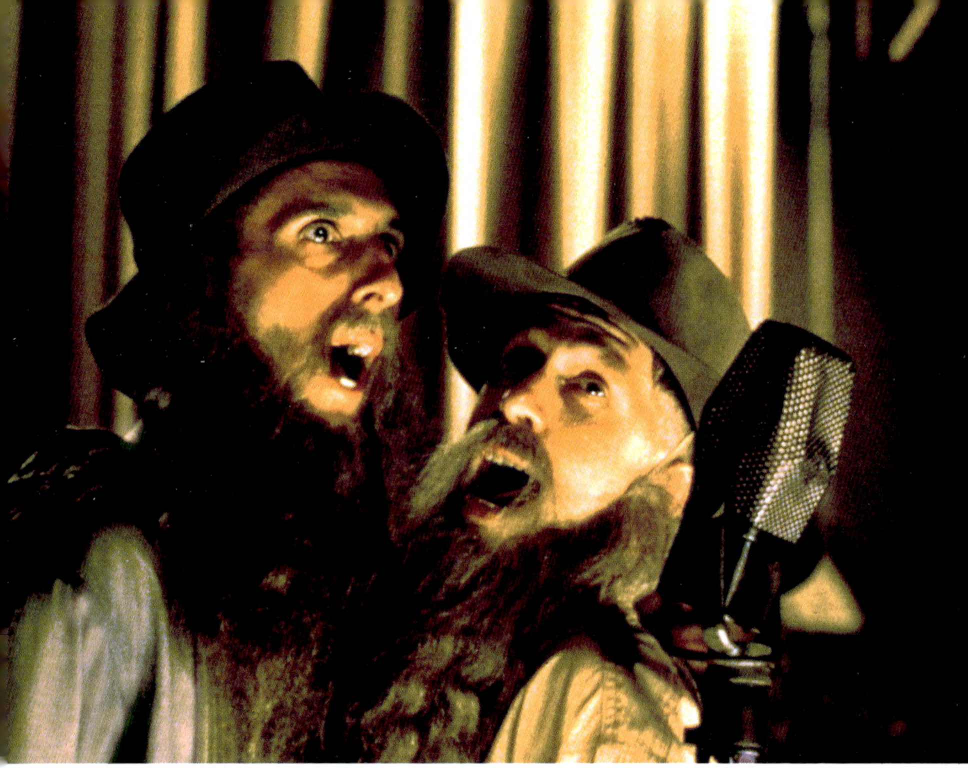

ABOVE: Unlike his co-stars, Tim Blake Nelson (right)
performed his own vocals in the movie.

But there was another ingredient the Coens added. Its special sauce, you could say. For this, they called up their *Big Lebowski* collaborator T Bone Burnett.

While Joel and Ethan did not envision *O Brother* as a full-blooded musical, they wanted their story immersed in the music of the era – bluegrass, roots, mountain music and gospel. 'It is compelling music,' said Ethan, 'harking back to a time when music was a part of everyday life and not something performed by celebrities.'

'The music is a huge part of the movie,' said Joel. 'You wouldn't call it a musical, but the songs all figure in the story naturally, performed by the characters.' There is the haunting rendition of

Coens in concert: *Down From The Mountain* (2000)

On completing *O Brother, Where Art Thou?*, the Coens and T Bone Burnett felt there was even more they could do to raise the profile of the folk sounds that fuelled their movie. They decided they should put on some kind of event, and it was Universal Nashville CEO Luke Lewis who suggested they make it a concert film. Directed by D A Pennebaker, *Down From The Mountain* documents a special concert put on at Nashville's Ryman Auditorium on 24 May 2000, whose proceeds went to the Country Music Hall of Fame and Museum. The film combines behind-the-scenes rehearsal footage with performance recordings of all the songs from *O Brother*, and features Alison Krauss, John Hartford, Ralph Stanley, Chris Thomas King (who plays guitarist Tommy Johnson in the movie) and the Fairfield Four, among many others. 'If you have any affection at all for traditional American music,' wrote A O Scott in the *New York Times*, 'the movie is pretty close to Heaven.'

'Down to the River to Pray', when Everett, Pete and Delmar encounter a Baptist procession, for example, or the Sirens' sultry lullaby 'Didn't Leave Nobody But the Baby', which precedes Pete's apparent transformation into a horny toad.

Having got on so well with Burnett on *The Big Lebowski*, the Coens involved him before they'd even finished the script for *O Brother*, asking the musical archivist for a playlist they could build their screenplay around. He set about resurrecting songs from the era and recording them afresh with modern country and folk musicians.

Many of the songs were pre-recorded and lip-synched by the actors. On the surprise hit record 'Man of Constant Sorrow', performed by the three hayseed heroes as The Soggy Bottom Boys, Clooney's vocal was provided by Dan Tyminski, who is part of Alison

Krauss' band. In other instances, the performances were recorded live on set, such as a cappella quartet The Fairfield Four's appearance as doleful gravediggers, singing 'Lonesome Valley' when Everett and co are about to be hanged, or Nelson's on-stage rendition of 'In The Jailhouse Now', during the climactic political rally.

O Brother's musical novelty was intrinsic to its widespread appeal and makes the movie their least cynical offering by a long stretch. It's hard to think of a more purely feelgood, punch-the-air moment in any Coen film than the scene where The Soggy Bottom Boys, disguised as bearded hobos, strike up 'Man of Constant Sorrow' on stage, and are greeted by a wildly enthusiastic crowd who, during the trio's adventures, have become hooked on their impromptu recording of the song. But the movie's substantial box-office success (grossing almost $72 million, it was their biggest hit yet) also had much to do with Joel and Ethan booking a bona fide star in George Clooney.

It was his performance in Steven Soderbergh's slick crime drama *Out of Sight* (1998) that had drawn the Coens to Clooney, and when they offered him the role he accepted without hesitation. They visited the star in Phoenix, Arizona, while he was shooting David O Russell's Gulf War heist movie *Three Kings*. 'They came to my hotel room, put the script on the coffee table, and I said, "Great, I'm in." They said, "Don't you want to read the script first?" I said, "No, I know what you guys do."' Having already clicked with Soderbergh and Quentin Tarantino, he was a man with good American-indie taste.

Joel and Ethan were convinced of Clooney's skill as an actor. But they were also pleased to discover a new, previously untapped side to him. 'What we didn't know at the time is that he's also a goofball, which lends itself to the part,' said Joel. 'George is pretty funny, in spite of how he looks. He's not given to vanity, either.'

Clooney's performance as Everett is a pure delight: his pretentious high-speed patter, his wild facial contortions during the first performance of 'Man of Constant Sorrow', his capacity for slapstick and pratfalls. Evidently, Joel and Ethan couldn't get enough of this newfound schtick, and would cast him another three times, in increasingly idiotic roles. 'Every time they send me a script, they say, "You're going to play a knucklehead," and I'm always willing to do it,' he said in 2016.

While Clooney and his co-stars nailed the ridiculous, cinematographer Roger Deakins was busy achieving the sublime.

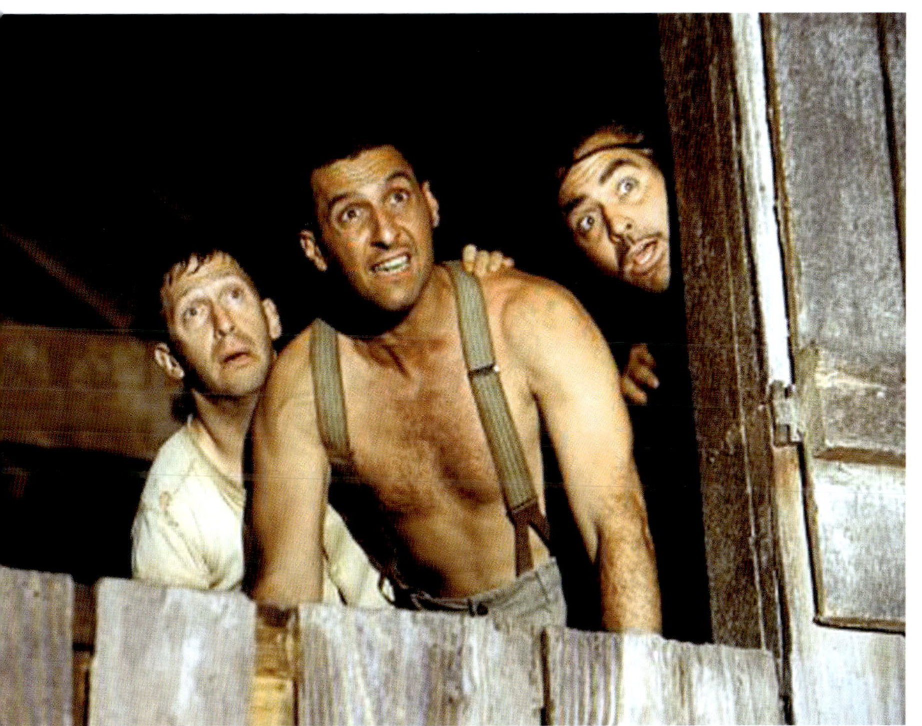

ABOVE: Everett and pals find themselves in a tight spot.

The Coens tasked their director of photography with giving the film the feel of 'an old, faded postcard', not so much sepia as imbued with a dusty, ochre quality that would more powerfully evoke its Depression-era setting than the lush greens of Mississippi during the summer they shot there. Having found that traditional chemical processes couldn't bring the image anywhere close to what the Coens were looking for, Deakins decided to take a punt with some new technology.

Aware that Gary Ross' 1998 film *Pleasantville* had brought modern colour to a Fifties sitcom world through the digital intermediate (DI) colour-timing process, he wondered if the same technique could turn all that green he'd captured on film to gold. It would involve digitizing everything he'd shot and carefully tweaking it in the computer – a long and painstaking process that had never before been done for an entire movie.

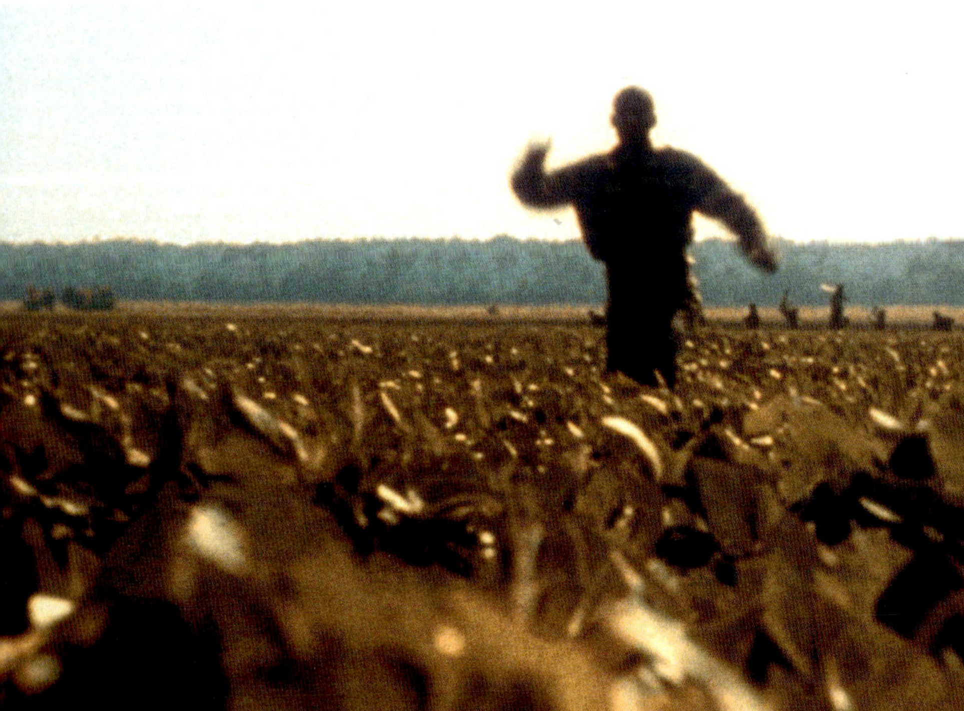

Deakins' effort and innovation paid off, resulting in the film's gloriously vivid aureate hues. As intended, it felt like an artefact retrieved from the distant past, despite being created through a state-of-the art approach.

O Brother was the Coens' third hit in a late Nineties/turn-of-the-century triple whammy that saw Joel and Ethan deliver an awards darling, a cult phenomenon and an all-out audience pleaser. Higher profile stars were keen to work with them, and studios, it seemed, were happier to back their projects (*O Brother* was made with money from both Disney and Universal). To paraphrase *Barton Fink*'s Jack Lipnick, people were loving that Coen-brothers' feeling.

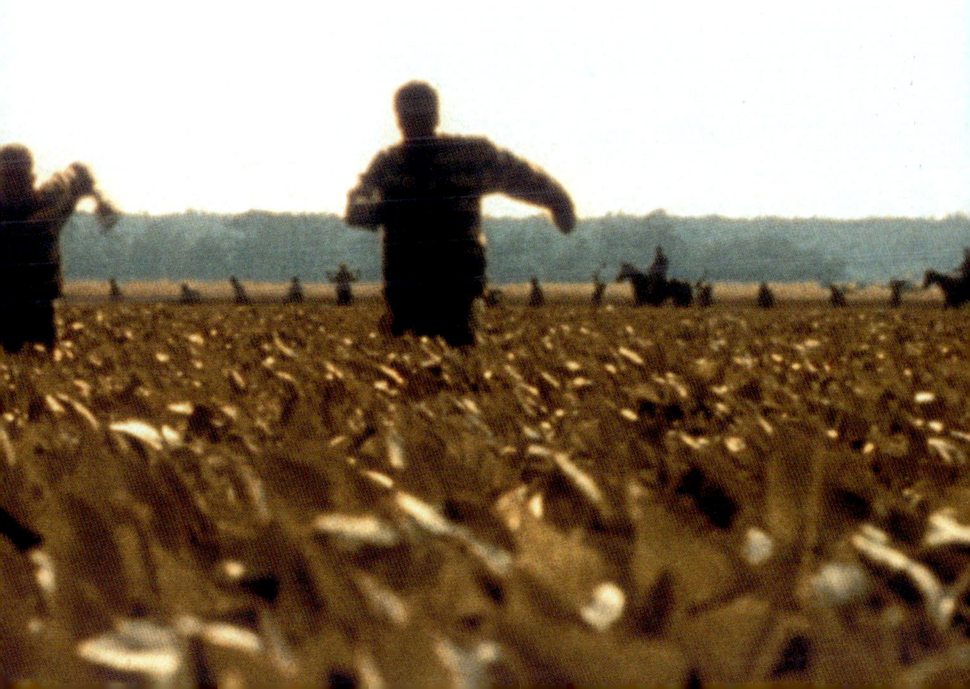

BELOW: The pioneering use of DI to colour-time *O Brother* soon became the industry norm.

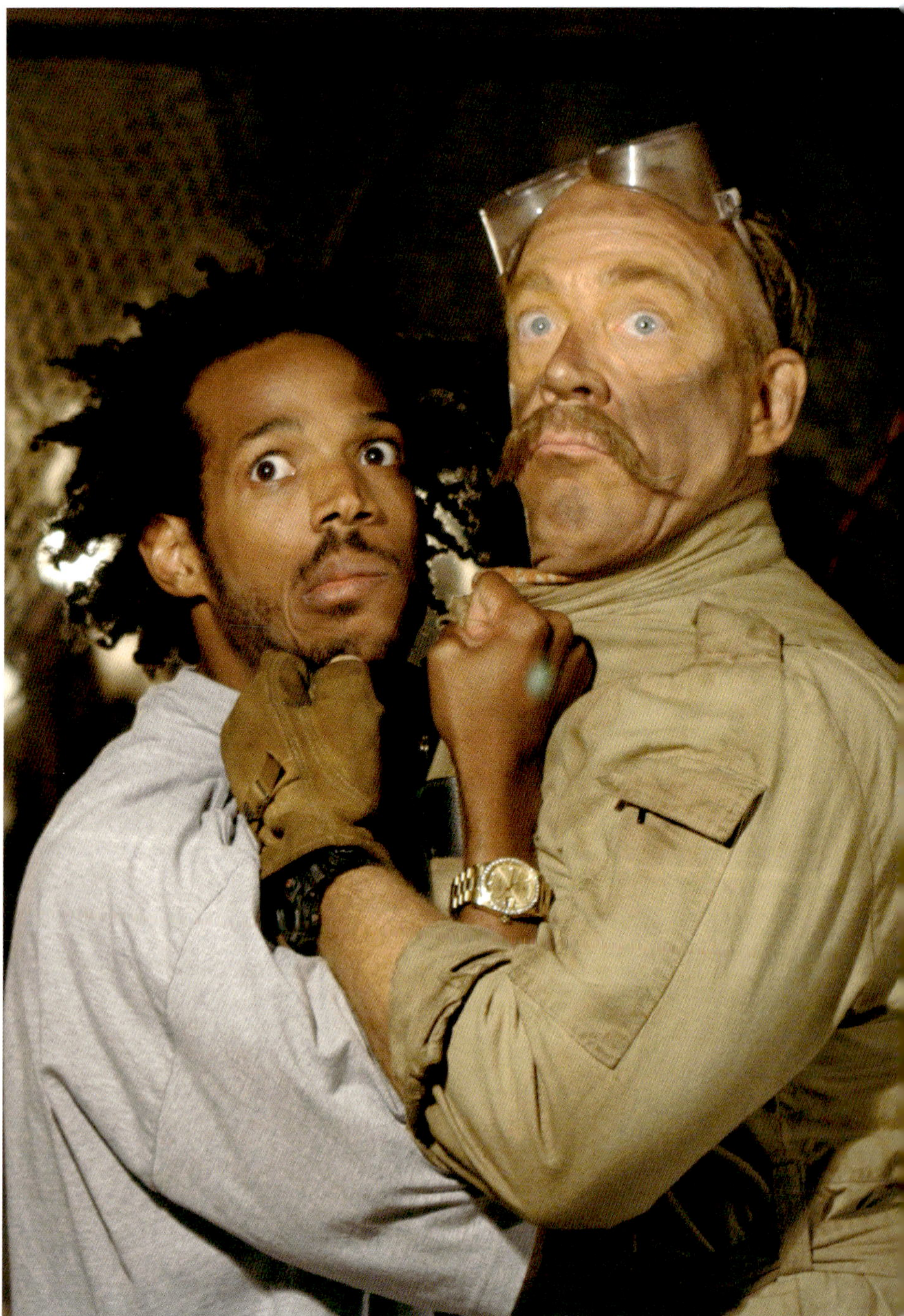

'Why, this is most irregular'

THE DIFFICULT YEARS

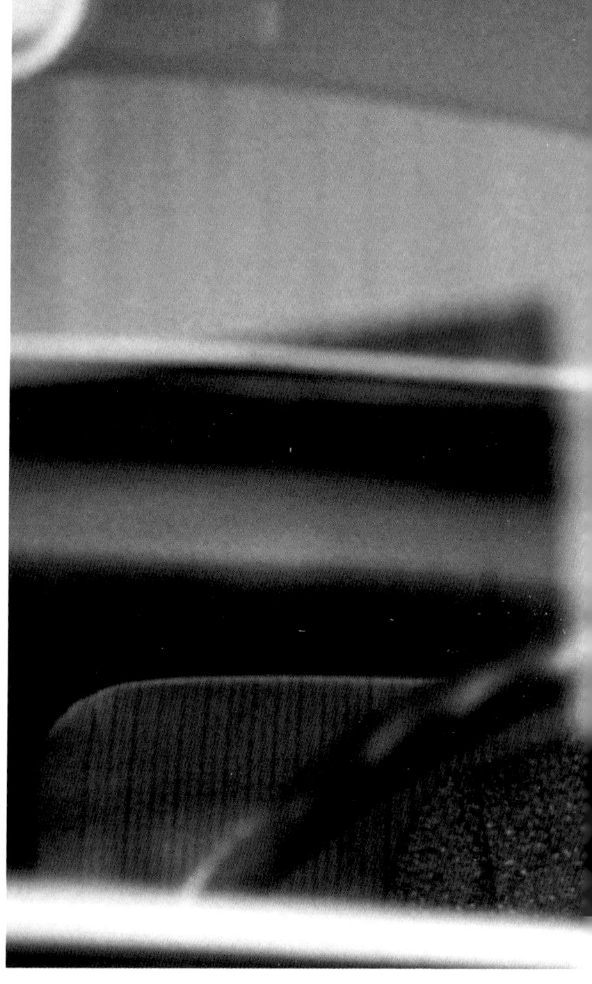

THE MAN WHO WASN'T THERE

2001

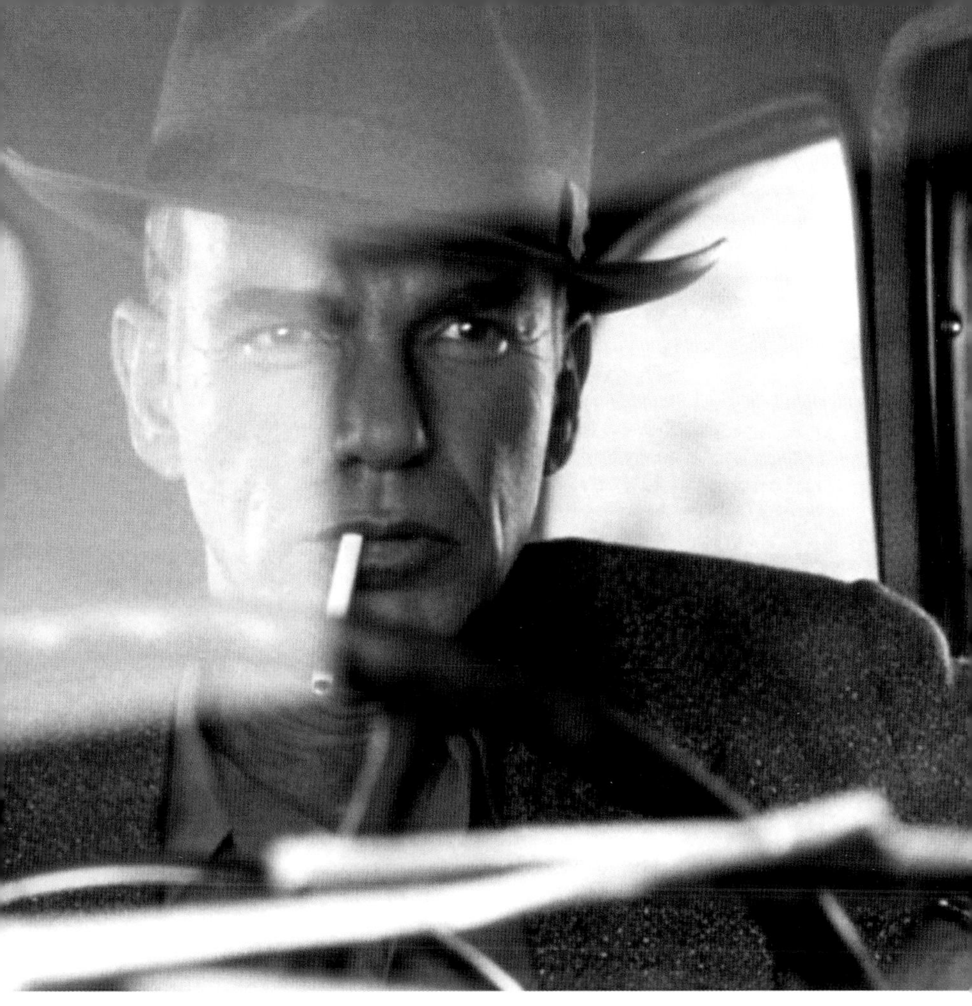

s *The Big Lebowski* revealed, the reception to a Coen movie – whether a *Hudsucker*-sized flop or a *Fargo*-scale triumph – has no bearing on what they do next. 'We don't trouble ourselves too much with what people might be expecting from this or that,' Joel once said.

So it proved again with *The Man Who Wasn't There*, a film whose abstruse nature became a joke for Joel and Ethan, even as they pitched it to people in the wake of *O Brother, Where Art*

Thou?'s success. Joel recalled describing it to Ann Richards, the governor of Texas, at a screening in Austin. 'She said, "What are you doing next?" I said, "We're making a movie about a barber who wants to be a dry cleaner." She looked at me. It was a long beat. And she said, "I'm trying real hard to get excited about that."'

This odd little 'barber movie' began with a prop. After shooting *The Hudsucker Proxy*, the brothers kept a poster of 1940s haircuts that had been used as set dressing, and which included all the cuts that would be referenced in *The Man Who Wasn't There* (the butch, the executive contour, the junior contour. . .). 'We started thinking about the person who did those haircuts,' said Joel. 'I mean, what is that about? Spending your whole day cutting hair like that.'

Hair has always caught the Coens' attention, even beyond the distinctly odd hairdos sported by characters such as Barton Fink (*Eraserhead* wedge), Walter Sobchak in *The Big Lebowski* (flat-top buzzcut) and Anton Chigurh in *No Country For Old Men* (sideswept mop-top). There is the false mystery of what happened to Rug Daniels' wig in *Miller's Crossing*, assumed to have been taken by his killer, but in fact nabbed by a passing urchin. There is Everett's obsession with the neatness of his coiffure in *O Brother, Where Art Thou?* and his petulant insistence on using a particular brand of pomade ('I'm a Dapper Dan man!'). And pomade is also used as a plot device in *Raising Arizona*, the means by which Leonard Smalls tracks the duck's-ass-styled Snoats brothers.

In *The Man Who Wasn't There*, hair gives Ed Crane (Billy Bob Thornton) not only his profession, but also a metaphor for his sense of existential disconnection. 'This hair, you ever wonder about it?' Ed asks his fellow barber and brother-in-law Frank (Michael Badalucco). 'It keeps on coming, it just keeps growing. It's part of us, and we cut it off and throw it away.'

Later on, via a voiceover that belies his blank, laconic nature, Ed will further identify himself with that thrown-away hair, saying he feels different to regular folk; an outsider, 'a ghost'. Yet he strives to make his mark on the world, whether that's through extorting his wife's lover Big Dave Brewster (James Gandolfini) to fund a dry-cleaning enterprise, or becoming a patron to a teenage pianist named Birdie (Scarlett Johansson) whom he believes to be a prodigy.

Of course, this being a Coen tale, both attempts fail: Ed's supposed business partner (Jon Polito) disappears – actually

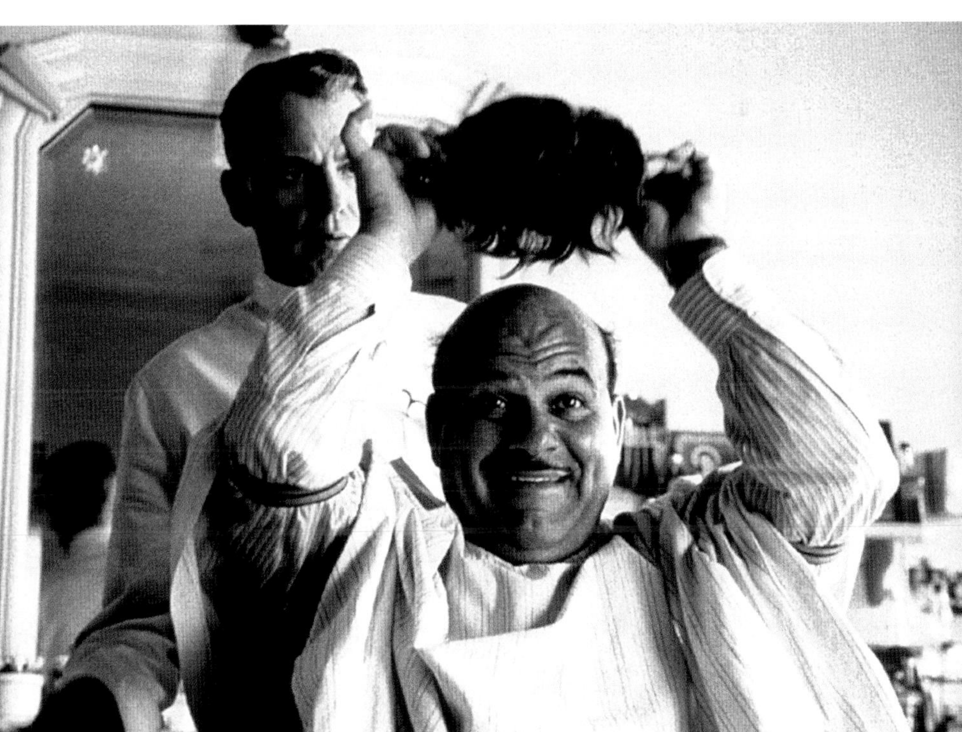

ABOVE: Jon Polito returned to the Coenverse as wig-wearing dry-cleaning pioneer Creighton Tolliver.

murdered by Big Dave, before Ed kills *him* in self-defence; a crime for which his wife Doris (Frances McDormand) is convicted, leading to her suicide. Meanwhile, in a cruel little twist, Birdie is revealed to be just an averagely proficient musician. After she clumsily attempts to thank Ed by fellating him while he's driving, he crashes his car and awakens to find *he's* been convicted of killing the dry cleaner. He is ultimately sent to the electric chair, having achieved nothing of worth, aside from writing an article for a men's magazine (which explains the post-mortal narration).

The film's noirish plot machinations brought the Coens back to the writer who inspired their debut: James M Cain. They effectively mash up *Mildred Pierce*, *The Postman Always Rings Twice* and *Double Indemnity* – all stories, Joel noted, where the day-to-day lives of the characters were 'rather banal'. *Mildred Pierce*, as he put it, 'is about a woman who starts a pie shop,' while *Double Indemnity* 'is about an insurance salesman'. But a more intriguing influence is a genre the brothers had previously claimed they would avoid. 'We were thinking about science-fiction movies from the early 1950s,' said Joel. 'You know, flying saucers and the pod people. We were interested in the whole idea of post-war anxiety: atom-bomb anxiety and the existential dread you see in 1950s movies.'

In *The Man Who Wasn't There* – which is set in 1949 – this is no mere undercurrent, like the swept-away hair cuttings. In one eerily lit scene, Big Dave's widow (Katherine Borowitz) claims to Ed that, based on her own close encounter during a camping trip, she believes her husband to have been abducted by aliens. Later, we see a hubcap from Ed's car crash transform into a flying saucer right out of something like *The Day The Earth Stood Still*, while a

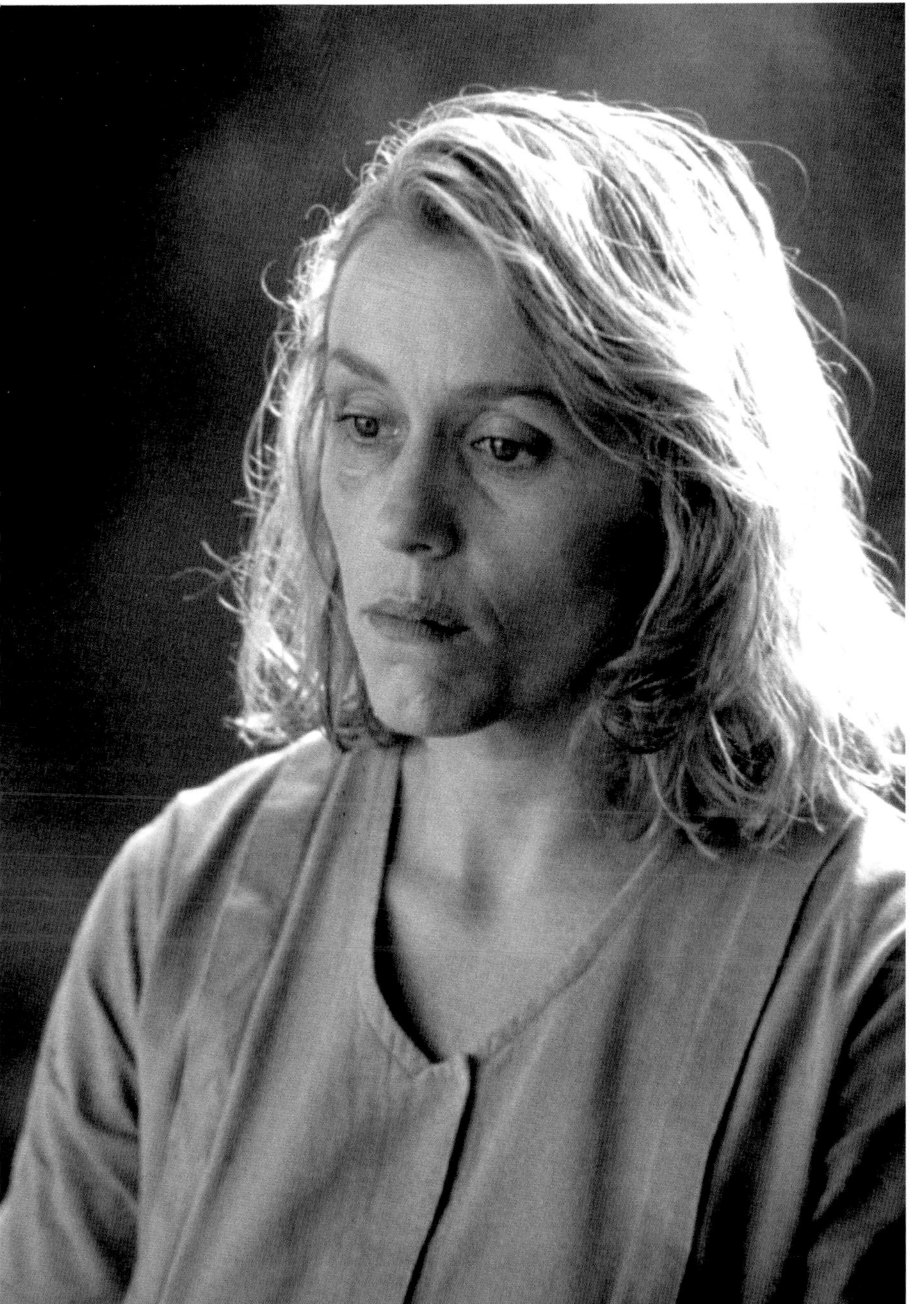

similar spacecraft appears to Ed, hovering in the sky, during a pre-execution dream sequence. Tellingly, it flies away without him, as if its unseen occupants found him insufficiently interesting to abduct.

The Man Who Wasn't There plays to the brothers' strengths, with its wry, offbeat approach to familiar genres, and with its focus on a character who – like The Dude, *A Serious Man*'s Larry Gopnik and Llewyn Davis – would be relegated to the sidelines in any other story. It also benefits from a striking visual approach marking, in this sense at least, a logical progression from *O Brother*, going

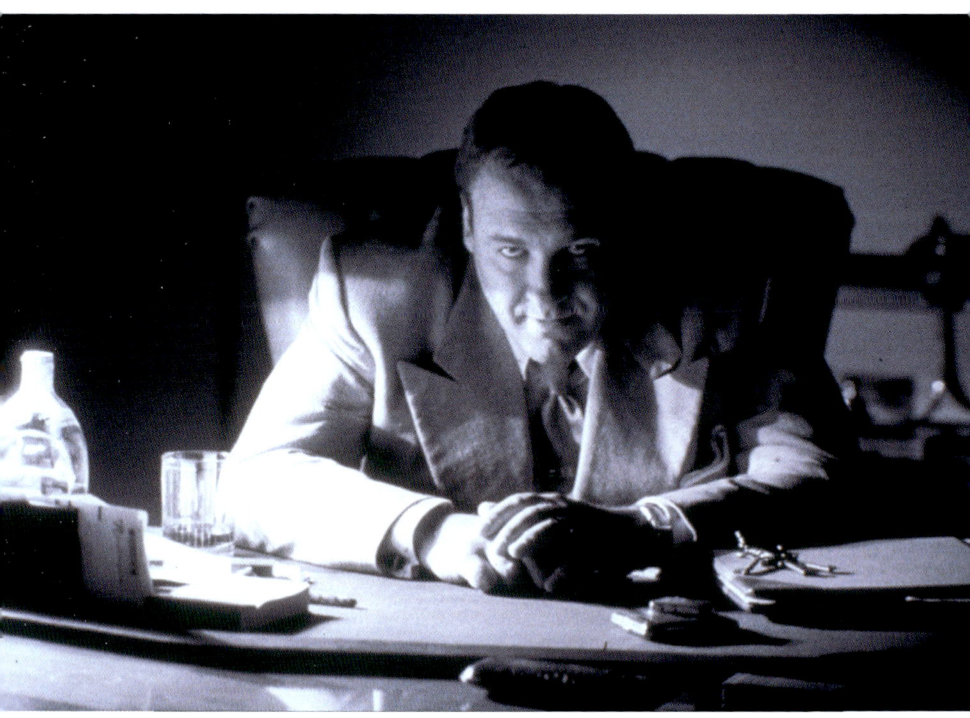

BELOW: *Sopranos* star James Gandolfini brings a touch of menace as Big Dave Brewster.

from postcard-sepia to high-contrast black-and-white, realized with typical panache by Roger Deakins.

However, the movie lacks the humorous punch of most other Coen films and, as well-delivered as it is, Thornton's croaky voiceover begins to intrude and feel over-used, even if it is the largely expressionless character's primary form of expression. It also doesn't help that so many key scenes depend on Tony Shalhoub, who takes on the same jarringly acerbic persona as he does in *Barton Fink,* except this time he's a big-shot lawyer, named Freddy Riedenschneider, rather than a big-shot producer. There is at least some ironic amusement to be found in his masterplan to base his defence – for both Doris and Ed – on Heisenberg's uncertainty principle. 'Our minds get in the way,' says Riedenschneider. 'Looking at something changes it. . .The more you look the less you really know.'

This last statement applies to the movie itself, too. As handsome as it is, it shares the hollowness of its protagonist, lacking any of the warm pockets we can find in, say, *Fargo* or *No Country For Old Men*; nor the comic relief we get in the similarly bleak *A Serious Man* and *Burn After Reading*. It is not without its fans, however. On release, *The Guardian*'s Peter Bradshaw described it as 'the best American film of the year,' while more recently, *Little White Lies*' Dan Einav made the case for it being 'the Coen brothers' most underrated movie'. But, like Governor Richards, audiences didn't get excited by it. It became Joel and Ethan's least successful film since *Hudsucker* (grossing less than $19 million against a $20 million budget), while also lacking the cult durability of their other movies.

It started to feel that Joel and Ethan were losing their way, that they had perhaps peaked in the late Nineties. Were we seeing these fascinating filmmakers in decline?

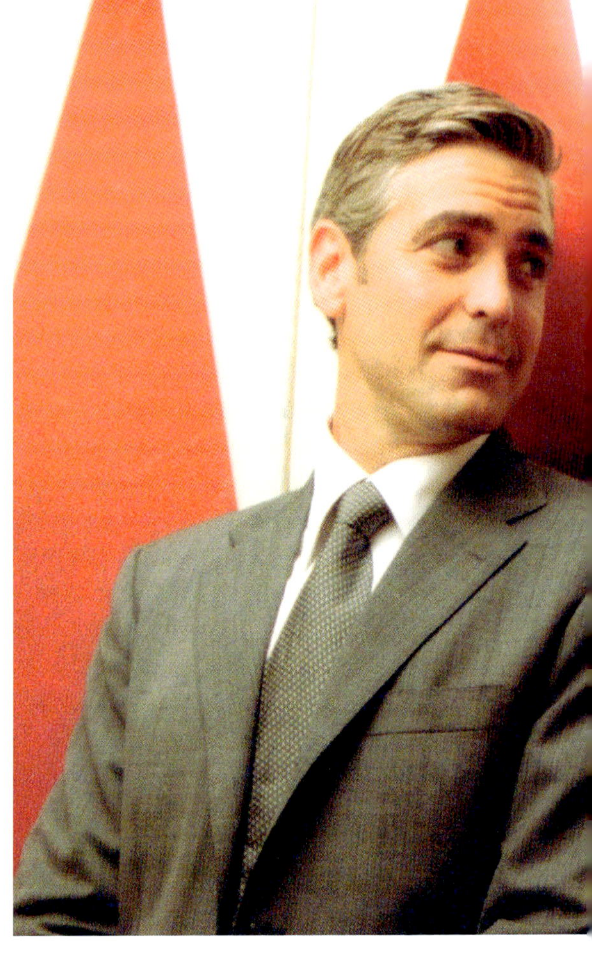

INTOLERABLE CRUELTY
2003

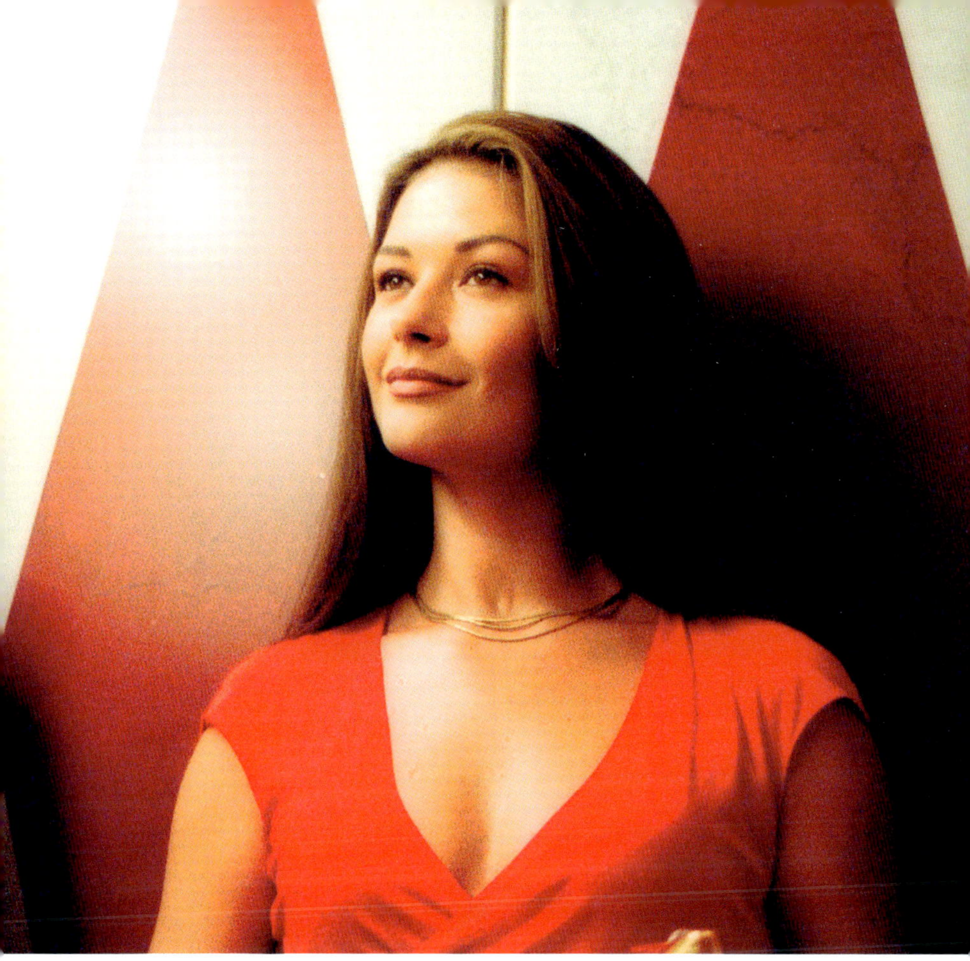

It was a big-budget, mainstream romantic comedy described by its high-profile producer Brian Grazer as 'a love story for anybody and everybody'. It paired George Clooney with so-hot-right-then Welsh actress Catherine Zeta-Jones, who'd just won an Oscar for playing Velma Kelly in *Chicago*. And it was set amid the glossy, opulent environs of Beverly Hills.

Intolerable Cruelty was a significant first for the Coen brothers. Never before had they directed a movie based on a screenplay they hadn't originated themselves. It was a project that had flitted around Hollywood for years, taking various forms as it was picked up then dropped. It started out as a story concept by John Romano (*The Lincoln Lawyer*, *The Third Miracle*) which was turned into a script by Robert Ramsey and Matthew Stone (*Destiny Turns on the Radio*, *Life*). The Coens were asked to rewrite it in 1994 – the first time they'd accepted a write-for-hire gig – before it went through various script doctors (including Carrie Fisher) and directors, including Ron Howard, Andrew Bergman and Jonathan Demme. During this time, it looked like it might coalesce as a Julia Roberts/Richard Gere reunion (the pair having previously made *Pretty Woman*), then a Tea Leoni/Will Smith reunion (following *Bad Boys*), then a Julia Roberts/Hugh Grant reunion (following *Notting Hill*).

Eventually, Universal Pictures sent the script to Clooney, who asked to see the Coens' 1994 draft and expressed an interest in starring if he could do *that* version – with his *O Brother* compadres Joel and Ethan. 'When we discovered that George was interested in doing it, that made us interested in making it,' said Joel. Originally, he and Ethan had hoped to follow up *The Man Who Wasn't There* with their planned adaptation of James Dickey's World War II thriller *To The White Sea*, but its funding had just fallen through, causing the project to collapse. They were at a loose end and, as Joel said, 'we always liked the script a lot.'

Universal was happy for the Coens to polish up their version and direct it, and the Coens were happy to work alongside Grazer just as they had with Joel Silver a decade earlier. So *Intolerable Cruelty* went into production in June 2002 with a budget of $60 million – by far the brothers' biggest to date.

There were no reports from the set, or from any point during the making of *Intolerable Cruelty*, of the studio meddling with the Coens' vision or process. They retained final cut, and have never

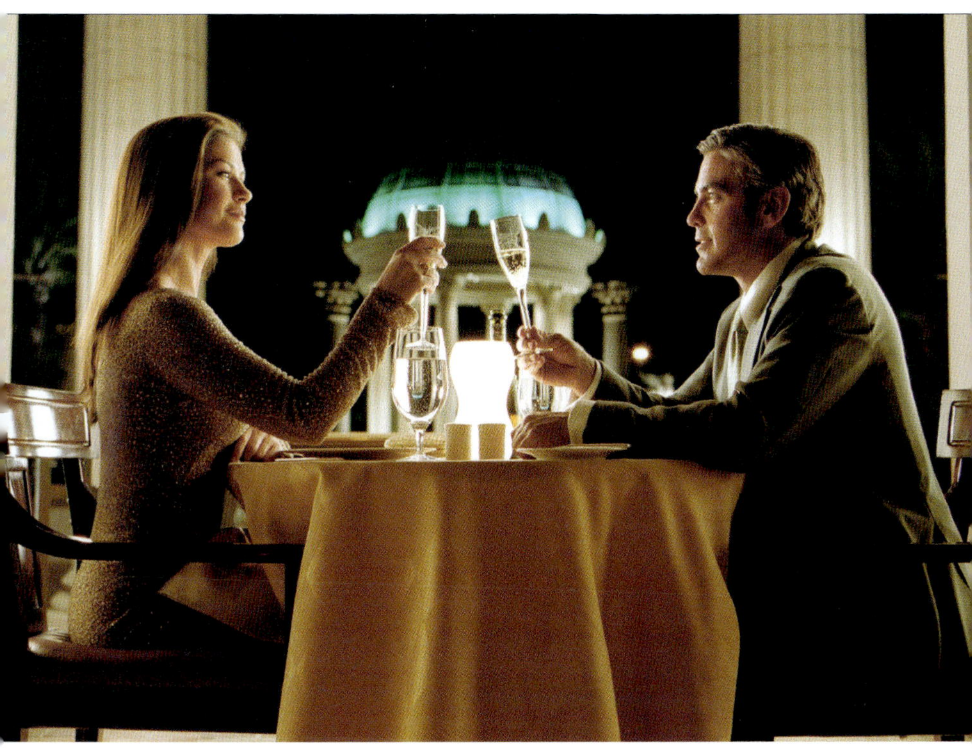

ABOVE: Marylin and Miles connect over a romantic meal, in one of the film's strongest scenes.

spoken of feeling any pressure to compromise. So we can only assume that it is their most mainstream movie by design. For the first time since *Blood Simple*, they used a modern-day setting, and for the first time in their oeuvre they set a story exclusively amid the glitz and glam of the ultra-rich, rather than playing among the mooks, losers, crooks and strivers on society's fringes.

The central conceptual gag is that it is a romance about divorce. Clooney plays hotshot Beverly Hills divorce attorney Miles Massey, renowned for his watertight prenup. Zeta-Jones is Marylin Rexroth, a serial divorcee, who makes her living elegantly fleecing her exes. The pair become attracted while Miles foxes Marylin's latest gambit in the courtroom, then fall for each other while Marylin executes a cunning long-con plan to regain her fortune and wreak revenge on Miles.

The film might dwell in a traditionally predictable genre, but is not without some Coen flourish. Miles was considered by Clooney to be a direct descendant of *O Brother*'s Ulysses Everett

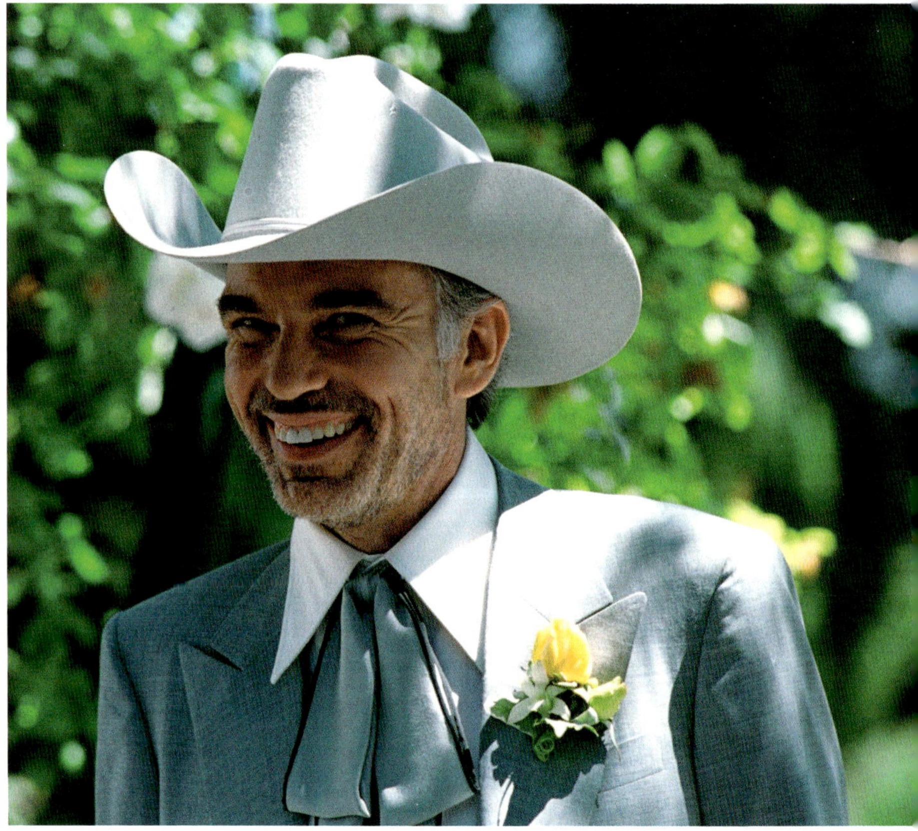

ABOVE: Billy Bob Thornton plays Marylin's latest husband/mark Howard D Doyle, who is as verbose as Ed Crane in *The Man Who Wasn't There* was laconic.

McGill, and has indeed inherited both his gift for the gab (albeit with less overtly thesaurus-raiding eloquence) and his preening vanity – though here it's dentally, rather than follically focused. Miles has a scarily decrepit boss, adding to the Coen gallery of grotesque and powerful men behind desks. The plot pivots into crime caper territory towards the end when a heartbroken Miles hires a gargantuan, asthmatic hitman named Wheezy Joe (Irwin Keyes) to kill Marylin. And there are absurd touches throughout, from a brief glimpse of a magazine titled *Living Without Intestines* to a lapdog-carrying surprise witness named Heinz, the Baron Krauss von Espy (Jonathan Hadary), who speaks with a ludicrous euro accent.

But there is a strange feeling of the brothers pushing too hard for laughs, while also delivering some of their weakest punchlines. The Wheezy Joe payoff is one of their biggest comedic blunders, when the supposedly professional killer mixes up his gun with his inhaler and blows his own head off while trying to quell an asthma attack. Then there's Miles' sidekick (Paul Adelstein), who cries at weddings. It's a corny gag repeated numerous times, much like the clumsy catchphrase given to the coitus-interrupting private investigator Gus Petch (Cedric the Entertainer): 'I'm gonna nail yo' ass'. Though the film follows in the Coen tradition of riffing on classic screwball movies in the Howard Hawks mould, and benefits from the cinematography of Roger Deakins and the lush scoring of Carter Burwell, it simply lacks the stylistic verve of their previous offerings.

Intolerable Cruelty doesn't even excel as a romantic comedy. Clooney and Zeta-Jones should have been a great pairing, but they never quite gel. Where he is full of cocksure energy (then later sheer desperation), she is gracefully sedate. This was a conscious choice by Zeta-Jones, who saw Marylin as 'the eye of the storm. . .All this craziness that happens around her, she just waltzes through it.

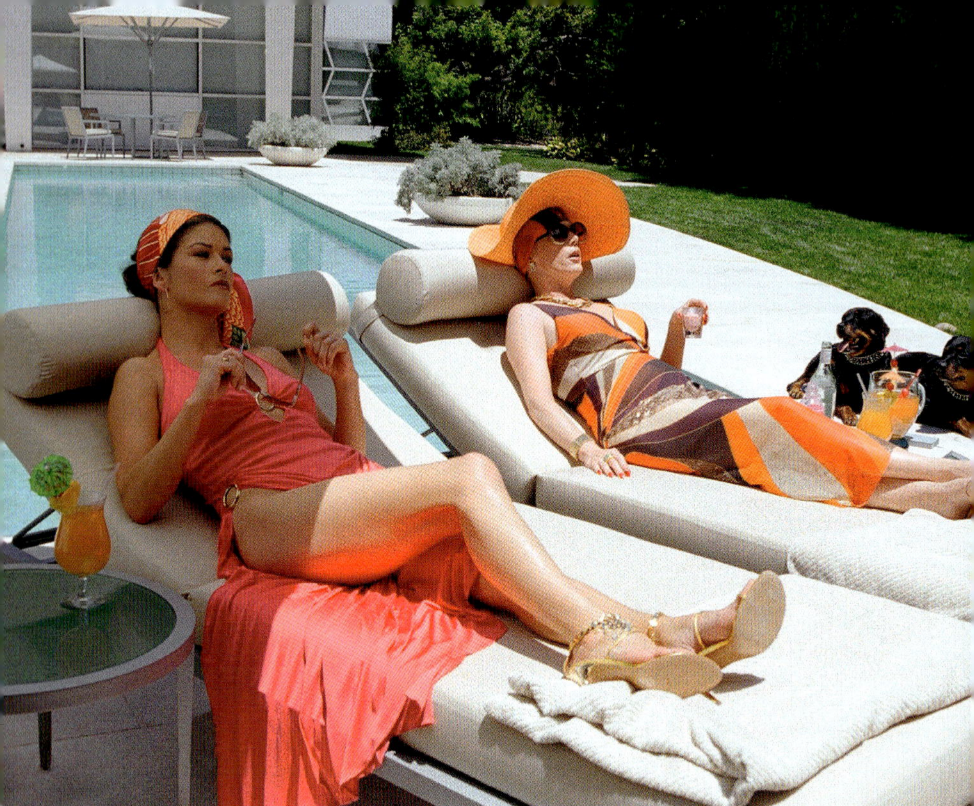

She really has no idea how much chaos she can create.' It's an approach that ultimately lacks the requisite zing to make us root for them to get together.

Of course, you could read the movie as the Coens' attempt to subvert the genre, though this was never their stated aim. There is a sense of this in the way that the film's biggest romantic gesture is ripping up a prenup, and also in its ending, which does not fade out on a kiss but epilogues with the revelation that Miles and Marilyn have invested in an unconvincing reality TV show, fronted by the ass-nailin' Gus, devoted to exposing infidelity for the sake of entertainment.

The critical response to *Intolerable Cruelty* was mixed, with many reviewers bemoaning its lack of heart. 'We, poor saps, who invested our emotion in this movie, are hung out to dry,' wrote Roger Ebert. But it did have its advocates. *Empire*'s Damon Wise described it as 'a superb hijacking of an ailing art form', and predicted that it should earn Joel and Ethan 'enough cash to make five more offbeat minor masterpieces'. With a worldwide gross of just over $120 million, it certainly outperformed *O Brother*. Yet it was a relatively modest result for a film of its type, taking only $35 million in its home country, just over half what it cost. Not that the Coens had a masterplan to take Hollywood by storm. Instead, they would follow up *Intolerable Cruelty* with the most perplexing movie of their entire career.

Unmade Coens: *To The White Sea*

Like most filmmakers, the Coen brothers' career is scattered with unrealized projects, but the lost movie that came closest to fruition – tantalizingly so – was *To The White Sea*. *Deliverance* writer James Dickey's 1993 novel followed the brutal journey of a downed US Air Force tail gunner named Muldrow, sneaking and murdering his way across Japan, from Honshu to Hokkaido, during World War II. The Coens' intention was to depict this bloody odyssey with virtually no dialogue, aside from unsubtitled Japanese (reflecting Muldrow's inability to comprehend the language), which would have made this a remarkable departure from their usually verbose approach. Brad Pitt was lined up to play Muldrow, and Universal Pictures seemed willing to back it. However, the Coens' requirement to shoot on location in Japan and recreate the firebombing of Tokyo by the US set a cost that the studio was ultimately unwilling to pay.

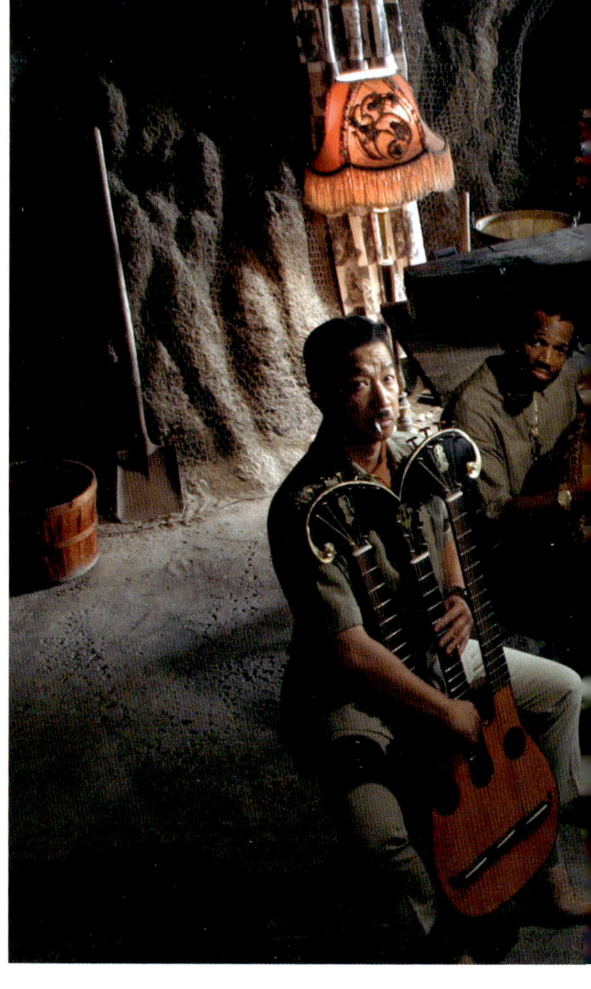

THE LADYKILLERS
2004

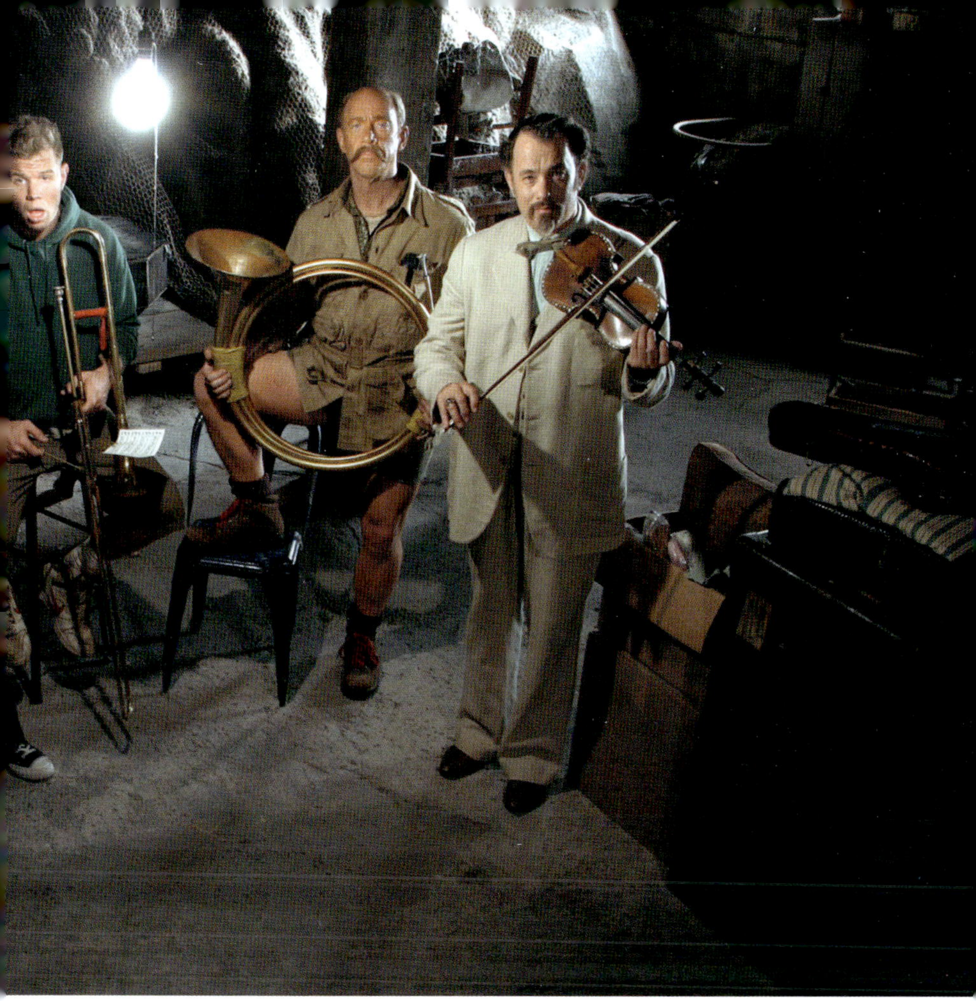

While promoting *Intolerable Cruelty* in June 2003, the Coen brothers appeared on Charlie Rose's PBS talk show with George Clooney and Catherine Zeta-Jones. As their interview wrapped up, Rose asked why Hollywood was so obsessed with remakes these days. Clooney shrugged and suggested, 'No new ideas,' before cheekily informing his host that Joel and Ethan's next movie was *The Ladykillers*. 'It's a really great Alec Guinness movie from the mid-Fifties that should never be remade,'

deadpanned Joel. 'Pointless to remake,' agreed a grinning Ethan, 'but we've just finished shooting.' Rose followed up by asking why they wanted to do it. 'Well,' replied Ethan, 'we had a lack of ideas.'

Look at any ranking of the Coens' movies, and you'll likely find *The Ladykillers* occupying the lowest spot. While, rather ironically, it was their first film to feature a joint writing, directing and producing credit, it is reasonably regarded as their creative nadir – the biggest blot on their record, treated with derision or, at best, disappointed embarrassment. And it wasn't even originally their idea at all.

BELOW: Gawain makes the first murder attempt on the heist-discovering Marva Munson (Irma P Hall).

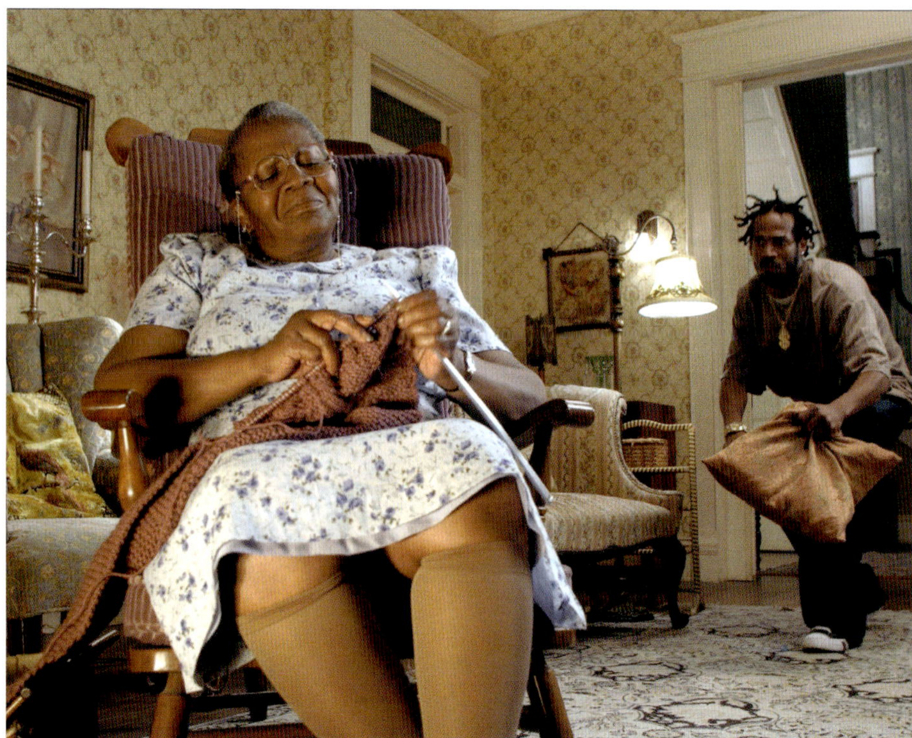

The Ladykillers started life as a write-for-hire gig. The impetus to remake Alexander Mackendrick's Ealing Studios classic – in which a gang of criminals rent a room from a kindly old widow while executing a heist at King's Cross station, then fall out when she discovers their ruse – came from one of Hollywood's biggest studios, Disney. The studio engaged Joel and Ethan's old pal Barry Sonnenfeld to direct, who asked the brothers if they'd like to write it. They agreed, savouring childhood memories of watching *The Ladykillers* on TV. And they felt it was ripe for a new take. 'We liked the bones of the story,' said Joel. 'It's got a great, strong concept and we thought it would survive our mucking about with it.'

While its darkly comic sensibility and crime-caper genre are an ideal match for the Coens, their 'mucked-about' *Ladykillers* displays little reverence. It is both modernized and Americanized, relocating the setting from Fifties London to contemporary Mississippi, marking a return to *O Brother?* territory – as does their decision to crowd the film with music, in this case African American gospel, once again supervised by T Bone Burnett.

The frail, bird-loving Mrs Wilberforce (Katie Johnson) becomes the pious and rather fearsome cat-owning Marva Munson (Irma P Hall), who does not suffer fools and even dishes out physical violence when offended, thus undermining her supposed vulnerability. The heist is now focused on a riverboat casino rather than a train station, while body disposal is provided by a trash barge instead of a passing locomotive. The criminal crew are similarly motley, but now include an ex-Vietcong tunneller (Tzi Ma), a foul-mouthed inside man (Marlon Wayans), a slack-jawed American football player called Lump (Ryan Hurst) and Garth Pancake, an IBS-inflicted film-effects technician (J K Simmons). Ringleader Professor Marcus, originally portrayed by Guinness as an Alistair Sim-inspired ghoul, is now Goldthwaite Higginson Dorr PhD, a garrulous, pretentious, Edgar Allan Poe-quoting Southerngent charlatan in the surprising form of two-time Oscar-winning star Tom Hanks, who at the time seemed committed to shedding his nice-guy on-screen image.

Hanks' involvement is an undoubted draw, if only for the novelty value of seeing him embrace an out-and-out villain role. He certainly found it a challenge. 'There was a huge amount of verbiage that went on and massive amounts of check-list stuff,' he said. 'You know: he's going to have a dialect, he's going to have to be able to rattle this stuff off. . .' Fortunately, he had the best part of a year between accepting the role and shooting to prepare – though none of this time was spent studying the Mackendrick *Ladykillers*. 'Being completely oblivious to the original made it possible for me to see it simply as a Coen brothers movie,' Hanks insisted.

Of course, the Coen brothers taking a beloved movie and making it completely their own should give no cause for complaint. Remakes are usually strongest when they boldly depart from the original. But Ethan's joke about their lack of ideas does start to feel like an admission when you look at how he and Joel specifically Coen-ized Mackendrick's film.

Aside from the retrodden Southern setting and the *O Brother*-esque invocation of Burnett, there is a distinct sense of self-plagiarism. *The Big Lebowski*'s rolling bowling-ball point of view is heavily echoed in Lump's introduction sequence, which presents a football game from his helmet-wearing perspective. Dorr's verbose and multisyllabic patter feels like a reheated version of Everett McGill's in *O Brother*. And, most egregious of all, they virtually repeat the iffy Wheezy Joe gag from their previous movie, when, after saying, 'Who looks stupid now?' (a line from the original, previously 'stolen' for *Blood Simple*), Lump looks down the barrel of a misfiring gun and blows his own head off.

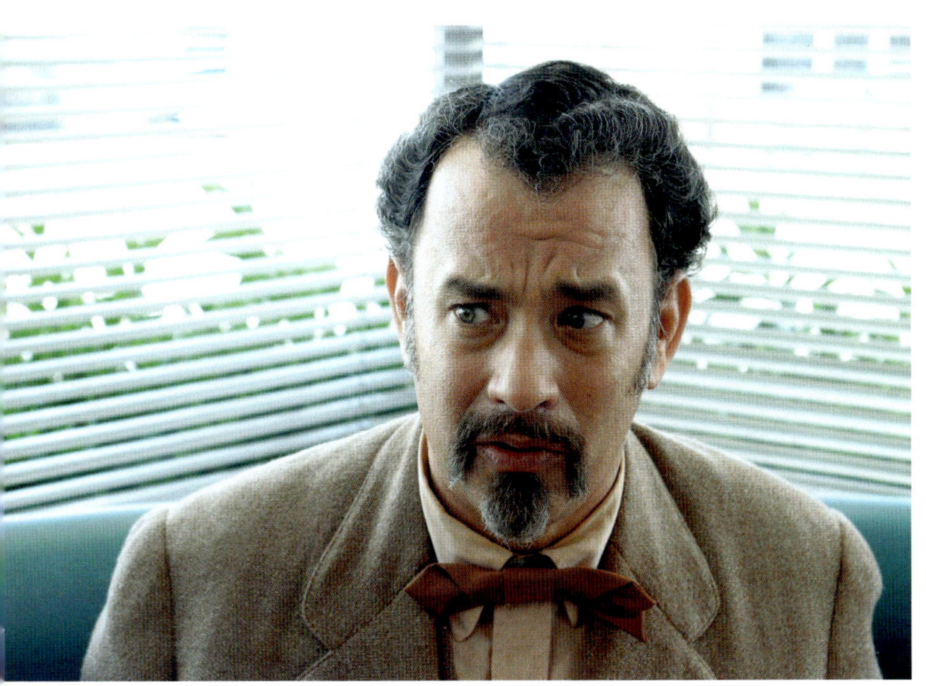

Other gags feel lazy and almost petulantly low brow. There is a fart joke, and J K Simmons is lumbered with portraying Gus' ferocious incontinence, taking a toilet break mid-heist. Then there's the device of showing the portrait of Marva's husband Otis with different facial expressions, reacting to various plot developments. It may be yet another tribute to *Sullivan's Travels* (in which the 'Dear Joseph' portrait reacts to his widow's attempts to seduce Sullivan), but it is wince-inducing even before it is repeated. To reluctantly borrow the film's bowel-related material, it is as if *The Ladykillers* was a kind of creative enema, whereby Joel and Ethan could flush out all their worst ideas, before taking a break and coming back refreshed. If so, judging by their next movie, it was – in this very specific way only – a resounding success.

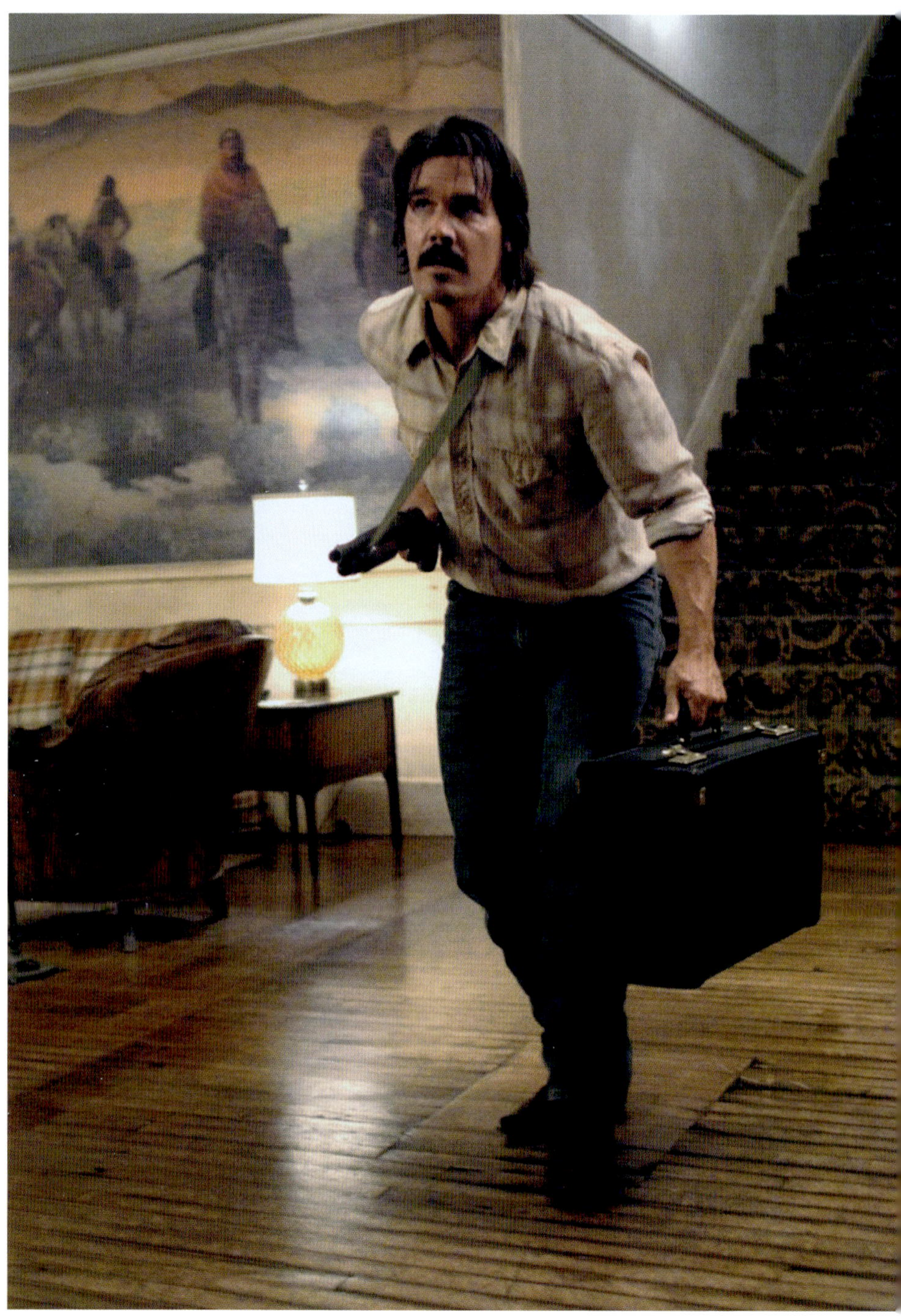

'What's the most you ever lost on a coin toss?'

A COMEBACK, AND HOW!

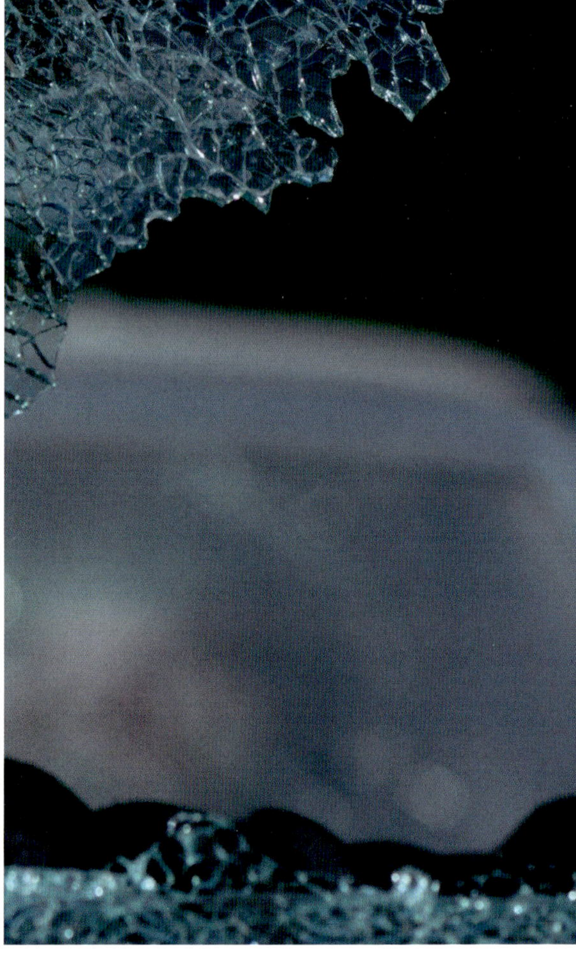

NO COUNTRY FOR OLD MEN
2007

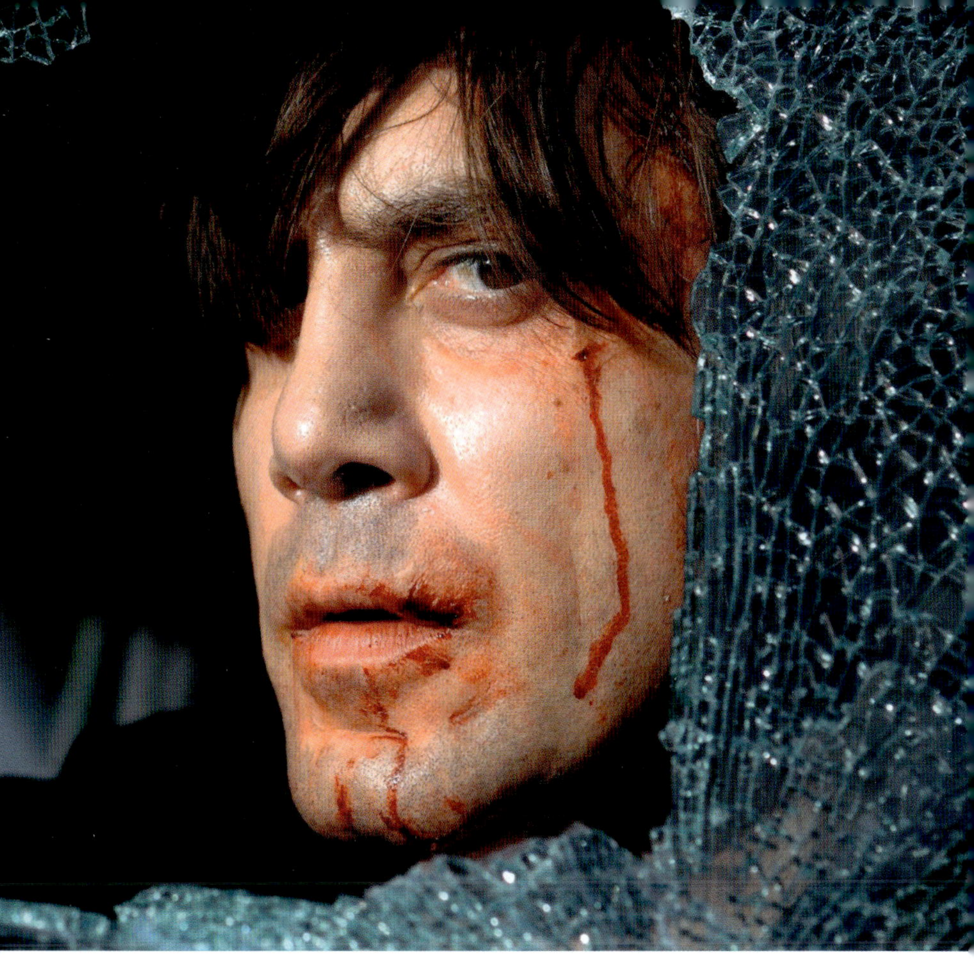

In 2004, it looked like the Coen brothers might have run out of steam. They were leaning too hard on star vehicles and other people's material. Then they returned in 2007 with *No Country For Old Men*, which won Oscars for Best Film, Best Director and Best Adapted Screenplay. Critically speaking, Joel and Ethan went from their nadir to their zenith in just one movie.

Based on the novel by Cormac McCarthy it takes place, like *Fargo*, in the relatively recent past (1980), and in a harsh environment, switching the horizonless snowscapes of the

Midwest for the dusty wind-scoured plains of West Texas. It is an ensemble piece based on a small set of main characters; one of whom is, like Marge Gunderson, a morally centred small-town law enforcer mystified by the extreme acts of violence that punctuate the narrative – here sparked by a hunter's discovery of a drug deal gone bad and a satchel stuffed with $2.4 million dollars. And it once again reins in the brothers' more showy, mannered tendencies, with a sparseness that extends to its dialogue.

The Coens claim not to have seen any similarity to *Fargo* when first reading the book, which producer Scott Rudin sent them in 2004, around a year before its publication. It was more the case that they saw in McCarthy's prose an opportunity to achieve what they hadn't been able to with *To The White Sea*. 'There were echoes of it in *No Country For Old Men* that were quite interesting for us,' Joel revealed. Specifically in 'the idea of the physical work that somebody does that helps reveal who they are. . .as opposed to any dialogue.'

But primarily they were impressed by how differently it read to McCarthy's previous novels: 'pulpier', as Joel put it. 'It was begging to be made into a movie,' said Ethan, who found it 'interesting in a genre way, because it subverts genre expectations. It's kind of a chase, but the bad guy never actually catches up to the good guy.'

They have characteristically joked that their adaptation process involved one of them holding the book open while the other typed it up. It is certainly a shining example of 'if ain't broke, don't fix it', allowing much of the novel's dialogue to reach the screen untouched. It also preserves the novel's structure and characters, who are notably cast outside the brothers' usual repertory (with the sole exception of Stephen Root, the blind radio station man in *O Brother, Where Art Thou?*). 'When we're writing our own stuff, part of the way of developing the character is thinking who might play it,' Ethan said. 'In this case the characters were ready-made, so our process of integrating old friends was bypassed. Actually, that was interesting and stimulating.' Reflective veteran sheriff Ed Tom Bell is played by Tommy Lee Jones, who hails from San Saba, close to where the story is set. Josh Brolin portrays capable but foolhardy hunter Llewelyn Moss. And Javier Bardem oozes menace as enigmatic killer Anton Chigurh, who uses a cattle-felling bolt gun as a horrifically eccentric murder weapon.

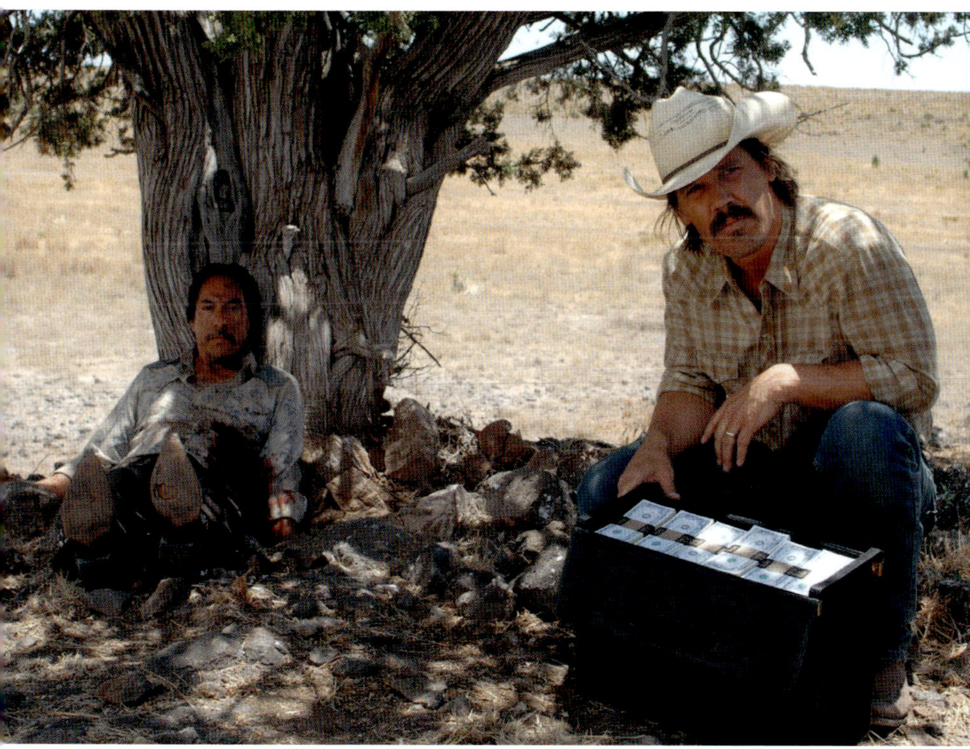

BELOW: Josh Brolin (right) as Llewelyn Moss, his breakthrough role as an adult actor, after starring in 1985's *The Goonies*.

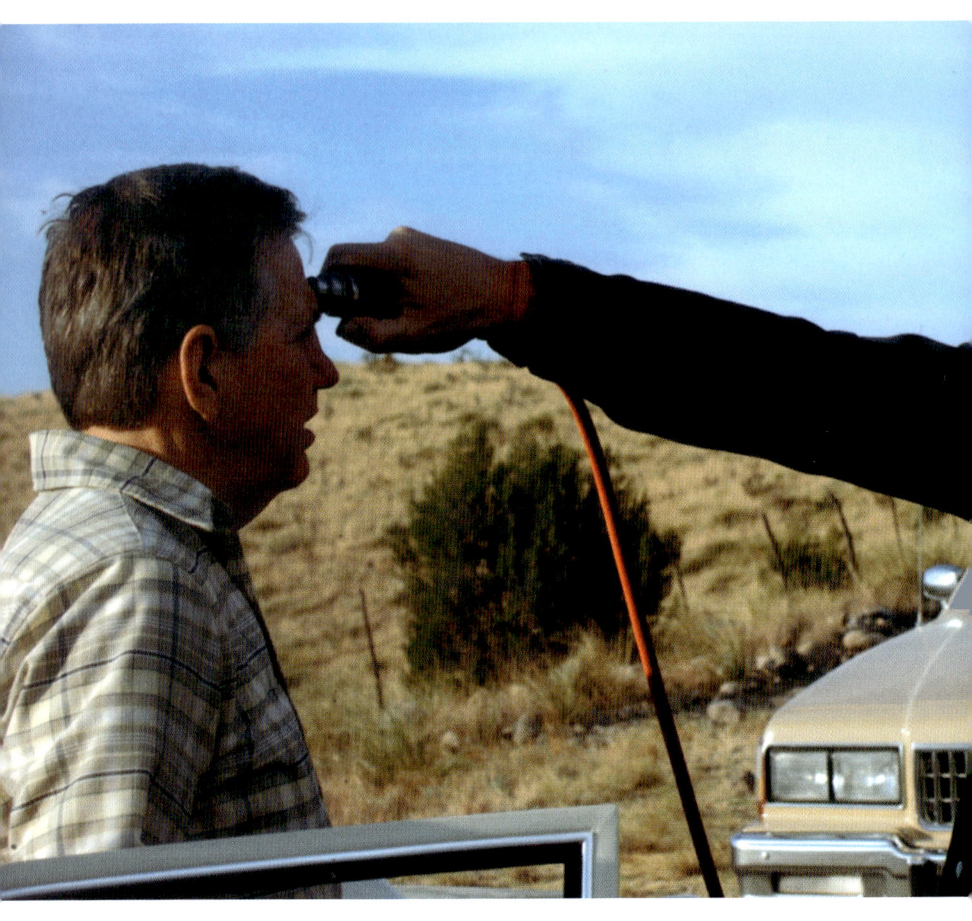

The Coens do, however, make some subtle changes to McCarthy's text. These include the removal of references to Sheriff Bell's soldiering days, and an astute tweaking of Chigurh's final-act confrontation with Llewelyn's young wife Carla Jean (Glaswegian actress Kelly Macdonald), who now refuses his invitation to toss a coin to determine whether or not she lives or dies. Chigurh is a rare figure in the Coen canon: a character whose symbolic significance they're happy to discuss (on account of him not being their creation). He is not so much evil incarnate.

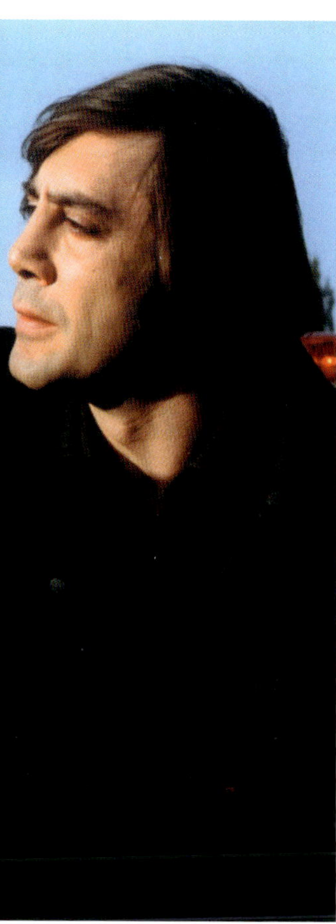

ABOVE: Chigurh uses his unconventional murder weapon – a bolt gun – on an unwitting victim (Chip Love).

He is more, Ethan says, 'a personification of the world, which is an unforgiving and capricious place'.

Joel and Ethan were sure to retain the original story's very specific location, judging it essential. 'The story is about where it takes place as much as anything else,' said Joel, 'so the location becomes a huge, important character, and it can't be separated from the story. It was very important to us that we shoot at least the stuff where you really get a feel for the landscape in West Texas.' Roger Deakins captures the region's inhospitable beauty, its scrubby expanses ominously shadowed by heavy, fast-moving clouds. It is a landscape that seemingly invites brutal acts, as its criss-crossing blood trails suggest. 'It's a harsh environment, not a picturesque landscape,' said Joel. 'It's not an easy place to live in, with a history of violence.'

While the Coens are hardly averse to depicting violence, *No Country For Old Men* is their most savage film, and features their highest body count. In a weird way, it is their first action movie, complete with foot chases, shoot-outs, explosions and car crashes. 'The almost excessive nature of the blood and the violence makes for some strange moments on the set,' laughed Joel during production. Ethan cited 'Steve

Root getting shot in the throat and gurgling' as one example, as well as Bardem 'performing field surgery on himself in a crappy motel room,' with a blood-spewing prosthetic wound. Then there is Chigurh's impactful introduction, where we see him arrested by an unwitting cop before throttling him to death with his own handcuffs. Their metal chain bites so deep into the victim's neck, it ruptures his jugular. Unsettlingly, the most striking aspect of the scene is the almost artful pattern of scuff marks that the cop's thrashing shoes leave on the floor.

Later in the movie, however, the violence shifts from being graphically depicted to occurring entirely off screen, including the deaths of Llewelyn (who isn't even killed by his hunter Chigurh in the end) and Carla Jean. This rankled some critics, who found it too casual and unsatisfying. But it is appropriate, in its own unconventional way. All this death and brutality is becoming normalized, everyday, mundane, almost. No wonder Sheriff Bell retires in the wake of Chigurh's spree, alienated by the cold-blooded chaos of this new narco-war-torn world.

Along with what goes unseen in the film, *No Country For Old Men* is also remarkable for what is unheard. When discussing how to score the movie, the Coens were stumped. 'Everything we could try to think about just seemed corny,' said Joel. 'Is it going to be Western stuff? Is it going to be cliché thriller stuff? Then looking at the movie when we cut it, we just went, "Okay, it works without [music]." The score is really just the wind.' Yet they did still engage Carter Burwell, who collaborated closely with supervising sound editor Skip Lievsay to underscore the action, and the tension, in the subtlest of ways.

OPPOSITE: Kelly Macdonald as Carla Jean Moss, another Coen-movie wife who meets a bad end.

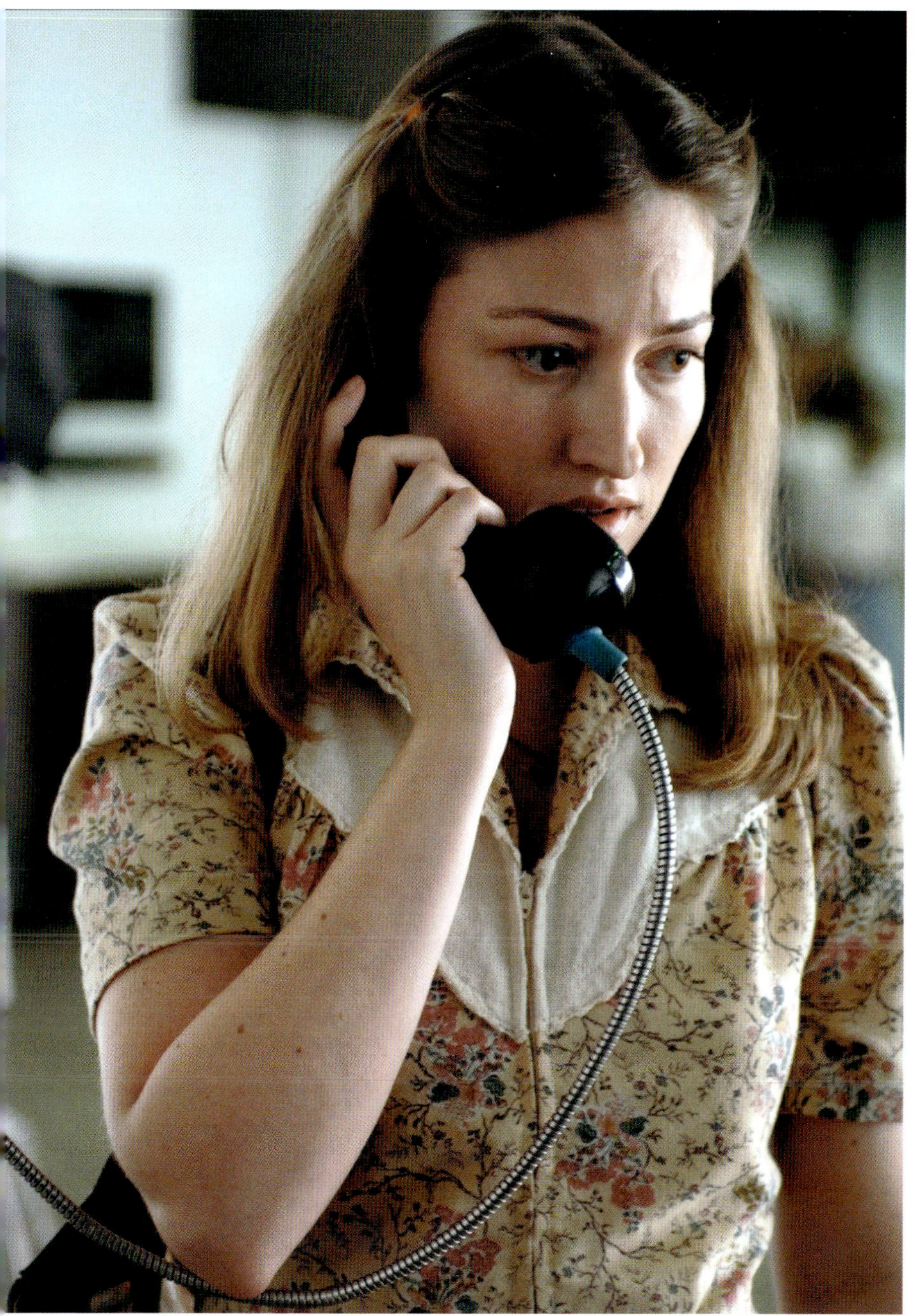

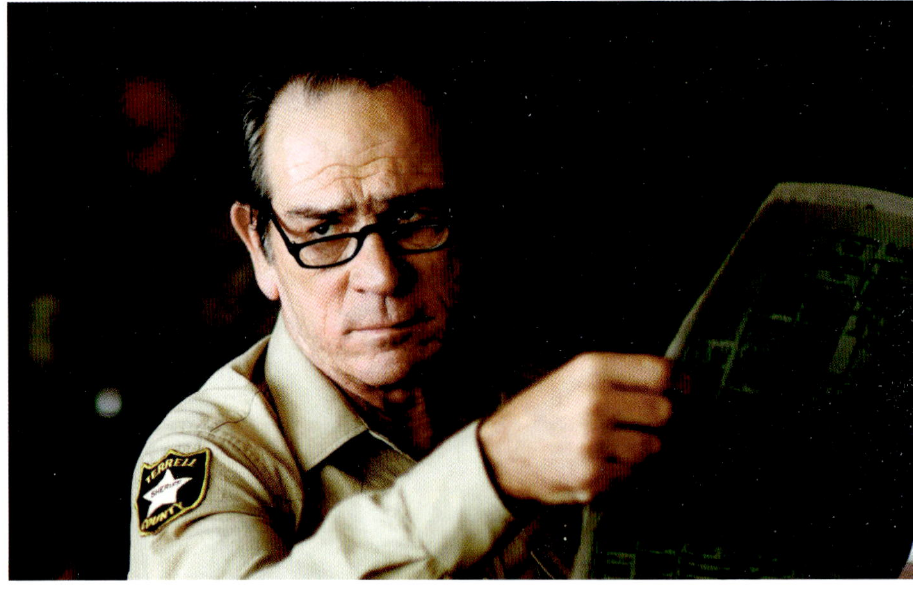

ABOVE: Tommy Lee Jones couldn't be more worldweary as Sheriff Ed Tom Bell.

In the gas station scene – probably the film's most memorable moment, where Chigurh first asks someone to bet their life on a coin toss – Burwell took the background hum of the refrigerator and added a slowly intensifying 60Hz tone beneath it. 'It gets louder and louder, and then it goes away when he reveals the result of the coin toss,' said Burwell. 'Only when it disappears do you notice there had been something there.'

Elsewhere, Burwell and Lievsay tinkered with the pitch of the wind, while the composer used sine waves and Tibetan singing bowls to create what he described as 'steady state sounds'. The only piece of music Burwell composed was for the final credits, after the Coens realized they had to have *something*, but didn't want a song to suddenly intrude on the mood woven by Tommy Lee Jones' final elegiac monologue, in which Ed Tom describes a dream of his dead father, waiting for him 'out there in all that dark and all that cold'. So Burwell used a shaker to pick up on the clock that's heard ticking in the scene, gradually easing the audience towards a guitar that doesn't come in until about a minute later.

Burwell's contribution to *No Country For Old Men* is symptomatic of the challenges the Coens created for themselves and their collaborators on this brilliantly unconventional film, with the result earning much well-deserved praise. It is regarded as their masterpiece and, like *Fargo,* reached a far wider audience than expected, grossing just under $172 million worldwide. There was a suggestion that Joel and Ethan had quelled their zanier tendencies and, finally, matured. Yet they claimed to feel unchanged by the fresh admiration of their peers. 'Y'know, life goes on,' said Joel of their Oscar win. 'It doesn't affect us in any substantive way on a day-to-day basis. It will be forgotten about in a few months.'

'There's something very odd about it,' added Ethan. 'It goes right in the "Life is Strange" box. It was never an ambition to grow up and win an Academy Award. So when it happens you go: "Weird!"'

Coens abroad: *Tuileries* (2006)

Until 2006, the Coens had never set a film outside the United States. They had explored their own country extensively, but their cinema had yet to travel abroad. That changed with *Tuileries,* the first of two short films they made in the space of a year. (The other was 2007's *World Cinema,* starring Josh Brolin.) Commissioned for French anthology movie *Paris, Je T'aime,* this rather contrived confection riffed knowingly on the brothers' resolute Americanness. It starred Steve Buscemi as a tourist in the Tuileries metro station, whose reliance on his guidebook doesn't help him when he becomes embroiled in a French couple's tempestuous tiff, resulting in a fierce beating that leaves him lying, bewildered, in a pile of Louvres souvenirs.

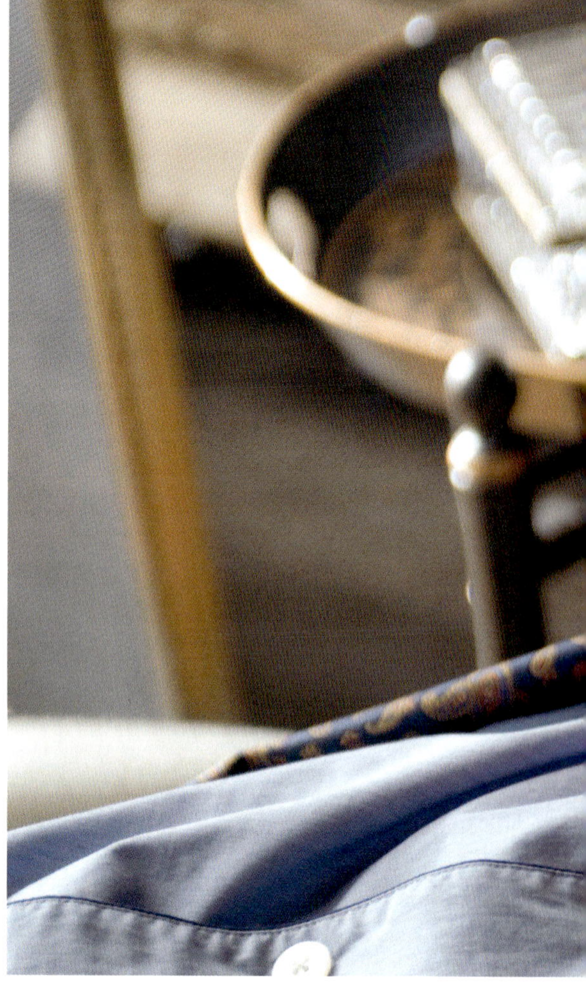

BURN AFTER READING
2008

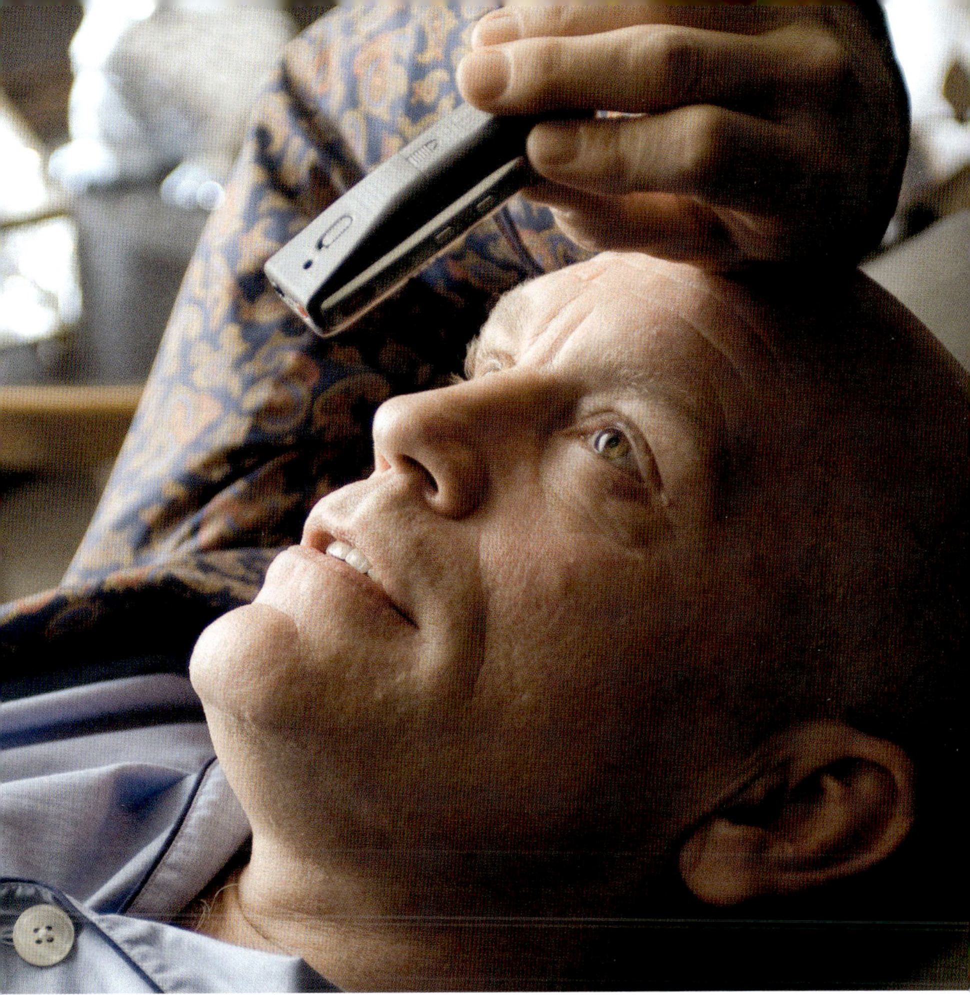

The primary reason Joel and Ethan claimed to be unchanged by their triumph with *No Country For Old Men* was that, by the time it was released, they were already in the thick of making their next movie, whose script they'd written simultaneously with their McCarthy adaptation.

The first original Coen script since *The Man Who Wasn't There*, *Burn After Reading* is about bad intelligence. Or to be more accurate, non-intelligence. It is also about physical fitness. And

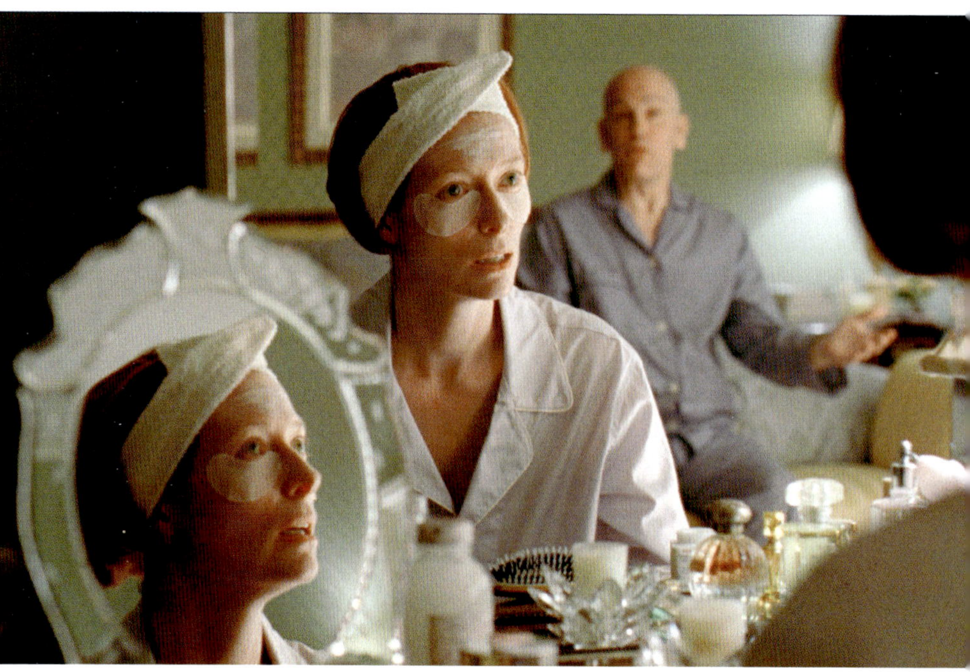

ABOVE: Tilda Swinton as Osbourne's frustrated wife Katie, who doesn't smile once during the whole film.

plastic surgery. And internet dating. And, giving it some unexpected connective tissue to *No Country For Old Men*, the theme of age. 'The movie is about middle-aged people,' explained Ethan. 'All undergoing some sort of crisis,' Joel continued. 'Personal. Sexual. Even touching on matters of national security.' It was, he said, 'a Washington story.' One that gave the brothers the chance to deliver their own spin on a genre they hadn't tackled before: 'Spy stuff and intrigue,' said Ethan, who compared it to the thrillers of Tony Scott and the Jason Bourne movies. Only, 'without the explosions'.

Despite being set in the United States' capital in the modern day, *Burn After Reading* is not intended as a political satire, or a commentary on War on Terror-era espionage. But it does subvert conspiracy theories, whose elaborate machinations provide great grist for Hollywood political thrillers – especially those of the Sixties and Seventies, which the Coens were consciously referencing. A common counterargument to conspiracy theories is that terrible things happen by mistake, not by design. This is known as the cock-up theory. So *Burn After Reading* could be described as Hollywood's first 'cock-up thriller': a catalogue of national-security-adjacent errors made by a grab-bag of dolts.

It is essentially a new twist on the Coens' love of crap criminals. 'If everybody knows what they are doing in the movie, if they are capable and everyone is on top of things, then what is going to happen that is interesting, or fun, or surprising?' reasoned Ethan.

In *Burn After Reading*, people couldn't be less capable. Its events are triggered when a mid-level CIA analyst named Osbourne Cox (John Malkovich) decides to write his memoirs after being fired for 'a drinking problem'. These are burned onto a disk, along with his financials, by his wife Katie (Tilda Swinton) as part of her preparation for divorce. She is having an affair with US marshal Harry Pfarrer (George Clooney), a serial philanderer who also hooks up with Linda Litzke (Frances McDormand), an employee at Hardbodies Gym who is unaware of her boss Ted's (Richard Jenkins) affection for her, and is desperately trying to afford cosmetic surgery. When Linda's inane but enthusiastic co-worker Chad (Brad Pitt) finds Katie's disk left in the gym, he presumes it is 'raw intelligence' and he and Linda hatch a plan to extort money from Osbourne, allowing Linda to fund her surgery. When this doesn't go as planned – Osbourne threatens them and punches Chad in the face – Linda tries to sell the disk to the bemused Russians, who realize it is 'drivel', and in turn inform a nonplussed CIA.

Eventually, through an intricate series of mishaps and misunderstandings, Chad is killed by Harry, Ted is axe-murdered by Osbourne, Osbourne is shot and rendered brain-dead, Harry flees to Venezuela, and Linda's surgery is paid for by the Agency to keep her quiet. At the rather abrupt close of the film, the CIA Superior (J K Simmons) asks his underling (David Rasche) what they've learned. 'I don't know, sir,' comes the reply. 'I don't fuckin' know either,' says the boss. Unlike the big curtain pulls we usually get in conspiracy thrillers, there is nothing to reveal here, nothing to learn. Just a mess that is probably best swept under the carpet.

Arriving in the wake of *No Country For Old Men*, *Burn After Reading* is easy to dismiss as a minor Coen. But where their last film was a distinctive departure, this one was a return to form. Despite its cruel streak – Ted's *Fargo*-like demise at the swing of an axe is one of the most upsetting moments in any of their films – it is their funniest caper since *The Big Lebowski*. And one of their most commercially successful, grossing almost as much as *No Country*. This is largely down to its impressively starry ensemble, for whom the script was precision engineered. 'We came up with the idea just thinking about different parts we might want to write for actors that we know, who we thought it might be fun to throw together,' said Ethan.

This stratagem allowed for Clooney to complete his 'trilogy of idiots' for the Coens (though it would become a trilogy of four with *Hail, Caesar!*), and to share scenes for the first time with fellow Coen regular McDormand, now on her sixth film for the brothers. It also enabled them to work for the first time with Malkovich, whom they'd only met once before but were keen to have as a collaborator. Plus it gave them the opportunity to finally have Brad Pitt in one of their movies.

Pitt proves he can be as much a character actor as he is a star, and is by far the most hilarious of all the film's various knuckleheads, especially during Chad's eye-narrowing, voice-deepening attempts to intimidate Osbourne over the phone.

With his feathery, patchily highlighted hairdo (inspired by a make-up mistake on a commercial he'd just done), he also joined the great tradition of badly coiffured Coen characters. 'We frequently give actors haircuts that they have to somehow disguise during their off-camera moments,' admitted Joel.

With their reputation fully restored, and the brothers now well into the strongest run of their career, it seemed like they could take their pick of virtually any Hollywood A-lister. But for their next three films, they took an alternative approach, recruiting for their lead characters either complete or relative unknowns.

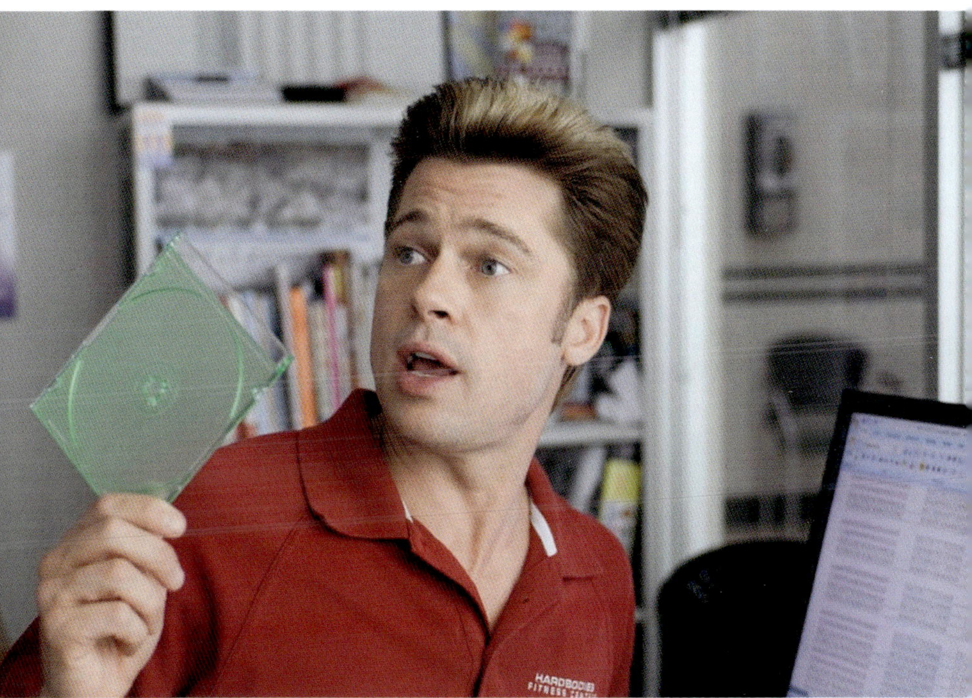

ABOVE: As Chad Feldheimer, Brad Pitt gamely sported a classic-Coen bad hairdo.

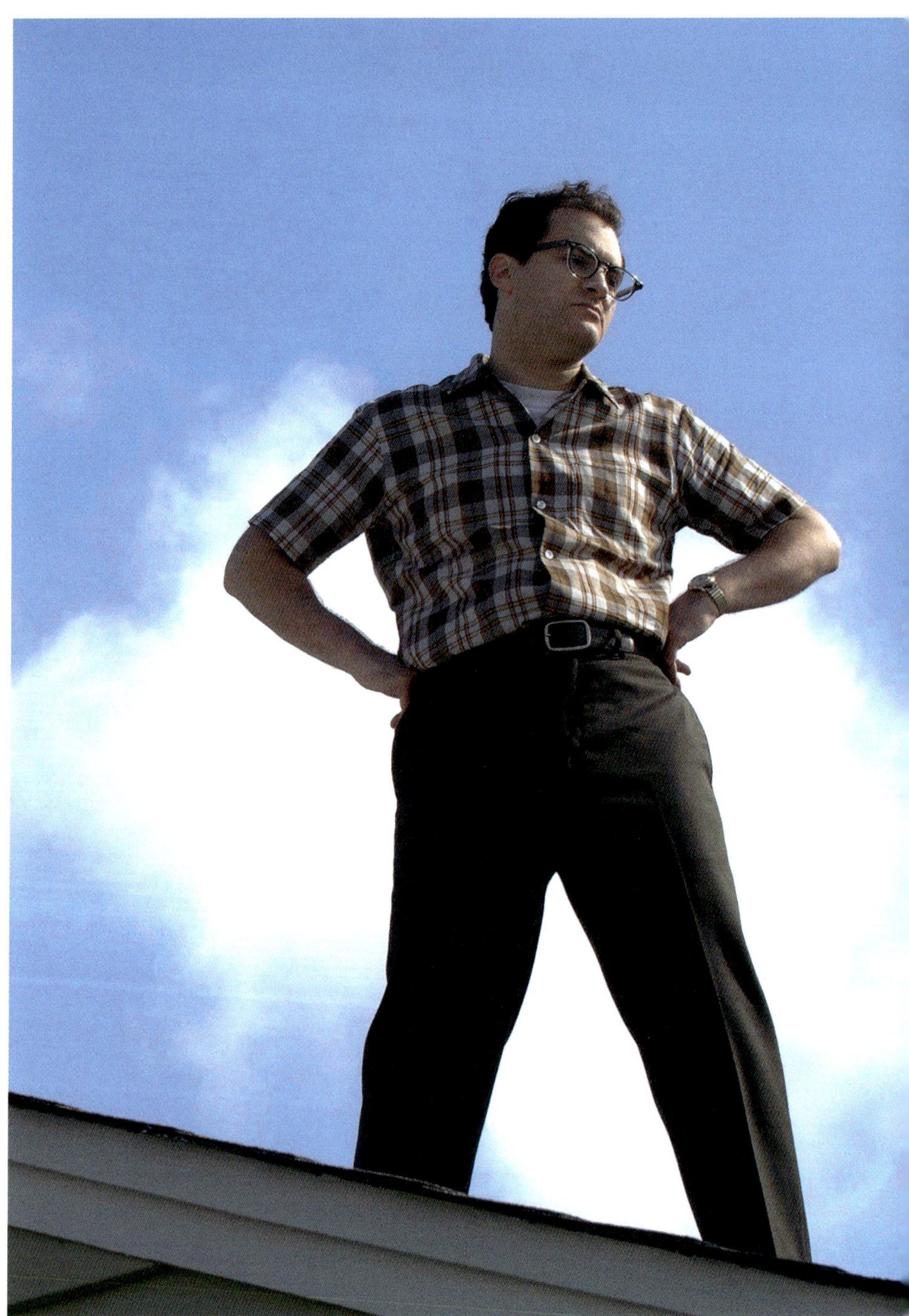

'*We can't know everything*'

SERIOUS MEN

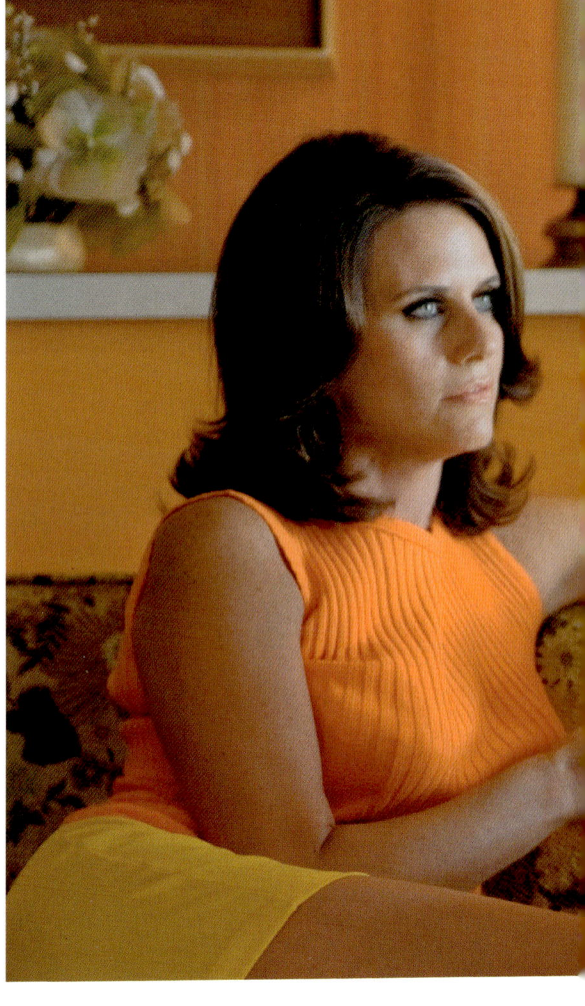

A SERIOUS MAN
2009

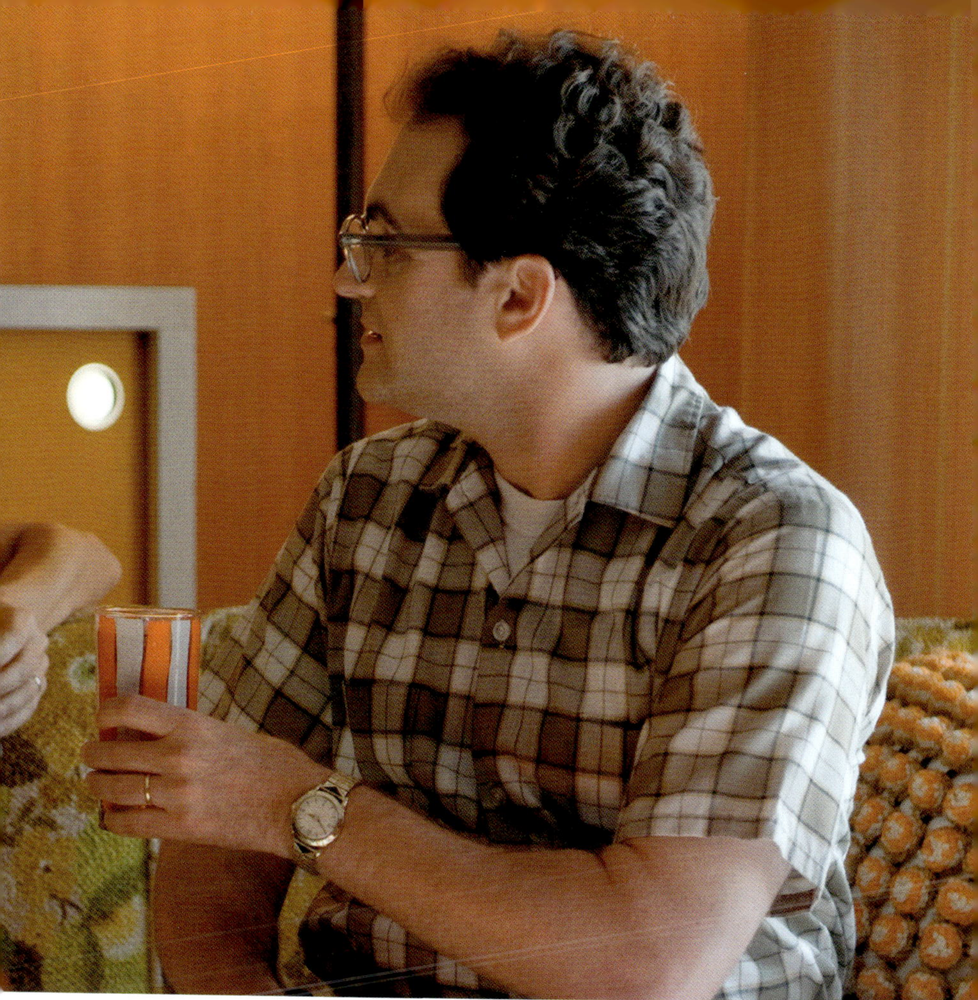

Since childhood, Joel and Ethan had shared a strong memory of a rabbi in their community – an elderly, mysterious figure, to whom boys were sent after their bar mitzvah. 'He was a sage,' recalled Ethan. 'He said nothing, but had a lot of charisma.'

Over the years, the brothers had planned to translate this memory into a short film. Gradually that idea mutated into something that more extensively drew on their early years amid the manicured-garden suburbs of late-Sixties Minnesota.

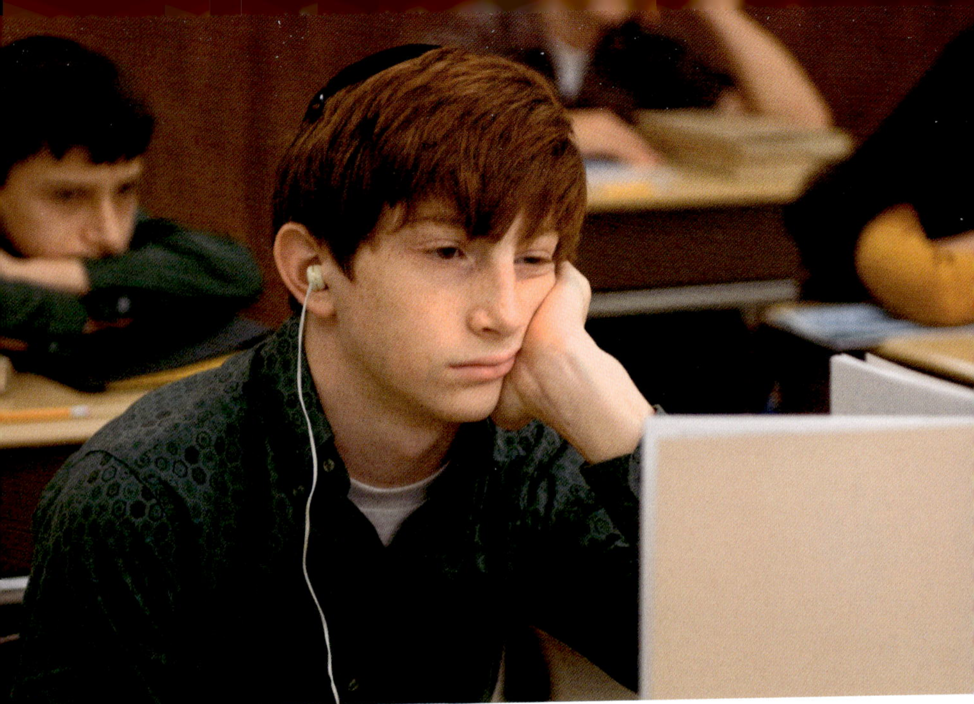

ABOVE: Teenager Danny Gopnik (Aaron Wolff) is more interested in rock music than studying Hebrew.

A Serious Man was the second revisitation of Joel and Ethan's old stomping ground, though it's notably lacking in 'Minnesota niceness'. As suggested by its semi-ironic title, it signalled a continuation of their 'mature' phase, and became their most personal – for want of a less sentimental word – offering to date.

It is fair to say there is little reverence from the brothers for the faith of their youth. First, there was Bernie Bernbaum in *Miller's Crossing*, whose treatment some commentators found a little disturbing; critic J Hoberman even drew parallels between Bernie's intended woodland execution and the Holocaust. Barton Fink's Jewishness was never really a plot point, though Jewish studio head Jack Lipnick tossed around the self-denigrating term 'kike', and the two cops expressed an antisemitic disdain for the screenwriter. And in *The Big Lebowski*, Walter Sobchak's incongruous commitment to the religion he converted to after marrying his Jewish wife (since divorced) is played for big laughs.

It was not ever something they took seriously. 'Like most kids who get spiritual instruction, religious instruction, Hebrew school and going to the synagogue was always a chore,' said Joel. 'We both stopped going as soon as our parents let us.' Even so, it affected them enough to use *A Serious Man* to explore their relationship with their religion – in an oblique, blackly comical manner that, they insisted, was 'not in any way autobiographical'.

The closest character to Joel and/or Ethan is young teenager Danny Gopnik (Aaron Wolff), who illicitly listens to rock music, is obsessed with watching Western sitcom *F-Troop*, owes the school bully money for marijuana, and must prepare for his bar mitzvah, which he eventually attends stoned. The Coens' intention was to devote half of the film to Danny, but during the writing process found themselves focusing more on his father Larry (Michael Stuhlbarg), who like their own father Ed is a university professor, though he teaches physics rather than economics. 'The fun of the story for us was inventing new ways to torture Larry,' said Ethan. 'His life just progressively gets worse.'

Larry's Job-like tribulations form the plot's spine, and unlike the problems characters suffer in their other movies, his are not self-inflicted. His wife wants to divorce him for an older man (Sy Ableman, played to oleaginous perfection by Fred Melamed), and insists he should move out. One of his students is trying to bribe him into increasing his grade. His racist neighbour wants to build on his garden. Someone is sending defamatory letters to the board considering his tenure at the university. His live-in brother Arthur (Richard Kind) is depressed and constantly getting in trouble with the law. A record club he never joined is chasing him for arrears. And he might be very, very ill.

To underpin what Ethan termed the 'incongruity of Jews in the Midwest,' the Coens drew on local talent for their cast, and recruited 'real Jews as opposed to the Hollywood ethnic type.' As a result, the film is admirably absent of Coen regulars, its most recognizable faces being Kind (then best known for *Spin City*) and Adam Arkin (from *Chicago Hope*) as Larry's lawyer. This gives it a strikingly different texture to the brothers' other films which, combined with its mostly location-based shoot, also makes it more relatable than it might otherwise have been. They found the ideal lead in Stuhlbarg, then little known outside the New York theatre world. As the Coens ratchet up the unpleasantness for Larry, Stuhlbarg applies impressive restraint, impeccably embodying a man only just barely keeping things together.

Being a physicist, Larry is used to figuring out solutions, as the chalk equations on his huge blackboard attest. But he can see no reason for why his life is falling apart like this, and so must seek them from his faith. The rabbis he talks to speak only in non-sequiturs. The first (played by Simon Helberg) hilariously invites him to 'look at the parking lot', while the second (George Wyner) tells a pointless yarn about a 'Goy' whose teeth are discovered by his dentist to bear the Hebrew message 'Help me, save me'. The third rabbi (Alan Mandell) – the senior one, plucked from Joel and Ethan's childhood – won't even see Larry. He's too busy 'thinking'. When we do hear him speak, it's to (the still stoned) Danny, and he just quotes Jefferson Airplane lyrics and tells him to be a good boy. Perhaps the most useful piece of advice Larry receives (but ignores) comes from the father of the student trying to bribe him: 'Please, accept the mystery.'

OPPOSITE: Jessica McManus as Larry's eye-rolling teenage daughter Sarah, who was inspired by Joel and Ethan's own older sister, Deborah.

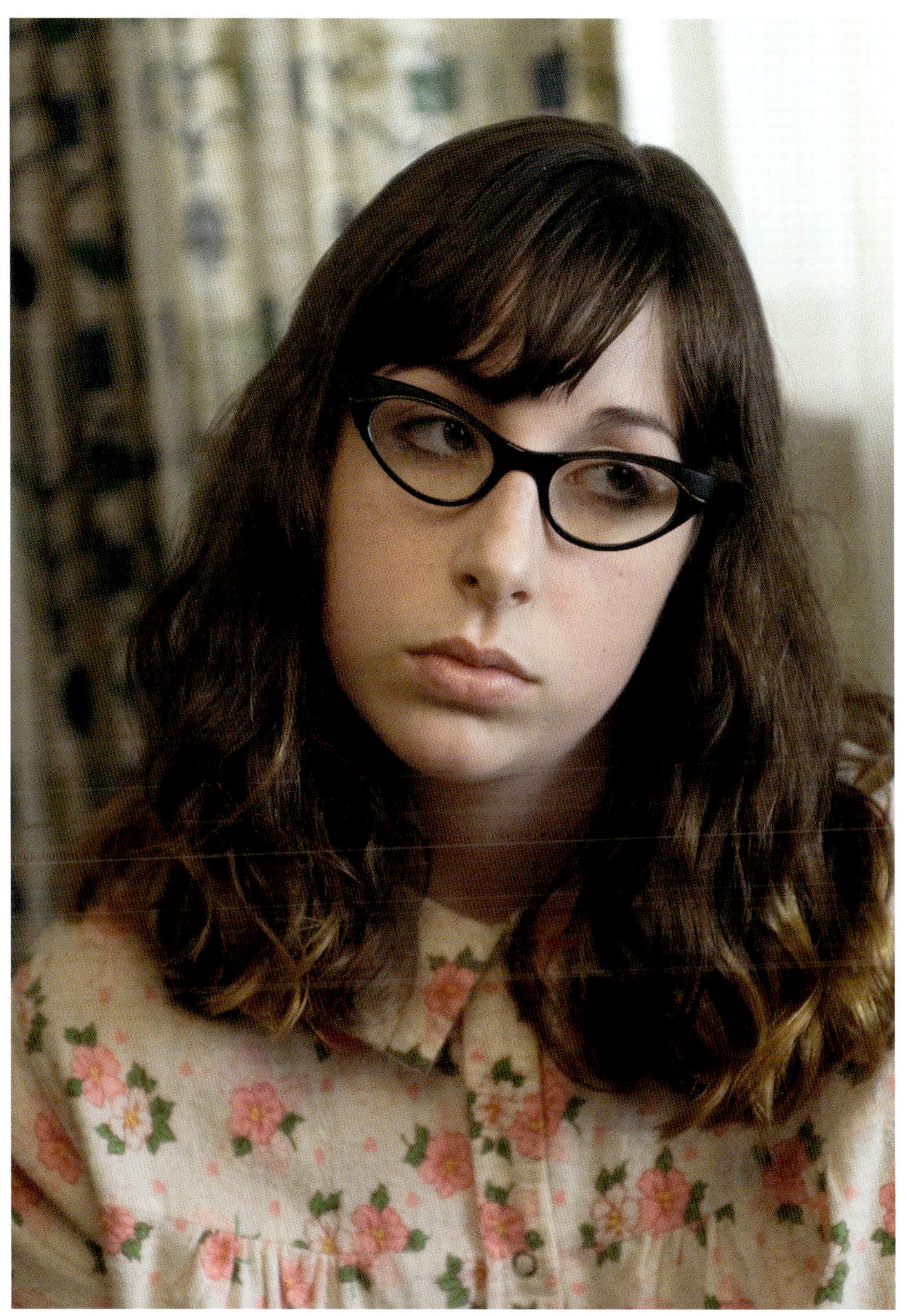

As must their audience at both the beginning and end of *A Serious Man*. The film opens with a prologue set in a 19th-century Polish *shtetl*, spoken entirely in Yiddish and concerning a supposedly dead man arriving for dinner at a couple's home and being fatally stabbed by the suspicious wife, who takes him for an evil spirit. A folk tale made up entirely by the brothers, it 'doesn't have any relationship to what follows,' Joel insisted. However, one might reasonably assume, as critic Roger Ebert did, that the couple are Larry's ancestors, creating the curse that will strike him.

At the other end of the narrative, *A Serious Man* ends on a double cliff-hanger, breath-taking in its portentousness. After Larry finally relents, accepts the bribe money and amends his student's low midterm grade to a C–, he receives a phone call from his doctor with his recent test results, insisting he immediately come in. Meanwhile, having been ushered out of class by a twister warning, Danny stands outside and beholds a huge, dark tornado coming directly towards him – like the manifest wrath of the Old Testament god.

A Serious Man is a funny, fascinating and fatalistic movie: a character-driven portrait of a very specific place and time, with little regard for cinematic convention. It earned the brothers their second Best Motion Picture nomination at the Oscars, along with much critical approval. But there was some ambivalence towards it among the community it portrayed. 'You're not making fun of the Jews are you?', they were asked during production. They weren't, 'but some will take anything that isn't flattering as an indication that we think the whole community or ethnicity is flawed,' said Ethan.

While some took offence, the film had its defenders, too. One of these was Rabbi Dan Sklar, a language and liturgy consultant on the production. 'It's the most Jewish movie I've ever seen,' he said. 'You leave the theatre with a host of questions, no easy answers

and, frankly, arguing about what it all means.' He even compared
the Coens with prophets, who 'speak truth to power and. . .speak
truth to the people. The Coens see right through the foibles of our
humanity. They turn their lens on "normalcy" and make the
mundane at once abnormal, beautiful and terrifying.'

It was high praise, but it's likely the ever level-headed Coens
took it as much to heart as they did the negative responses. They
certainly weren't going to take it too seriously. As the end credits
knowingly joke, 'No Jews were harmed in the making of this
motion picture.'

Ethan on page

The previous Coen work that bears the closest kinship to *A Serious Man*
is 1998's *Gates of Eden*, a collection of 14 short stories Ethan had been
working on over the previous decade.

Compared with the polished dialogue of his and Joel's scripts,
most of these feel like sketches that draw on many of the same themes
and references as their movies. His love for pulp detective fiction, for
example, shines through in the hard-boiled noir pastiche of 'Fever
in the Blood', the oldest story in the book, in which a private eye has
one of his ears bitten off. In 2002, this was adapted by Andrew Pulver
into a short film.

More interesting are the stories that are clearly drawn from
Ethan's childhood. As *The Guardian*'s Jonathan Romney wrote in 2000,
these 'hint at the personally revealing movie the Coens have yet to
make – although in all honesty, it's hard to imagine them coming up
with a screen evocation of a synagogue-going Jewish upbringing in
Sixties Minnesota.' Little did he know. . .

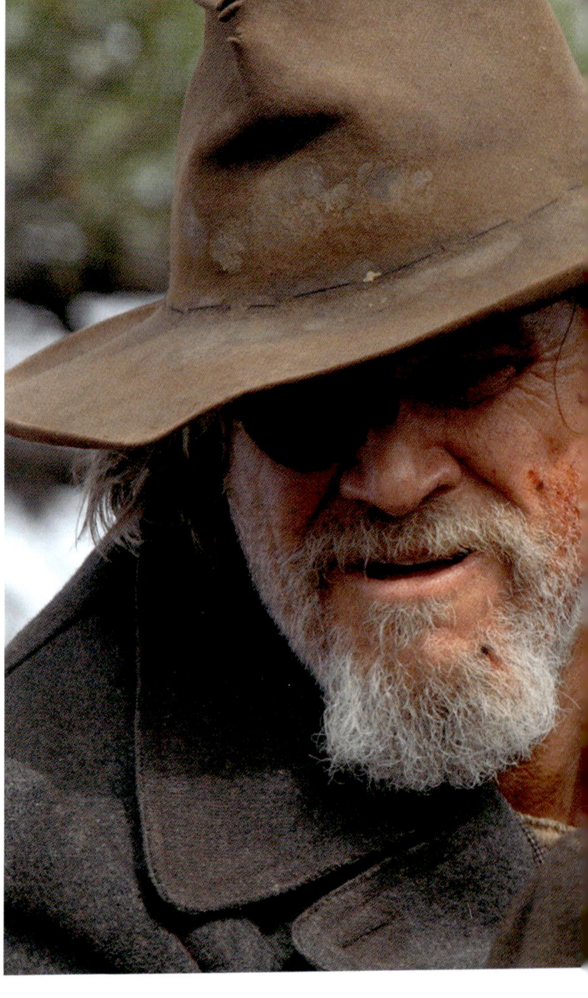

TRUE GRIT
2010

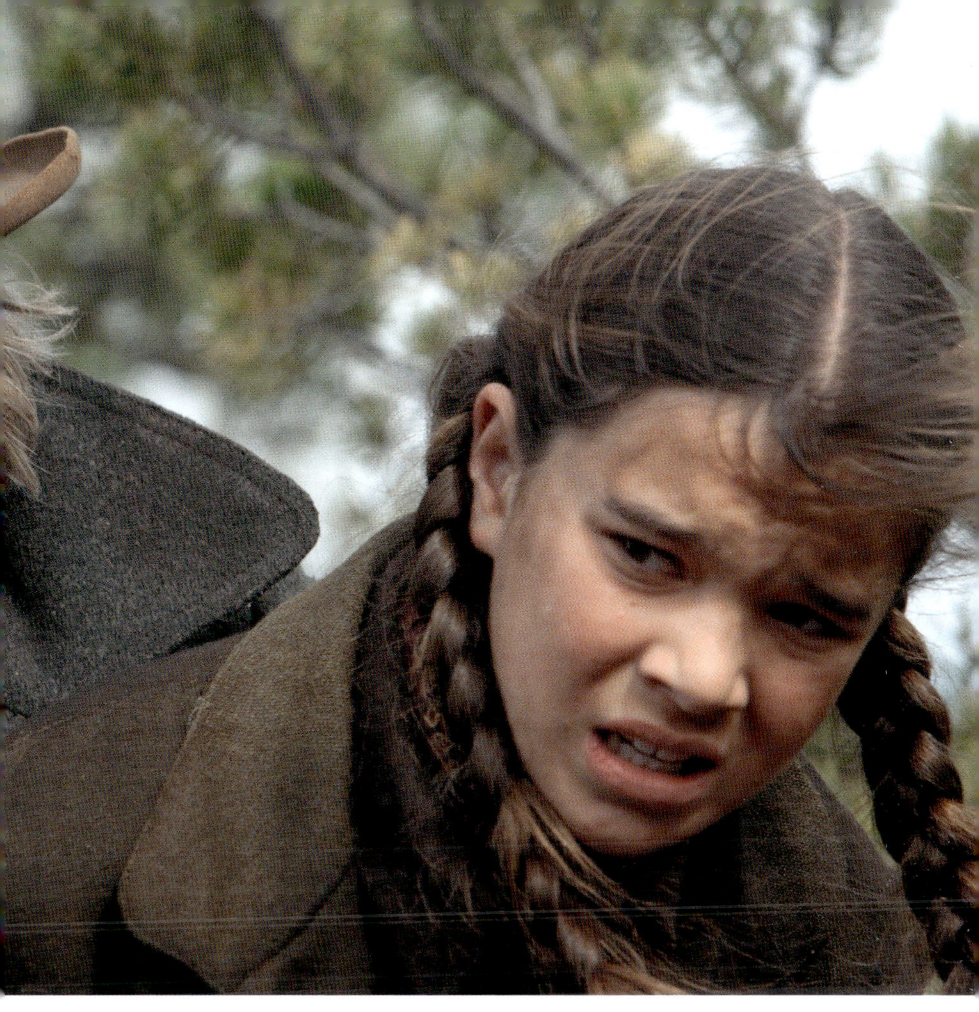

When Joel and Francis McDormand's son Pedro was little, Joel would, like most fathers, read him bedtime stories. But unlike most fathers, one of the stories he chose was Charles Portis' 1968 Western novel *True Grit*, a first-person narrative about a determined, godfearing girl named Mattie Ross, who enlists grizzled marshal Rooster Cogburn to help track down her father's killer in Indian Territory (now Oklahoma). 'As I was reading it I thought, "this would make a good movie",' recalled Joel years later.

Of course, it had already made a good movie: Henry Hathaway's 1969 Western of the same title, which starred John Wayne as the one-eyed Rooster and earned The Duke his first and only Oscar, at the ripe old age of 62. But Joel didn't really care about that. 'As I was reading, I thought, "I know what I would do, and I know it's not what they did before." I thought that would be fun to do. I didn't know whether or not it would be successful. . !

As it turned out, Joel and Ethan's *True Grit* was their biggest-ever movie, considerably outperforming all their others with a worldwide box-office haul of over $250 million and ten Oscar nominations, though it didn't win any. Not bad for a Western – hardly the most commercial genre in the 21st century – starring an unknown teenager (Hailee Steinfeld). Although, it did benefit from its popular provenance and a savvy Christmas holiday release. Plus, it boasted the impressive presence of Jeff 'The Dude' Bridges as Rooster, with Matt Damon co-starring as the puffed-up Texas Ranger LaBoeuf, who joins the manhunt, and *No Country For Old Men*'s Josh Brolin in the minor role of their quarry, Tom Chaney. But the main reason for *True Grit*'s phenomenal success was a simple one: it was perhaps the Coens' most straightforward and traditional picture yet.

Hathaway's solid 1969 take on Portis' novel was hailed at the time as a welcome blast of Old Hollywood, arriving just as the US film industry was undergoing a countercultural revolution in the wake of films like *Bonnie and Clyde* (1967) and *Easy Rider* (1969). The same night Wayne was awarded his Oscar, *Midnight Cowboy* (1969) became the first ever X-rated movie to win Best Picture. On the surface, then, it seems surprising that its source material

OPPOSITE: This was Steinfeld's first movie. Only 13 at the time, she was a year younger than her character, Mattie Ross.

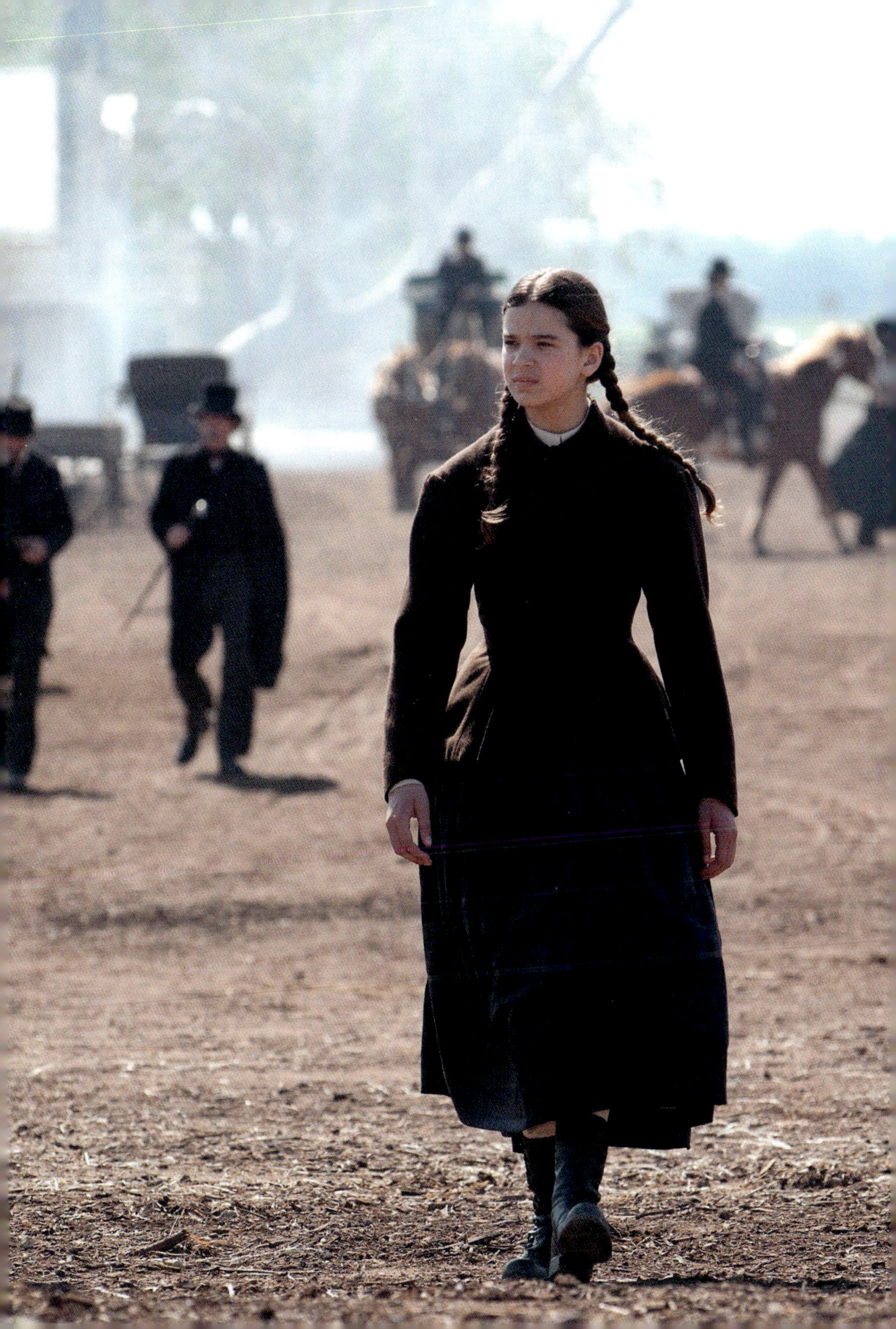

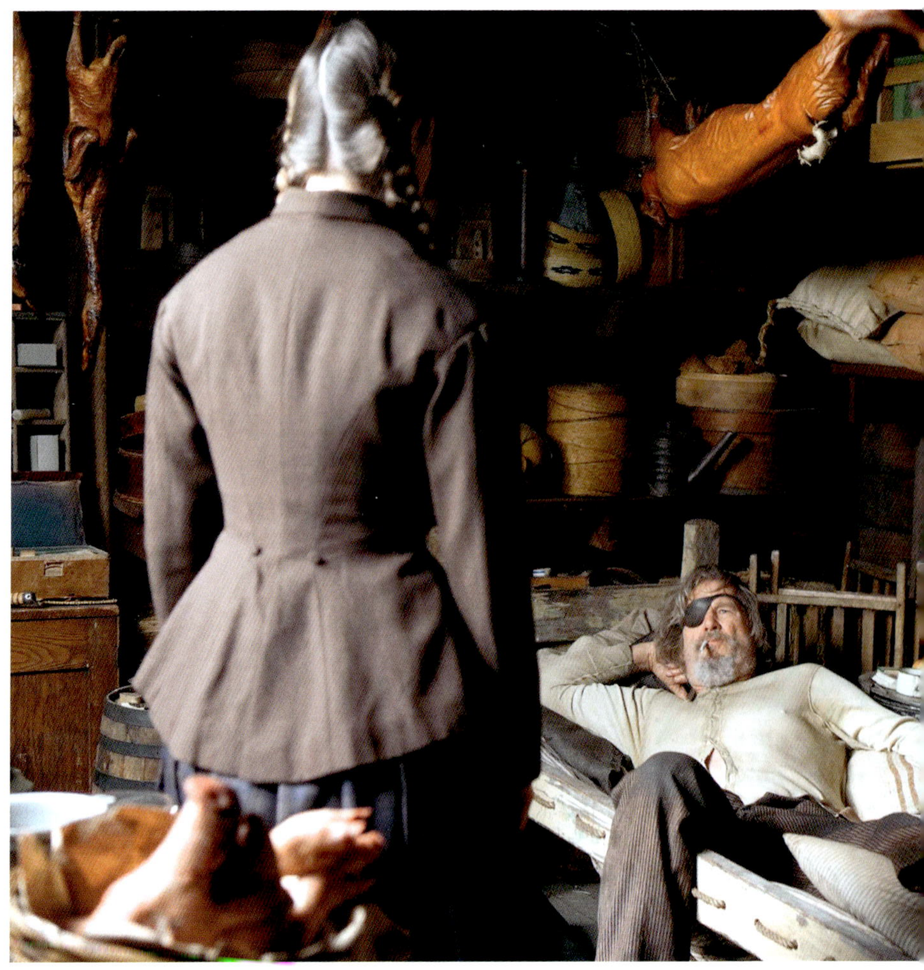

should have so appealed to the hardly conventional Joel and Ethan, especially as Hathaway had already adapted it with such success. But to the Coens it wasn't so much a matter of following where Hathaway had already trodden as pulling Portis' novel out from his film's wide-brimmed shadow. 'The novel is fantastic,' said Damon. 'It was a big American novel when it came out. Then the John Wayne movie came out and the book got forgotten about.'

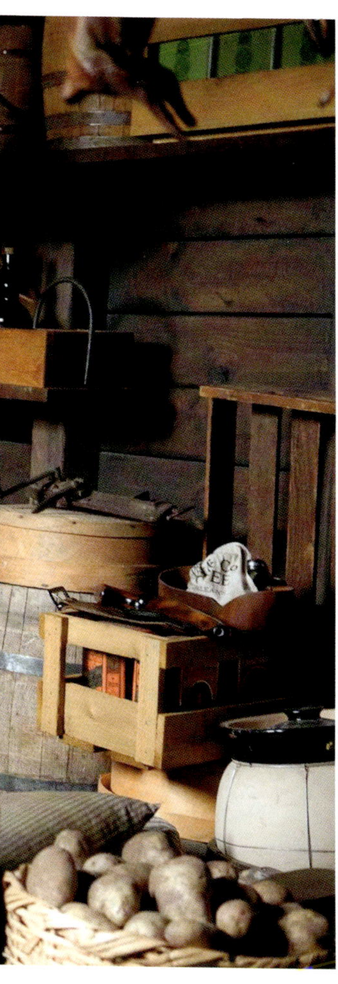

ABOVE: Appropriately for The Dude, Bridges played up Cogburn's slovenly side.

What had mostly been forgotten was just how rich and droll Portis' dialogue was. 'I would not put a thief in my mouth to steal my brain,' says Mattie when Rooster offers her some liquor; a line that could have been written by Joel and Ethan. Indeed, as Bridges noted when he read the book, 'I could see why the brothers wanted to do it. It reads like something they might do.' Writer Roy Blount Jr, a huge admirer of Portis, hit the nail on the head when he said the author 'could be Cormac McCarthy if he wanted to, but he'd rather be funny.' It was certainly Portis' sense of humour that won Ethan over. 'It's much funnier than the [1969] movie,' he said. 'I think, unfortunately, they lost a lot of humour in both the situations and in [Mattie's] voice.'

Once again, the Coens' adaptation process took the 'one holds the book open while the other types' approach, revelling in Mattie's precocious, Bible-honed voice. 'The whole Presbyterian–Protestant ethic in a 14-year-old girl was interesting to us and sounded fun,' said Ethan. They also preserved Rooster's gasbag tendencies, LaBoeuf's drawling superciliousness, and the book's vividly violent outbursts – surprising for what we'd now call a young adult novel. The confrontation in Greaser Bob's cabin suddenly turns bloody when one outlaw cuts off another's fingers and

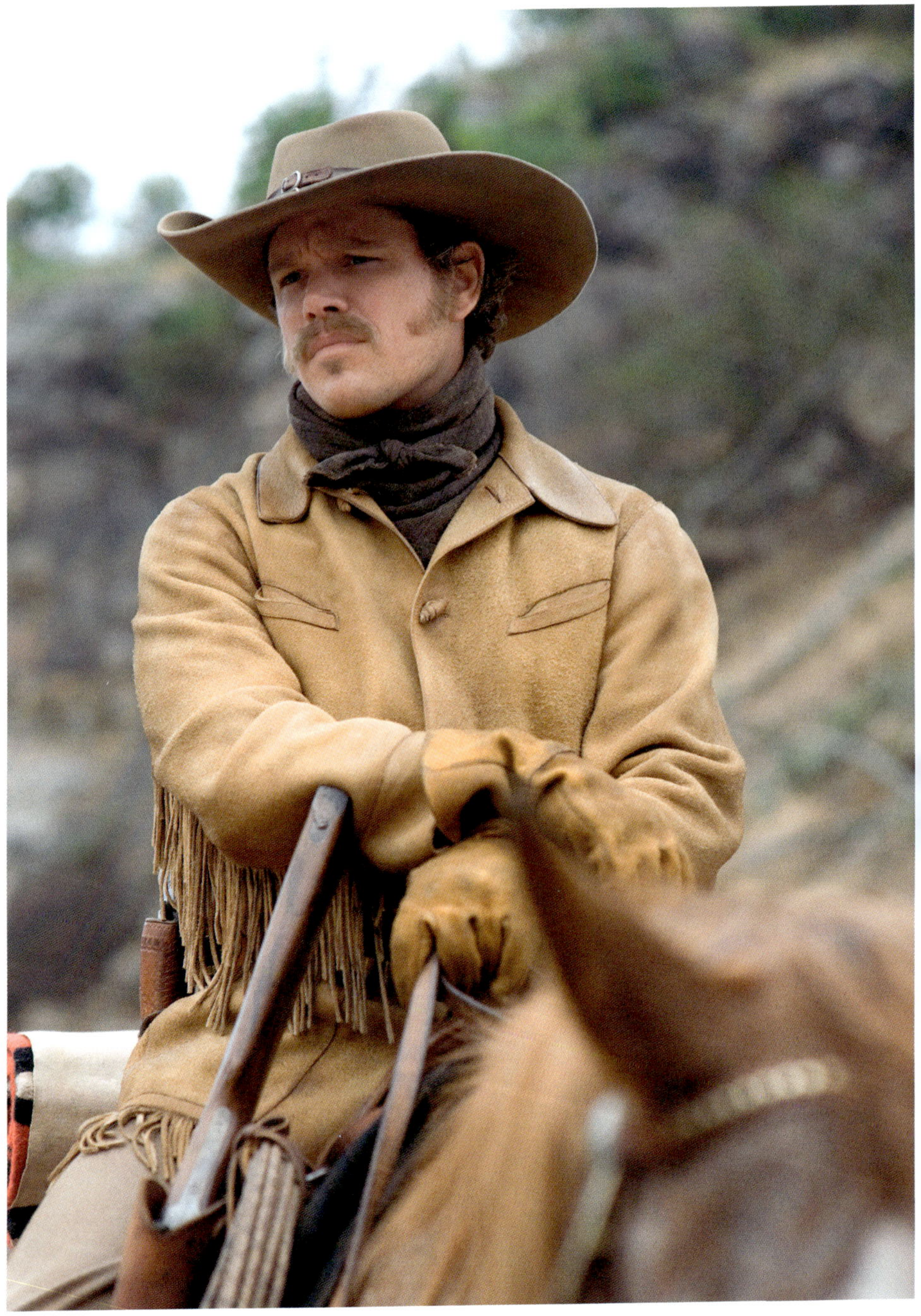

stabs him in the sternum, before Rooster puts a bullet through the attacker's face. This all takes place directly in front of Mattie, whose relatably wide-eyed reaction makes the scene's impact far more keenly felt than any previous Coen-choreographed savagery.

There are some added Coen touches, such as a rider who surreally wears a bear-rug costume and asks, 'Do any of you need medical attention?', and a mysterious body that Mattie and Rooster find hanging impossibly high in a tree. But it is a faithful adaptation, and all the better for it – especially as the brothers were insistent that Mattie (to whom the novel's title truly applies) not be side-lined by the cycloptic lawman, as she is in Hathaway's version. Unlike the 1969 Mattie, who was played by 25-year-old Kim Darby, they felt it essential to find someone Mattie's age.

Hailee Steinfeld was one of more than 15,000 girls who answered a casting call posted on 27 October 2009. It sought a 12–16-year-old, 'who's tough, strong and tells it like it is.' Not until very late in the day – weeks before filming – did the Coens discover her, with the help of casting directors Rachel Tenner and Ellen Chenoweth. 'It wasn't a given that we were going to find the person who could do the movie,' said Ethan. 'It's a great part for a 14-year-old, but it could have turned out to be beyond all real-life 14-year-olds.'

It wasn't beyond 13-year-old Steinfeld, however. Exhibiting an appealingly steely determination as Mattie, she proved more than capable of holding her own in complex dialogues, while her callowness is still allowed to shine through. Sometimes it's sweet, such as in the campfire scene where she tries to quell the alpha-male tensions between Rooster and LaBoeuf by telling them the ghost story of The Midnight Caller. Damon went as far as to

OPPOSITE: Self-absorbed Texas Ranger LaBoeuf (Matt Damon) becomes both ally and rival to Mattie and Rooster.

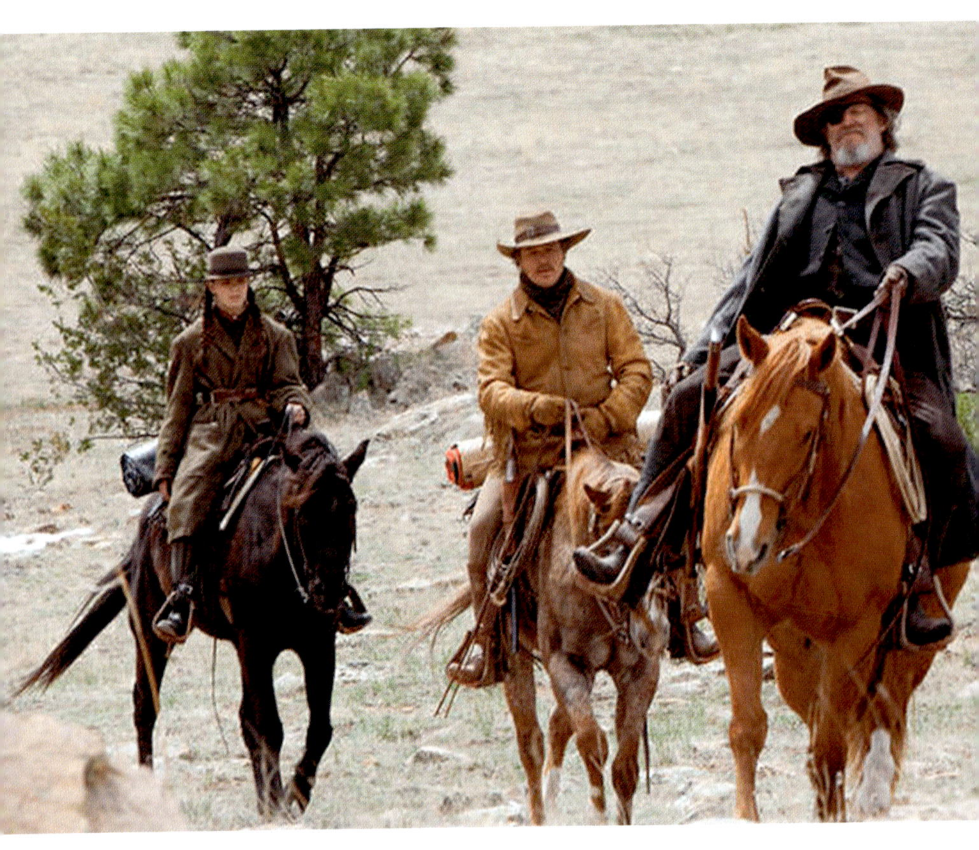

compare her with Jodie Foster, no doubt thinking of Foster's similarly textured first turn in *Taxi Driver*. 'She's that kind of centred,' he said. 'She's a special kid.'

She also bore up well during what was a difficult and physically taxing shoot for the Coens, largely based around Santa Fe, New Mexico. This was mainly due to the wintry weather conditions necessitated by the brothers and Roger Deakins' brittle, overcast vision of the West, including a bitter blizzard that foxed their first day of shooting and forced a 150-mile relocation. But 'stuff like that just adds to the challenge,' said Steinfeld while promoting the film, already sounding like a seasoned pro.

For Joel and Ethan, the challenge persisted into the edit. The toughest aspect, they realized, was achieving the correct balance between the perspectives of Mattie and Rooster. What made it especially difficult was the masterstroke of making their Cogburn The Dude rather than The Duke. Slovenly, saggy and slurred, Bridges saw some connection between his *Big Lebowski* character and the ageing marshal. 'Both The Dude and Rooster are very true to themselves,' he said. 'They're both at home with who they are, and not really interested in improvement or anything like that!'

The main difference, of course, is that Rooster is a 'pitiless man' who's killed 23 men in four years, and is capable of executing 'a cold-blooded bushwhack'. Bridges is no less adept at portraying that side of the character; in fact, Rooster feels far more ruthless in his hands than Wayne's. He's more of a natural-born killer than an icon with deliberately scuffed edges, particularly in the rousing climactic showdown with the criminal gang led by Lucky Ned Pepper (Barry Pepper), when he rides at them with the reins in his teeth, firing a revolver in each hand (just as Wayne did, with both movies closely following the text in this instance).

Coming after the closure-free trio of *No Country For Old Men*, *Burn After Reading* and *A Serious Man*, *True Grit*'s traditionally framed narrative only stands out more. Even stylistically, it was reined in. It was a surprise that their first proper Western (as opposed to neo-Western *No Country For Old Men*) should not be an attempt to reinvent the genre, or marry it with another. And it's all the stronger for it. More palatable for a wider audience, too: an audience the Coens didn't usually reach. As Ethan joked, 'Yes, you can probably bring Grandma to this one!'

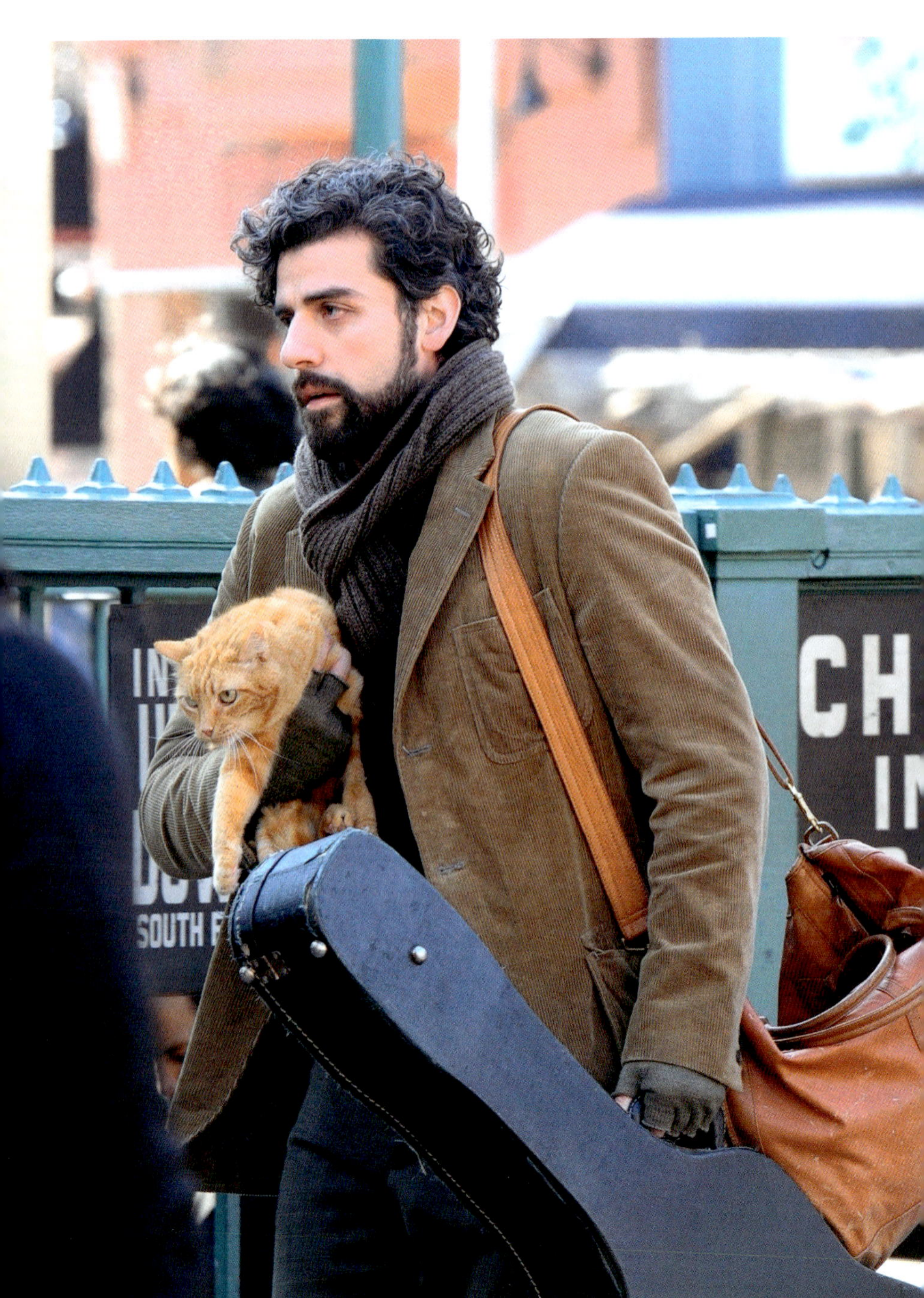

INSIDE LLEWYN DAVIS
2013

Over the course of their career, the Coen brothers have worked with dogs (including a worryingly speedy pit bull in *No Country*), horses (*True Grit*), a marmot (*The Big Lebowski*), a pig (*The Man Who Wasn't There*), even a trained vulture (*True Grit* again). But their greatest animal challenge came with *Inside Llewyn Davis*.

'The whole exercise of shooting a cat is pretty nightmarish,' said Ethan, 'because they don't care about anything. They don't want to do what you want them to do. As the animal trainer said to us, "A dog wants to please you; a cat only wants to please itself." It was just long, painstaking, frustrating days shooting the cat.' In describing their feline-related headache Ethan strikes a familiar note. Couldn't he and Joel be said to not care about anything when it comes to fulfilling others' expectations? Haven't they always been creatively driven to please themselves first, rather than anyone else?

Inside Llewyn Davis is a case in point. If the brothers were instead driven by a dog-like compulsion to please others, it is unlikely they would have made a film based on a largely forgotten figure in what was possibly history's least sexy music scene.

The Coens' 16th film didn't start with a feline. It originated in a very culturally specific (and obscure) notion, voiced by Joel one day in their New York office. 'Okay, suppose Dave Van Ronk gets beat up outside of Gerde's Folk City,' he said to Ethan. 'That's the beginning of a movie.'

Known as the Mayor of MacDougal Street, former Merchant Marine Van Ronk was a luminary of the late Fifties/early Sixties folk music revival in New York's Greenwich Village, who would, like so many on that scene, become eclipsed by Bob Dylan. Where most filmmakers would be drawn to Dylan's game-changing effect, Joel and Ethan were more interested in the moment that came just before, and the people who were left behind.

Though it lifts elements from Van Ronk's memoir, and its title from his 1964 album *Inside Dave Van Ronk*, the movie is no biopic. The singer was a loose model for their own fictional, and far less amiable, folk artist Llewyn Davis (played by newcomer Oscar Isaac). Having lost his musical partner to suicide, Llewyn is trying to make it as a solo performer, but the fact that he is homeless indicates that is not going well. In fact, similar to Larry Gopnik in *A Serious Man*, nothing is going well for Llewyn. But in true Coen tradition, it is largely the fault of his own bad decisions and shortcomings. And his actions hardly encourage our sympathy.

The story takes place in the Village during a wintry week of Llewyn's life which, in an echo of *The Hudsucker Proxy*'s structure, elliptically begins and ends with the aforementioned and arguably deserved beating, while in the background Dylan makes his career-making stage appearance. During this time, Llewyn will discover he's possibly impregnated his friend's girlfriend (Carey Mulligan), and try to borrow the money for the abortion from said friend (Justin Timberlake). He will lose the cat of a kindly academic couple who let him sleep on their couch, then treat them horribly at a social gathering. He'll collaborate on a novelty pop record (the

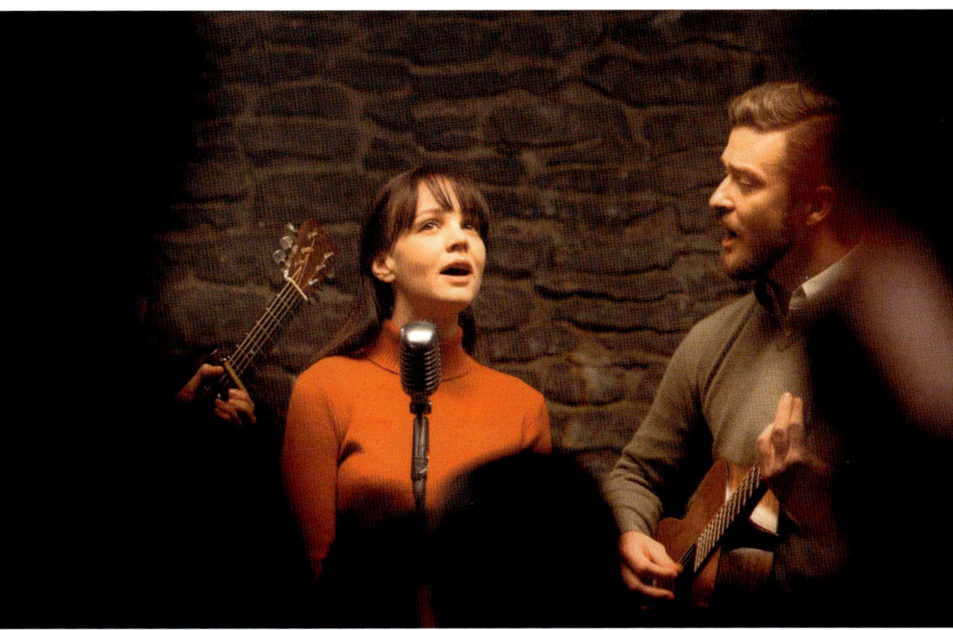

ABOVE: Carey Mulligan as Jean, performing '500 Miles' with Justin Timberlake as her partner Jim.

fantastic 'Please Mr Kennedy'), then turn down the chance of earning royalties for the sake of an immediate pay cheque. He will embark on a road trip (with John Goodman cameoing as a folk-hating, heroin-addicted jazz musician) for a potentially career-changing audition with a major music manager (F Murray Abraham), and perform possibly the least commercial, most depressing song he knows ('The Death of Queen Jane') – before spurning the manager's offer to join a Peter, Paul and Mary-like trio. He'll discover he has a child in Akron, then drive right past the town later in the film. And he'll even mess up his plan B of returning to the Merchant Marine by throwing out the necessary papers.

Llewyn Davis is the architect of his own failure, and the Coens leave it to their audience to decide if he really is an unrealized genius, or just an average musician with a superiority complex.

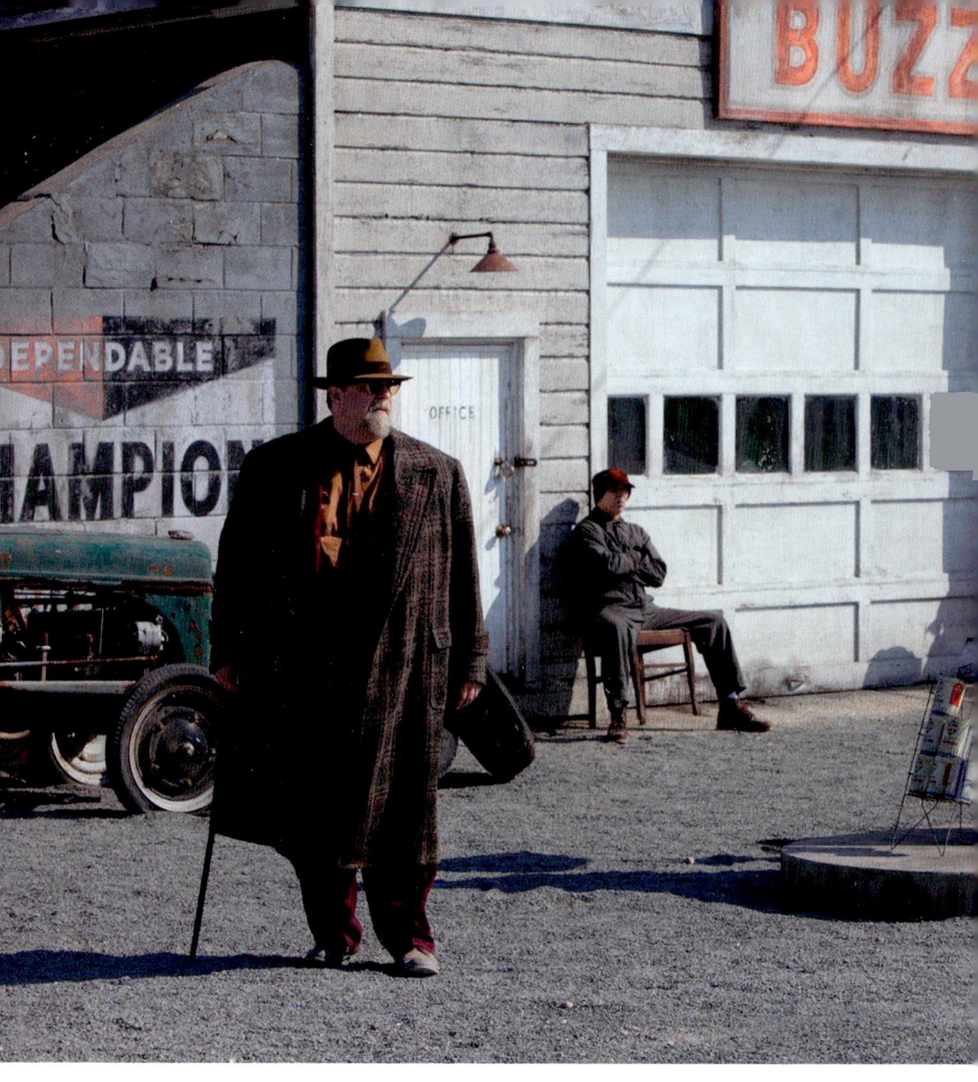

Either way, he is rather like the animal he spends much of the film carrying around. Llewyn doesn't want to do what others want him to. He only wants to please himself. Which makes him one of the closest characters we've ever had to the Coens themselves. Only, as the box of unsold LPs of his solo debut suggest, not nearly as successful.

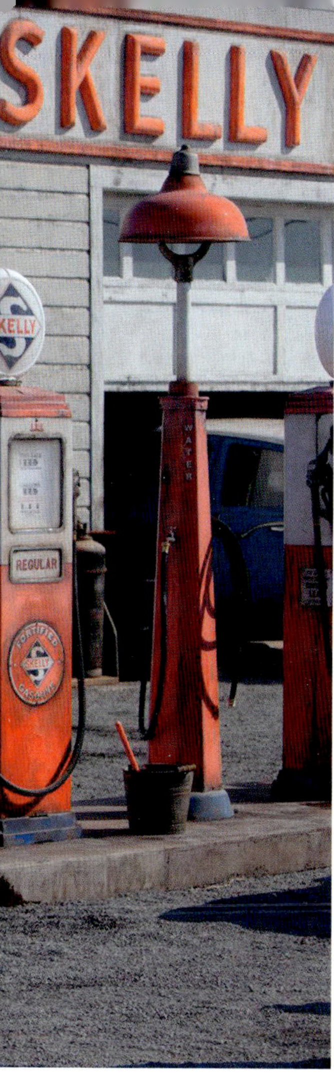

ABOVE: John Goodman makes a memorable cameo during the film's road-trip segment as jazz musician Roland Turner.

Despite Llewyn's similarity to them (intentional or otherwise), Joel and Ethan weren't exactly connoisseurs of his chosen genre, though they shared fond memories of their mother playing folk records when they were kids. So, once more, the brothers recruited T Bone Burnett for his music-archivist expertise, and he was the first person they sent the script. Burnett likened its circular structure to a folk song: 'You get to the last verse and it's the same as the first verse, except you've learned quite a bit along the way.'

As well as digging up some deep folk cuts for the film, Burnett adapted The Gold Coast Singers' 1962 song 'Please Mr Kennedy' from a Vietnam draft protest piece to a space-race sceptic's anthem ('Uh-oh! I don't wanna go into outer space'), and recruited Marcus Mumford of Mumford & Sons (Mulligan's husband) to co-produce the soundtrack and provide the vocals for Llewyn's dead partner, Mike Timlin. Burnett also spent months working with Isaac before production, having 'a character conversation,' he said, about 'how he carried his guitar case, his wardrobe, hair, everything.' Together, they shopped around and found Llewyn's guitar, a 1924 Gibson, and played together, too. 'At one point T Bone told me to just sing like I was singing to myself on my couch,' Isaac said. 'That not only opened up the music but the character. That's how I played the character as well.'

From the start, the Coens knew that the movie, like *O Brother, Where Art Thou?*, would need to feature musical performances. But this time they wanted them all to be sung live by the actors, rather than dubbed. Initially, they tried to find a musician who could play Llewyn. 'But this character's literally in every scene of the movie, so we realized we were going in the wrong direction,' said Joel. 'We started seeing actors who could play, as opposed to musicians who could act.' That was how they alighted upon Issac, whose biggest previous role had been a scene-stealing turn as King John in Ridley Scott flop *Robin Hood*. An accomplished singer and guitarist, Isaac so impressed Burnett with his audition tape, Burnett told the brothers he thought he was 'actually a better musician than a lot of the studio guys I work with.'

As with *A Serious Man* and *True Grit*, the brothers' decision to cast for talent rather than profile paid off with glowing reviews. In fact, the critical reaction to *Inside Llewyn Davis* was better than for either of those films, and even more rapturous than the response to *No Country For Old Men*. It remains their highest-ranked film on reviews aggregator Metacritic, with a Metascore of 93, compared with *No Country*'s 91.

The movie's downbeat tone and cold-snap atmosphere, though beautifully photographed by French cinematographer Bruno Delbonnel, did cause disgruntlement among folk singers who fondly remembered the Village scene as being more positive and vibrant. But this was by now just part and parcel of a Coen movie's reception among members of those very specific communities they chose to depict, as with *Fargo* and *A Serious Man*. When, after all, did the Coens ever set out to flatter?

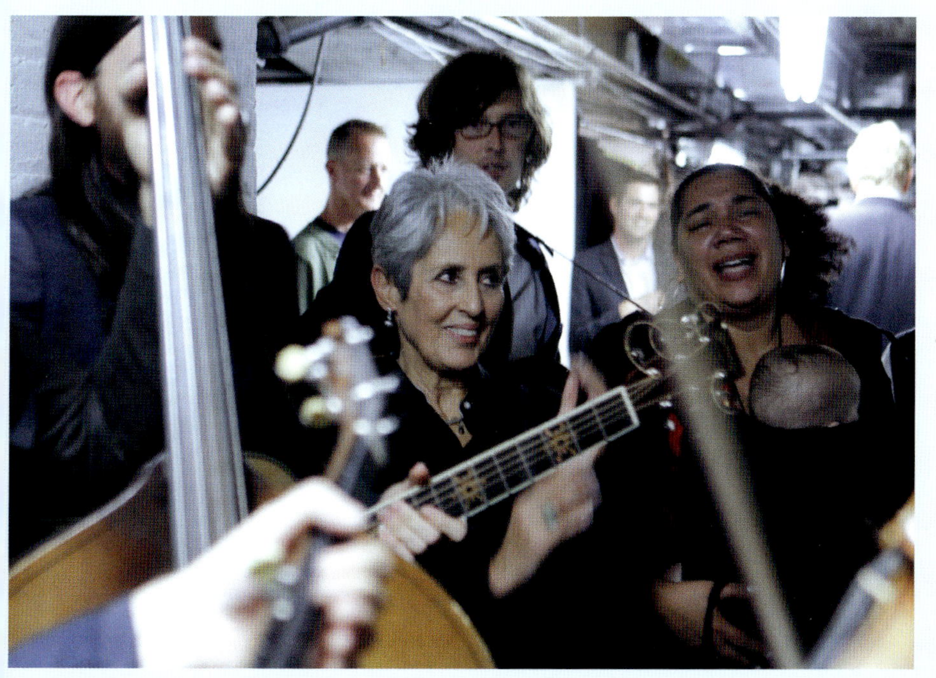

Coens in concert: *Another Day, Another Time* (2013)

Given the phenomenal success of *O Brother Where Art Thou?*'s soundtrack, it made sense to repeat that film's post-release pattern and put on a concert of *Inside Llewyn Davis*' music. Documented as a film produced by the Coens and Burnett, and directed by Christopher Wilcha, the event was televised on *Showtime* a week after *Inside Llewyn Davis*' release. While not ultimately enjoying the same reach and impact as *Down From The Mountain* and *O Brother*'s soundtrack, Wilcha's *Another Day, Another Time: Celebrating the Music of Inside Llewyn Davis* does feature an august roster of on-stage talent, with Marcus Mumford, Jack White, Patti Smith, Joan Baez and the Avett Brothers joining stars Oscar Isaac, Carey Mulligan and Adam Driver. Pictured above is a backstage scene from the documentary, featuring Joan Baez (centre).

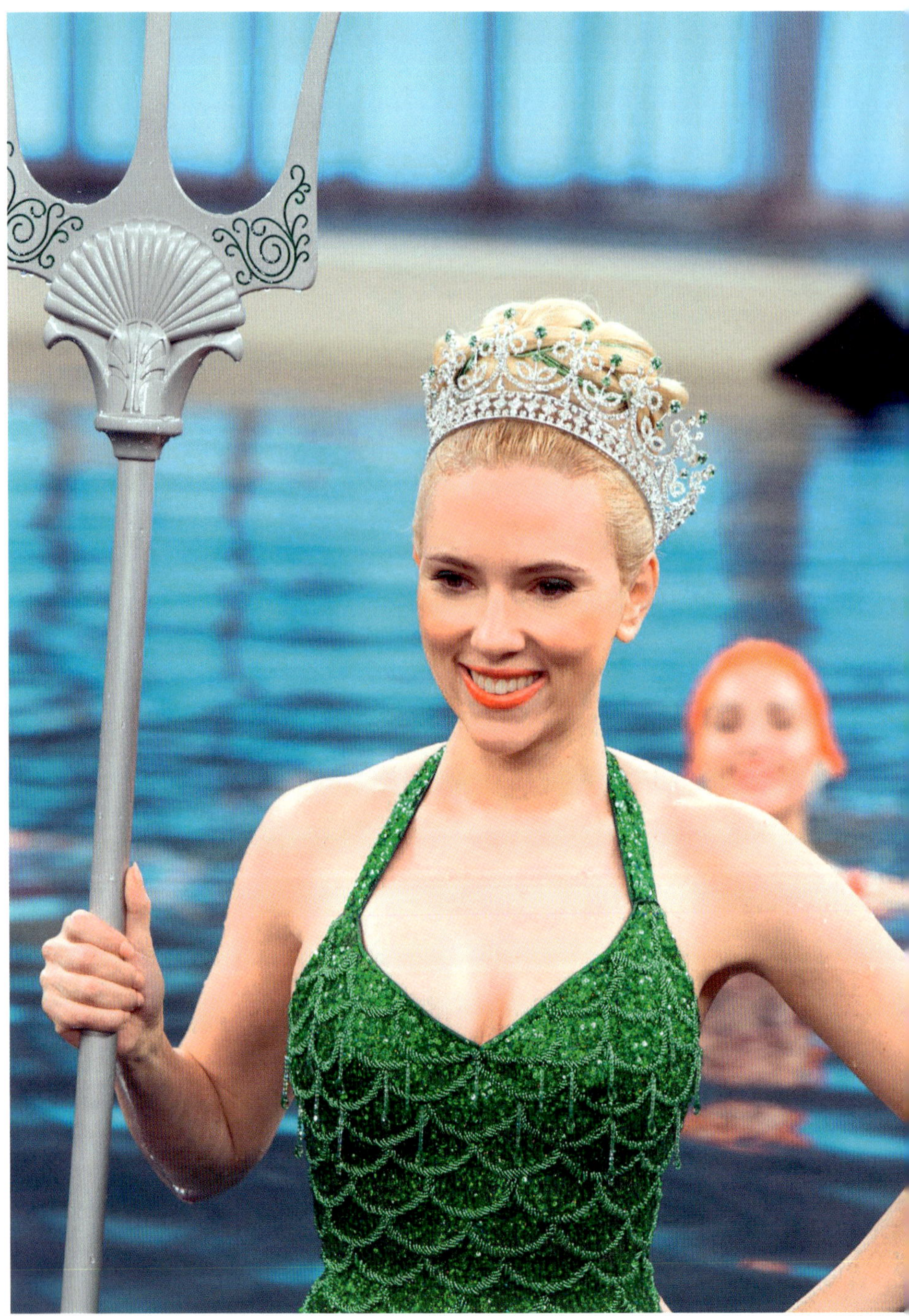

'Go out there and be a star!'

BACK TO HOLLYWOOD

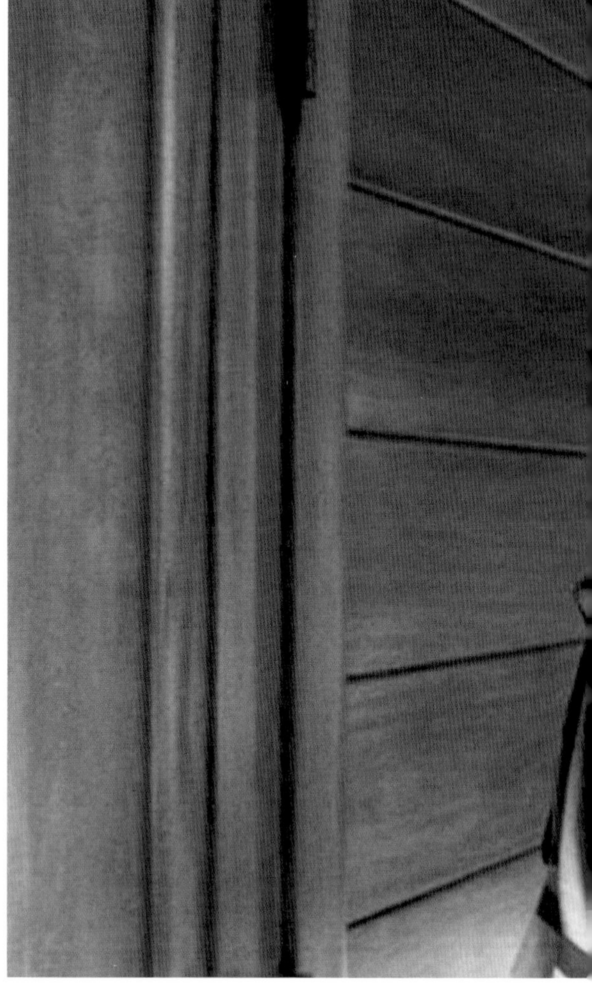

HAIL, CAESAR!
2016

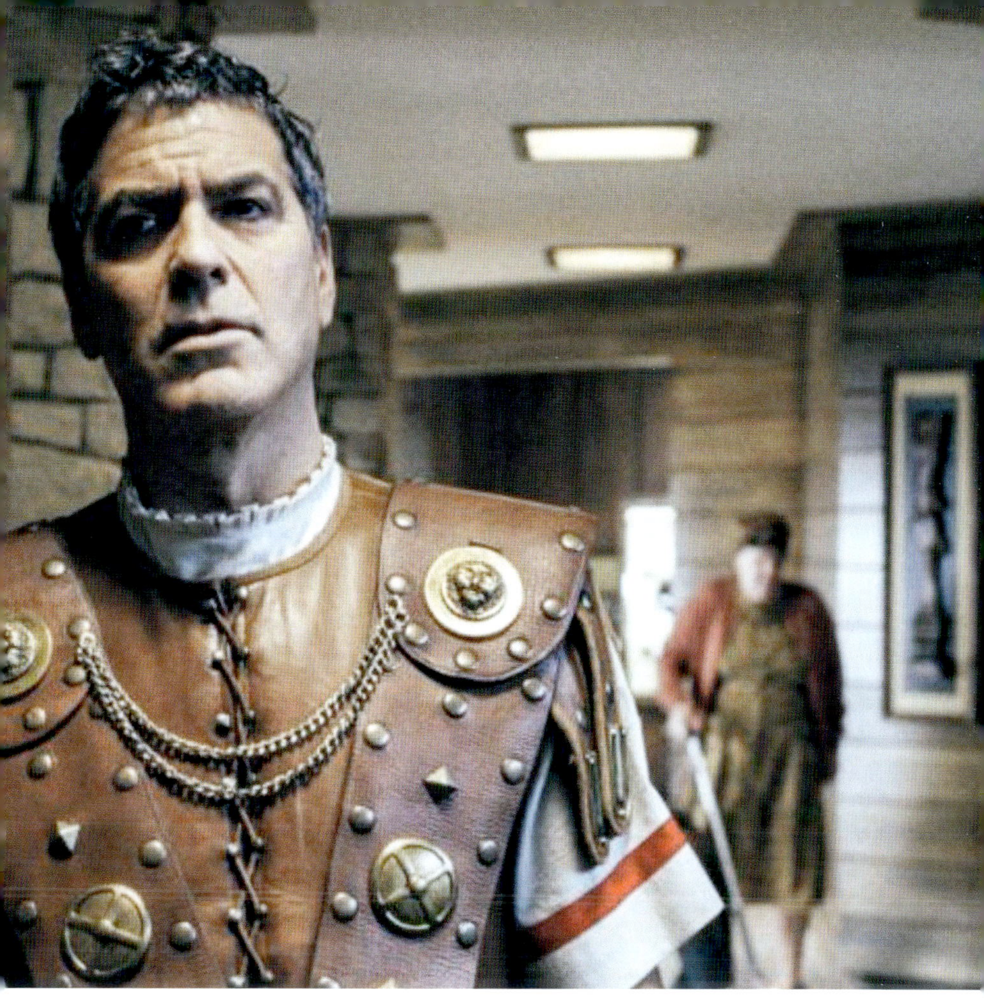

On the last day of filming *Burn After Reading*, George Clooney turned to Joel and Ethan Coen and said, 'Okay, that's it. I've played my last idiot.' Their response was simply to break out that shared Coen-brother chuckle and say, 'We guess you won't be working with us again!'

But there was unfinished knucklehead business between Clooney and the Coens. As far back as 1999, when they first clicked on *O Brother, Where Art Thou?*, the siblings told him about

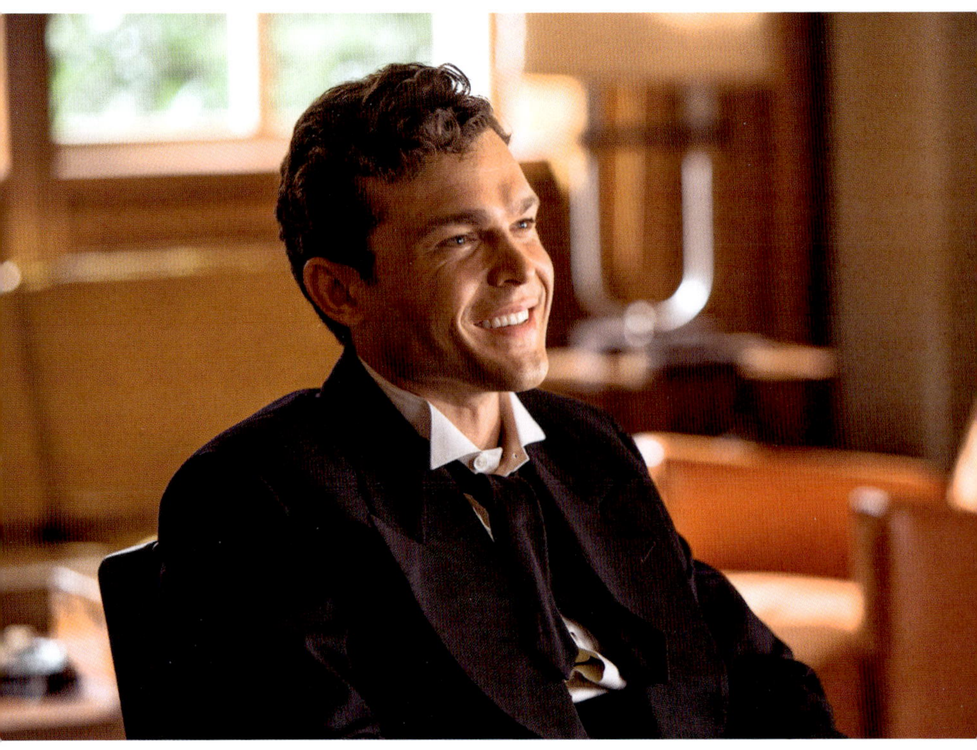

ABOVE: Alden Ehrenreich brings fresh-faced charm as the cowboy who can't adapt to a comedy of manners.

an idea they'd had which they thought he'd be great for: *Hail, Caesar!*, a movie about the star of a 1920s Biblical epic who gets kidnapped. 'They had about three pages of plot written down and a few terrific lines,' Clooney remembered. 'That's it.'

When the film finally materialized more than a decade later, the plot still involved a Biblical-epic star who gets kidnapped – Clooney, as the guileless Victor Mature-like Baird Whitlock – but the Coens brought it forward to the 1950s when, much like the folk scene in *Inside Llewyn Davis*, the Hollywood studio system was on the verge of great change. With television starting to chew into its box office, and the 1948 Supreme Court's antitrust decision forcing major studios to divest the exhibition side of their business, the US film industry was fighting hard to keep its audiences and preserve its profits. Movies got brighter, budgets grew bigger, and glamorous escapism became the order of the day, especially as the real world had recently fallen under the shadow of the Cold War and the atomic bomb.

This was satirically ripe material for the Coens, who embodied the embattled business-of-show in the burly, homburg-topped form of Head of Physical Production Eddie Mannix (Josh Brolin). They based him on the real-life MGM studio fixer with the same name and from the same era, but relocated him to *Barton Fink*'s Capitol Pictures, while also making Mannix a far more sympathetic character, with an almost sweet Irish Catholic guilt complex over breaking his no-smoking promise to his wife (Alison Pill).

Mannix's job is to keep productions running smoothly and maintain their stars' pristine public image by covering up any private indiscretions. In other words, he is Hollywood's protector. So it is Brolin, not Clooney, who leads the film's ensemble – bringing them back to the starrier, zanier idiom of *Burn After Reading*, only less cynical – with Whitlock's disappearance just one of a number of fraying threads that the sometimes heavy-handed fixer has to tie up over the course of a couple of days.

Really, this was all just an excuse for the Coens to both have fun with, and pay tribute to, some of the Golden Age's most bombastic genres. 'The way these things were done is lost,' said Joel. So making *Hail, Caesar!* became 'this funny exercise – how do you reverse engineer those things with modern technology and digital effects so that you can make them look like they were?'

Scarlett Johansson reunited with the brothers to play an Esther Williams-style mermaid who's become pregnant and needs a husband fast – a storyline that gave them the chance to outdo

The Big Lebowski's Busby Berkeley number with a full-on aquatic extravaganza. (Shot in the very same tank Berkeley used for Williams movies.) Complete with a mechanical whale, the sequence transforms its synchronized swimmers into a stunning human kaleidoscope.

Newcomer Alden Ehrenreich heads up a delicious fish-out-of-water vignette as Hobie Doyle, an amiable but inarticulate cowboy star who is ordered by Mannix to appear in a sophisticated drawing-room comedy, much to the frustration of its director Laurence Laurentz (Ralph Fiennes). This enabled the Coens to pastiche the overwrought refinement of the comedy of manners as Hobie singularly fails to land even one line, while also indulging in the saccharine silliness of the singing-cowboy genre, with a snippet of Hobie's latest movie, *Lazy Ol' Moon*.

Elsewhere, Channing Tatum adds tap dancing to his skill set as Burt Gurney, a blend of Gene Kelly and Troy Donahue, who fronts an *On The Town*-style sailor-boy dance number with a not-so-hidden homoerotic undercurrent, all superbly choreographed by Tony-award winner Christopher Gattelli. Gurney is later revealed to be a communist traitor and the instigator of the Whitlock plot, which, in yet another satirical twist, Eddie must hide from twin-sister gossip writers, both played by Tilda Swinton as the two halves of a bitter sibling rivalry that's clearly based on feuding Golden Age columnists Hedda Hopper and Luella Parsons.

And then, of course, there is *Hail, Caesar!* itself, a pompous Technicolor spectacle that shares its subtitle – *A Tale of The Christ* – with *Ben-Hur*. This required production designer Jess Gonchor, now on his sixth Coen movie, to construct some of the brothers' most expansive sets since *The Hudsucker Proxy*. After all, it is Capitol Pictures' biggest tentpole. The studio takes it so seriously that Mannix even brings in a selection of fractious religious leaders for a sense check on its theological elements. 'I thought the chariot scene was fakey,' contributes the Eastern Orthodox clergyman, unhelpfully.

This amusing little sketch is contrasted by Baird's dialectics with his surprisingly cordial kidnappers, a tweedy enclave of blacklisted writers. But rather than being wrongfully accused left-

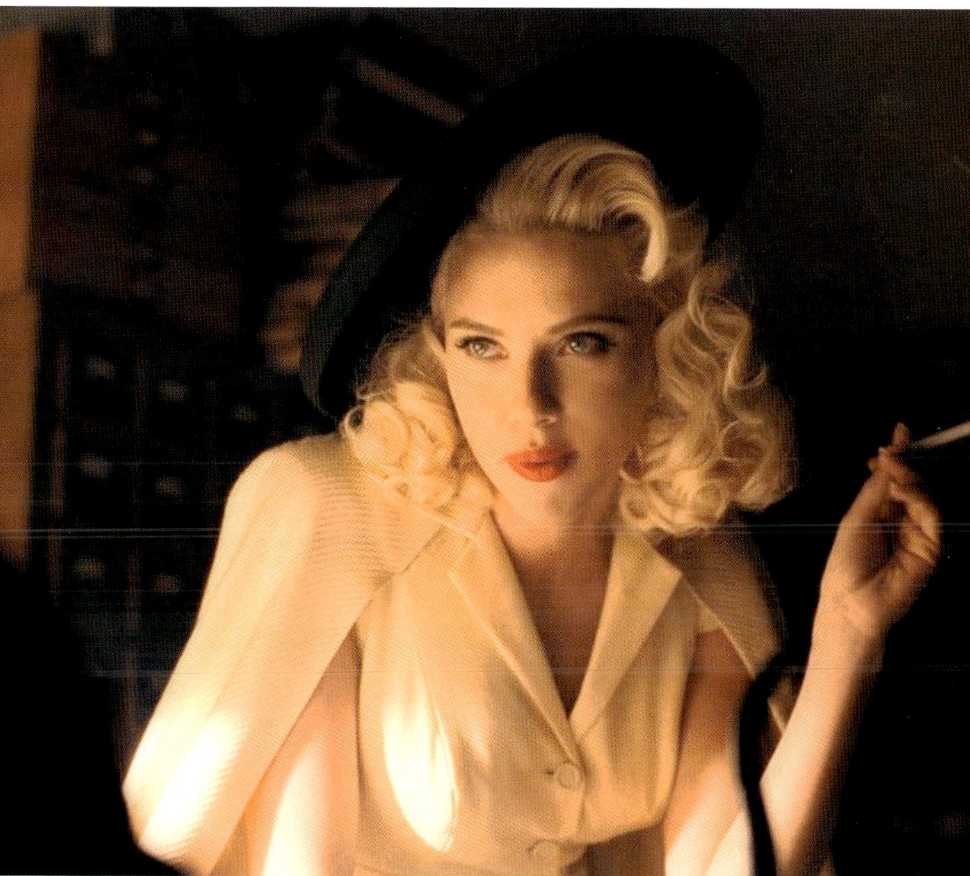

ABOVE: Scarlett Johansson as surprisingly coarse mermaid DeeAnna Moran.

wingers, they are in fact fervent, godless communists who seek to bring down his studio, which they describe as 'a pure instrument of capitalism'. (The clue is in the studio's name.) By the time he's rescued by Hobie, and Burt Gurney has dramatically defected on a Russian submarine (accidentally dropping the ransom money into the Pacific – another example of a lost Coen fortune), Baird is convinced.

If this represents a battle for Hollywood's very soul, then it's quickly won on behalf of capitalism – and Catholicism – by Mannix, who slaps some sense into Baird and sends the cringing actor back to set. Though perhaps he hasn't had all the red beaten out of him. When fluffing his big final speech as the Roman officer converted after an encounter with Christ, the word he can't remember is 'faith'.

Hail, Caesar!'s deeper thoughts are mostly drowned out by its slick showmanship. It is a tongue-in-cheek studio tour organized by a pair of filmmakers who have never really discerned between their enjoyment of trash and their love of true art. The films they devoured on television as children were, Joel recalled, 'an eclectic mix. . .There was no distinction between very sophisticated auteur-driven European films and the crassest commercial movies that were being made. To us, they were the same thing. They were just different kinds of expression.'

Early in their career, they exhibited this unconventional grounding in cinema by switching from noir-horror to madcap family comedy to a gangster film in just three movies. Now they were inflicting genre whiplash within a single picture, with entertaining if not entirely cohesive results. This atomized approach was one the brothers would take even further in their next movie, which went from saluting Hollywood as a myth-making machine to exploring one of its most potent myths.

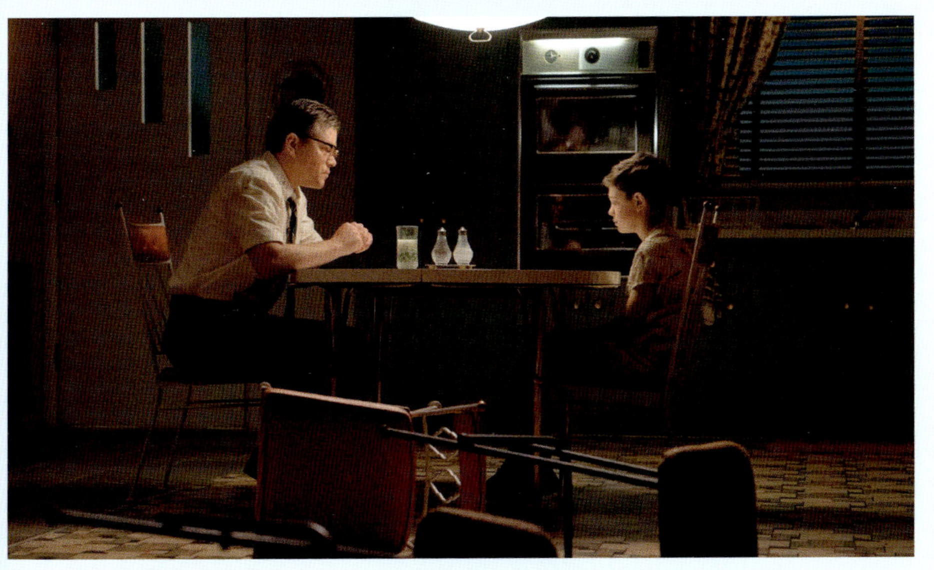

Coens on script: *Gambit* (2012), *Unbroken* (2014), *Bridge of Spies* (2015) and *Suburbicon* (2017)

In the 2010s, Joel and Ethan reached the peak of their scriptwriting-for-hire activities. First came *Gambit*, a sadly unsatisfying remake of the 1966 Michael Caine/Shirley MacLaine heist caper that mismatched Colin Firth and Cameron Diaz. This was shortly followed by a re-write for Angelina Jolie-directed World War II survival movie *Unbroken*, based on the real-life travails of Olympic runner Louis Zamperini (Jack O'Connell). Next came another based-on-fact period piece featuring a plane crash. Steven Spielberg's Cold War drama *Bridge of Spies* starred Mark Rylance as Soviet spy Rudolf Abel, and Tom Hanks as the lawyer who must negotiate his trade with captured U-2 pilot Francis Gary Powers (Austin Stowell).

Directed by George Clooney, *Suburbicon* (pictured) was a murder mystery set in a fictional, supposedly idyllic 1950s town, based an old Coen script, originally written in 1986. Clooney rewrote it (with Grant Heslov) to add a based-on-fact subplot about an African American family who are harassed by the community. Sadly, Clooney's well-meaning political commentary and the Coens' irony-laced noir failed to gel, and despite a strong cast (Matt Damon, Julianne Moore, Oscar Isaac), the film was Clooney's least successful as a director to date.

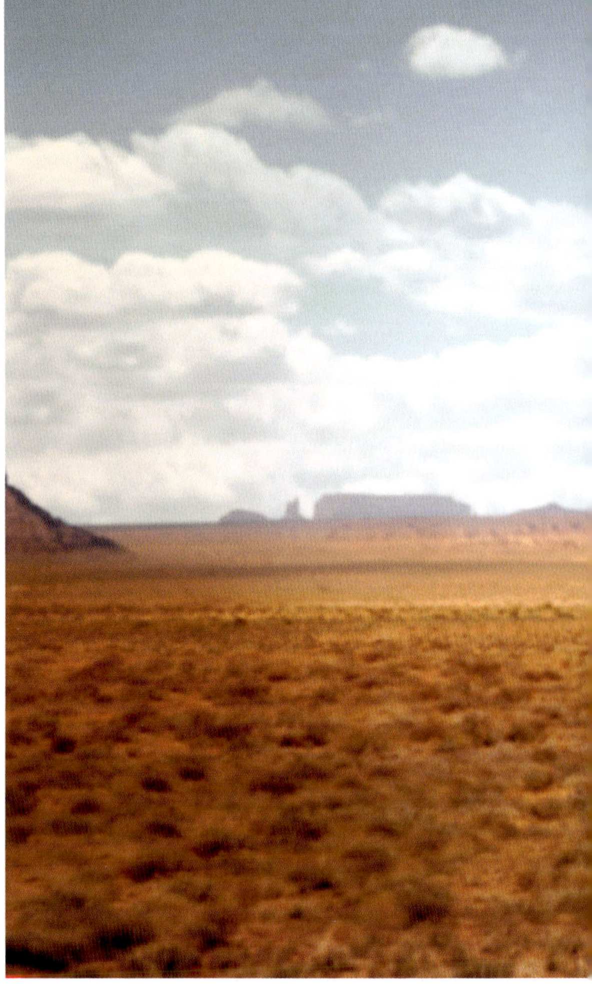

THE BALLAD OF BUSTER SCRUGGS

2018

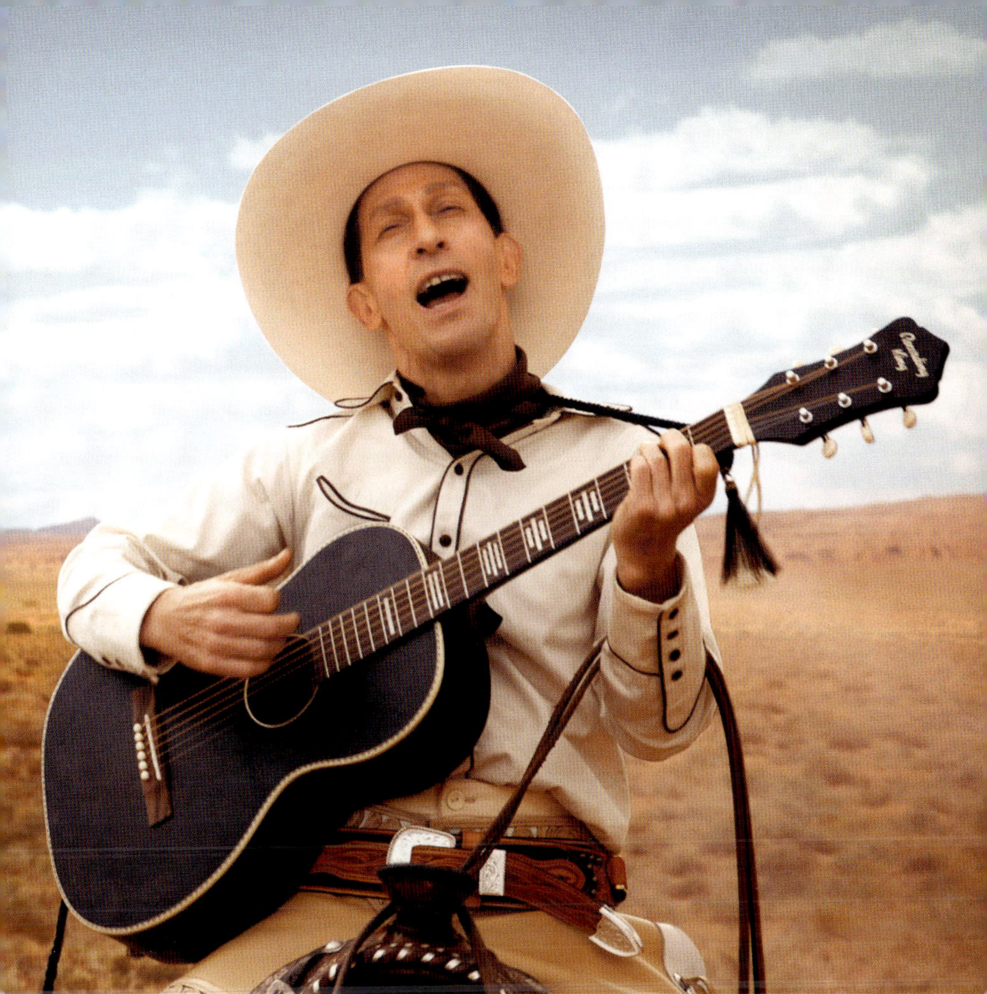

One of the six shorts that comprise the Coen brothers' last feature together – Western anthology *The Ballad of Buster Scruggs* – is an odd and disturbing tale titled 'Meal Ticket'. It involves a quadriplegic orator (Harry Melling), carted around winter-bitten mining towns by a gruff, laconic impresario (Liam Neeson). The repertoire of this 'Wingless Thrush' includes Percy Bysshe Shelley's *Ozymandias*, the book of Genesis (specifically the story of Cain and Abel), Shakespeare's *Sonnet 29* and the

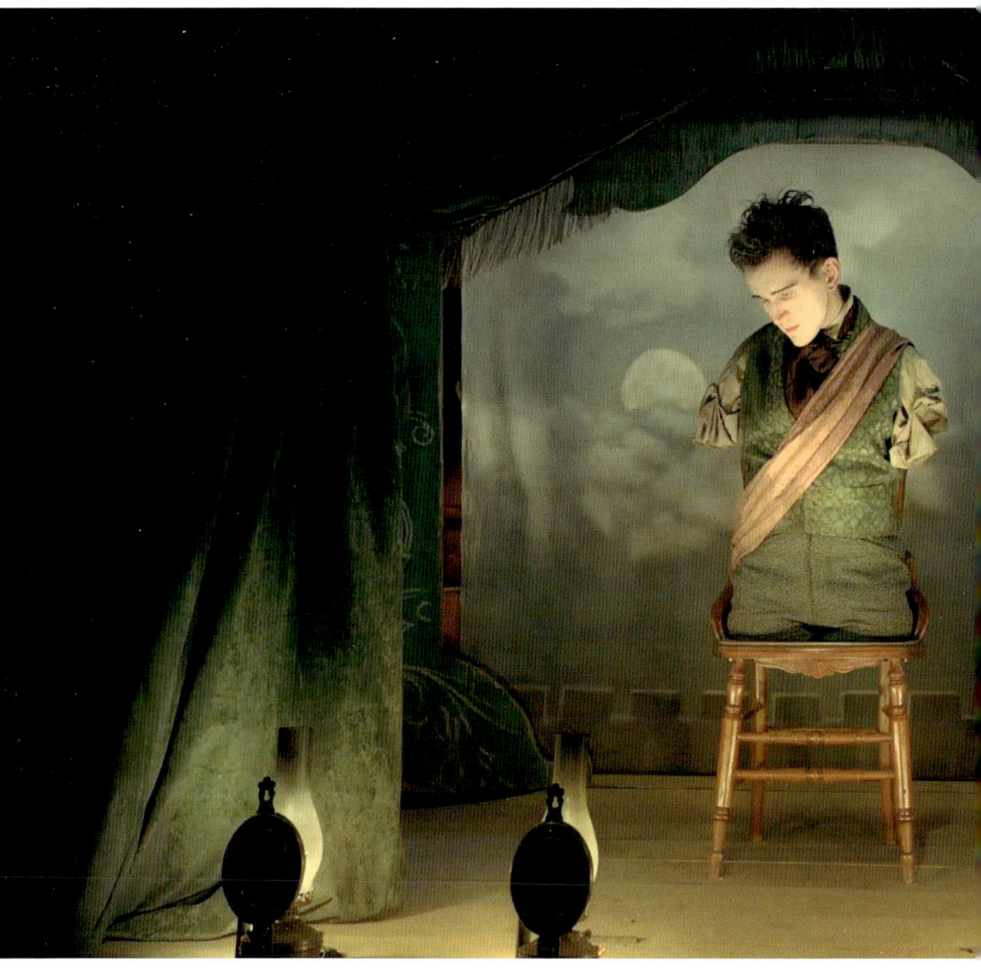

Gettysburg Address. But as the tour continues, the crowds dwindle and the impresario discovers another show that's clearly far more popular: a chicken that can do arithmetic. The story concludes with him purchasing this 'peckin' Pythagorean' and, we're given to believe, hurling the poor limbless orator into a ravine. Culture has been brutally supplanted by novelty, art discarded to make way for low-brow entertainment.

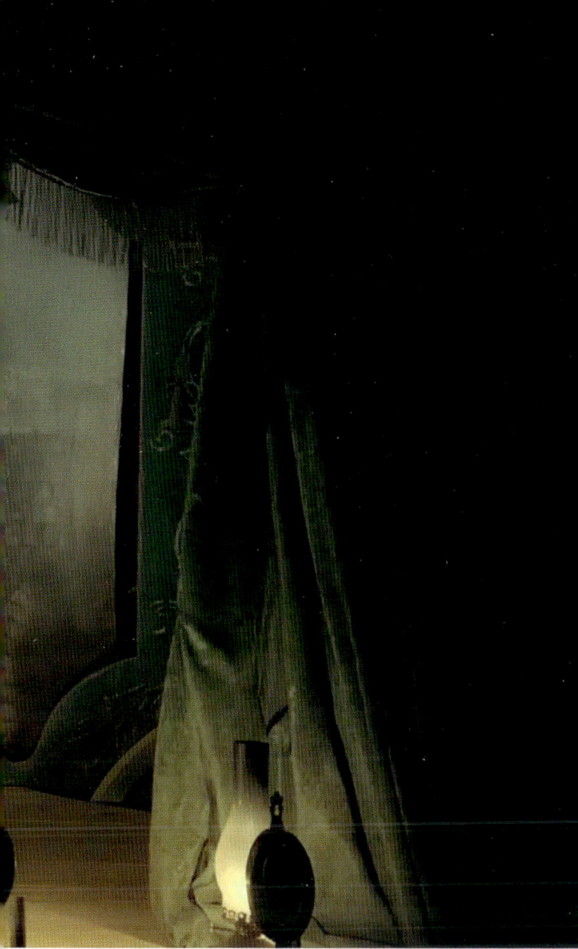

It's easy to interpret this as a metaphor for how the Coens saw themselves in the modern era of cinema: an odd, rarefied act, more concerned with wordplay than action, trying to persist in an environment where impressively loud and kinetic superhero movies dominate the multiplex.

But, while it has a démodé genre and format, the film does represent the Coens' adaptability as filmmakers. It was their first movie shot digitally (with cinematographer Bruno Delbonnel), rather than on celluloid. 'This seemed like a reasonable movie to give it a try,' explained Joel of a shift they'd been resisting for some years. 'There were 800 visual effects shots, and when you're doing a lot of visual effects shots, it's easier if the raw material has been shot digitally as opposed to on film.'

It was also their first project made for a streaming service, rather than a traditional studio. Reasoning that much of their early success was owed to the home video market, they figured they shouldn't complain about their new film being aimed straight at the small screen. Although they did break new ground for Netflix by insisting on a limited theatrical run before *Buster Scruggs* dropped on its platform (a streaming release pattern that is now common).

Netflix seemed happy to respect the brothers' independence during production, and Joel and Ethan vocally appreciated its support, without which, they believed, *Buster Scruggs* would never have existed. 'They're the people who are stepping up and spending money on movies that aren't Marvel Comics movies or big action franchise movies, which is pretty much the business of the studios now,' said Joel. Added Ethan, 'We never even went to a movie studio with it, because we knew that a studio would never finance this.'

The film was, both siblings recognized, 'a weird animal'. So much so, it was widely mis-reported that it had originally been conceived as a limited TV series. But in fact *The Ballad of Buster Scruggs* slowly came together over a quarter of a century, with Joel and Ethan conceiving each of its six chapters as a stand-alone short film, starting with the one they chose to open the anthology and provide its title. Starring *O Brother, Where Art Thou?*'s Tim Blake Nelson as a white-hatted, Gene Autry-style crooning shootist, this vignette subverts the singing-cowboy subgenre by making its

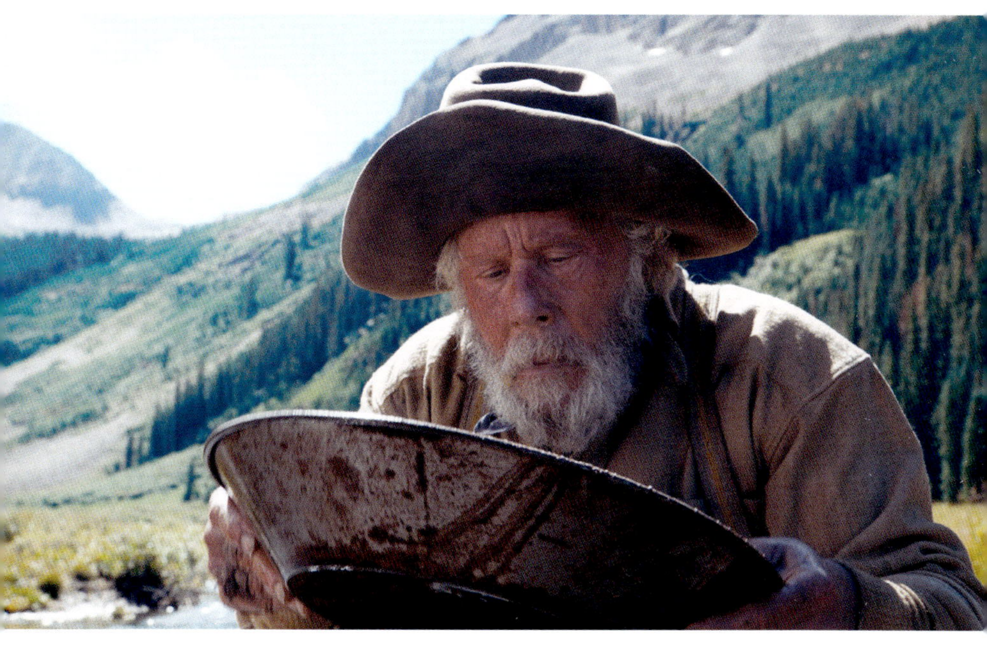

ABOVE: Tom Waits patiently prospects for treasure in the Jack London-inspired 'All Gold Canyon'.

eponymous protagonist deliver some extreme Sam Peckinpah-level gun violence. Although, with its almost cartoonish sense of humour, it bears a closer resemblance to Sam Raimi's own highly stylized take on the Western, 1995's *The Quick and the Dead*.

Neither brother has explained exactly why they fixated upon the Western for each of these six tales. Despite tackling the genre head-on in *True Grit*, they claim not to have been enamoured of it during childhood. With an exception: Sergio Leone's operatic spaghetti Westerns, whose influence can be most obviously felt in the harsh, arid second chapter, 'Near Algodones', in which a cocky bank robber (James Franco) escapes a hanging for a crime he did commit, before being caught and hanged for a crime he didn't.

Still, for decades the Western was the predominant genre in American cinema, providing excitingly mythic material for audiences, who observed their nation's 'manifest destiny' wrought by ruggedly heroic individuals on the perilous frontier. Though located in a very specific time and place, it was a highly malleable genre, which fitted a multiplicity of settings, styles and themes under its ten-gallon hat. And Joel and Ethan's appreciation for this is implicit in the way that each of *Buster Scruggs*' chapters has a different Western flavour.

Following the singing cowboy antics of the first story, the Spaghetti style of the second, and the *McCabe & Mrs Miller*-esque mining-town milieu of the third, the anthology's fourth episode, 'All Gold Canyon', affectionately adapts a Jack London story about a prospector (Tom Waits) discovering gold in a lush, bounteous landscape, where he must contend with a 'measly skunk' who tries to murder him for it.

Meanwhile, the fifth chapter, 'The Gal Who Got Rattled', is a classic 'wagons West' narrative in the vein of 1930's *The Big Trail*, though much of it was drawn from a 1901 story by Stewart Edward White. This is the longest and strongest of the set, unhurriedly presenting a surprisingly sweet and affecting romance between a lonely young woman (Zoe Kazan) and a gentle

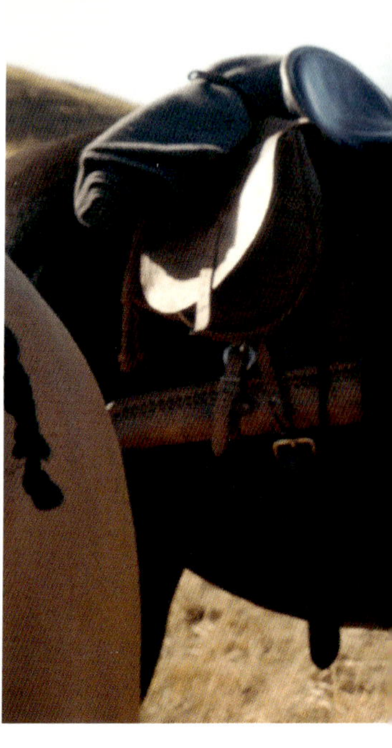

ABOVE: Zoe Kazan as Alice Longabaugh, who will sadly never complete her westward journey in 'The Gal Who Got Rattled'.

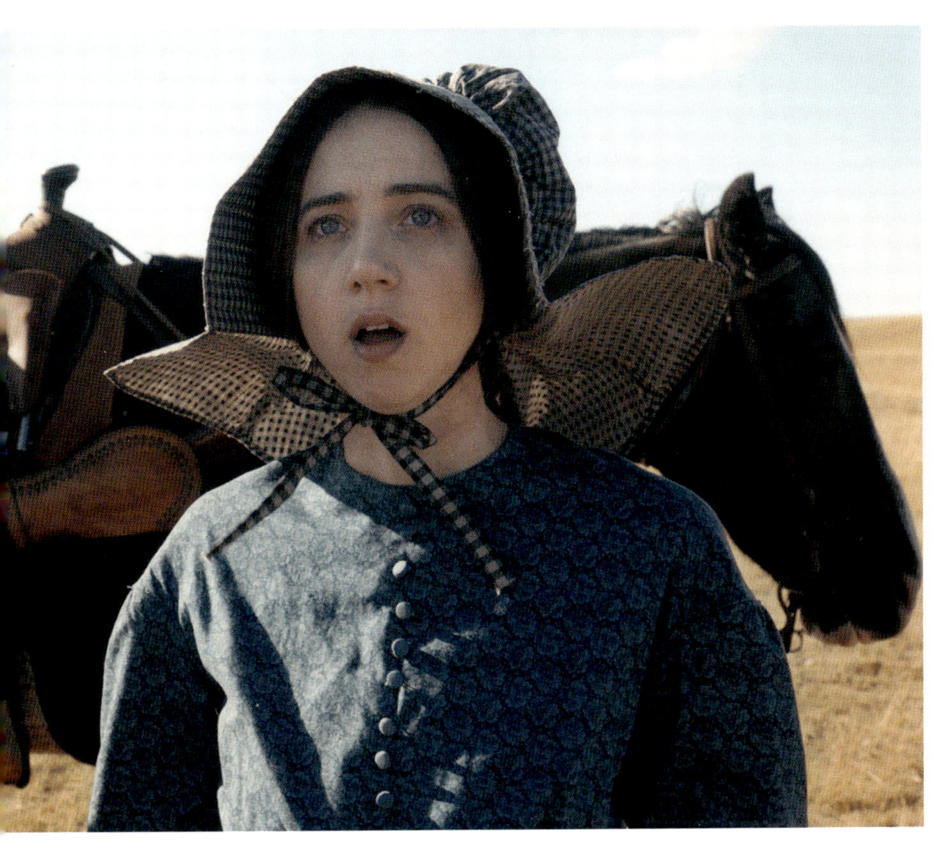

wagon master (Bill Heck). But then tragedy strikes when Native Americans attack and Kazan's character is badly advised to shoot herself rather than be abducted.

The final part, 'The Mortal Remains', is a stagecoach drama that veers into *Twilight Zone* territory. Gradually, it becomes clear that three of the cramped travellers (Tyne Daley, Saul Rubinek and Chelcie Ross) are recently departed souls, ferried to the afterlife by a pair of 'reapers', played by Brendan Gleeson and Jonjo O'Neill, the latter providing a chilling call back to 'The Midnight Caller', the ghost story mentioned by Mattie Ross in *True Grit*. We like to relate to people in stories like this, he sardonically points out, 'so long as the people are us, but not us. Not us in the end, especially. The Midnight Caller gets *him*, never *me*. I'll live forever. . .'

The suitability of these six shorts to a single anthology didn't become apparent to the Coens until they'd written the first five. Aside from all being Westerns, 'they seemed to relate to each other,' said Joel, 'but kind of retrospectively.' This was when they began to consciously consider the theme that tied the stories together. 'Clearly that was death,' said Ethan – as 'The Mortal Remains', the final script they wrote, so eloquently underlines.

Fate is fickle, the film tells us, and nothing is certain. Except death. Uncertainty 'is appropriate for matters of this world,' philosophizes Heck's wagon master in 'The Gal Who Got Rattled'. 'Only regarding the next are vouchsafed certainty.'

The Ballad of Buster Scruggs was possibly the Coens' toughest movie to make. Six productions rolled into one, it was, said Ethan, 'a weird mental exercise and mentally stressful in that way.' It was also a physically demanding shoot, with much of it filmed on exposed exterior locations in Colorado, Nebraska and New Mexico: 'four months of 12- to 14-hour days of either freezing or scorching weather,' said Joel. Mounting the wagon-train segment, with all those huge carts, and horses, and non-compliant oxen, was especially taxing. 'It might have been a good idea on paper, but as we discovered when we went out to shoot this wagon-train movie, it was just an incredible pain.'

In the end, it seemed, it was just too much for the brothers as a filmmaking team. Not long after the release of *The Ballad of Buster Scruggs*, Ethan decided to hang up his movie-making spurs to focus on writing for theatre. The experience of film production had become 'more of a grind and less fun,' he stated. 'The last two movies we made were really difficult in terms of production. So, if you don't have to do it, you go at a certain point: why am I doing this?'

This announcement only deepened the analogous relation of *Buster Scruggs* to the brothers themselves. Its theme of death, one could argue, now foreshadowed the end of their own shared career. But then again, we shouldn't forget the film's other assertion: nothing is certain.

Who is Mike Zoss?

At the very beginning of *The Ballad of Buster Scruggs*, the film's stories are presented as the contents of an old cloth-bound book of 'Tales of the American Frontier'. On its second page, we briefly see that the copyright for the publication is held by Mike Zoss & Sons, with, below it, a drawing of a horse viewed from the rear.

This horse is the ident for Mike Zoss Productions, credited on every Coen movie since *O Brother, Where Art Thou?* However, Zoss himself is never credited as a producer. He was, in fact, the owner of a pharmacy on Minnetonka Boulevard in St Louis Park, Minnesota, where Joel and Ethan grew up. Mike Zoss Drugs was where the brothers liked to hang out as kids while their mother went shopping, and they appreciated how he never told them off or turfed them out onto the street. So when they founded their own New York-based production company in 1992, they named it after him as a tribute.

Zoss also received a further tribute from the Coens in *No Country For Old Men*: the drugstore that Chigurh raids is named Mike Zoss Pharmacy.

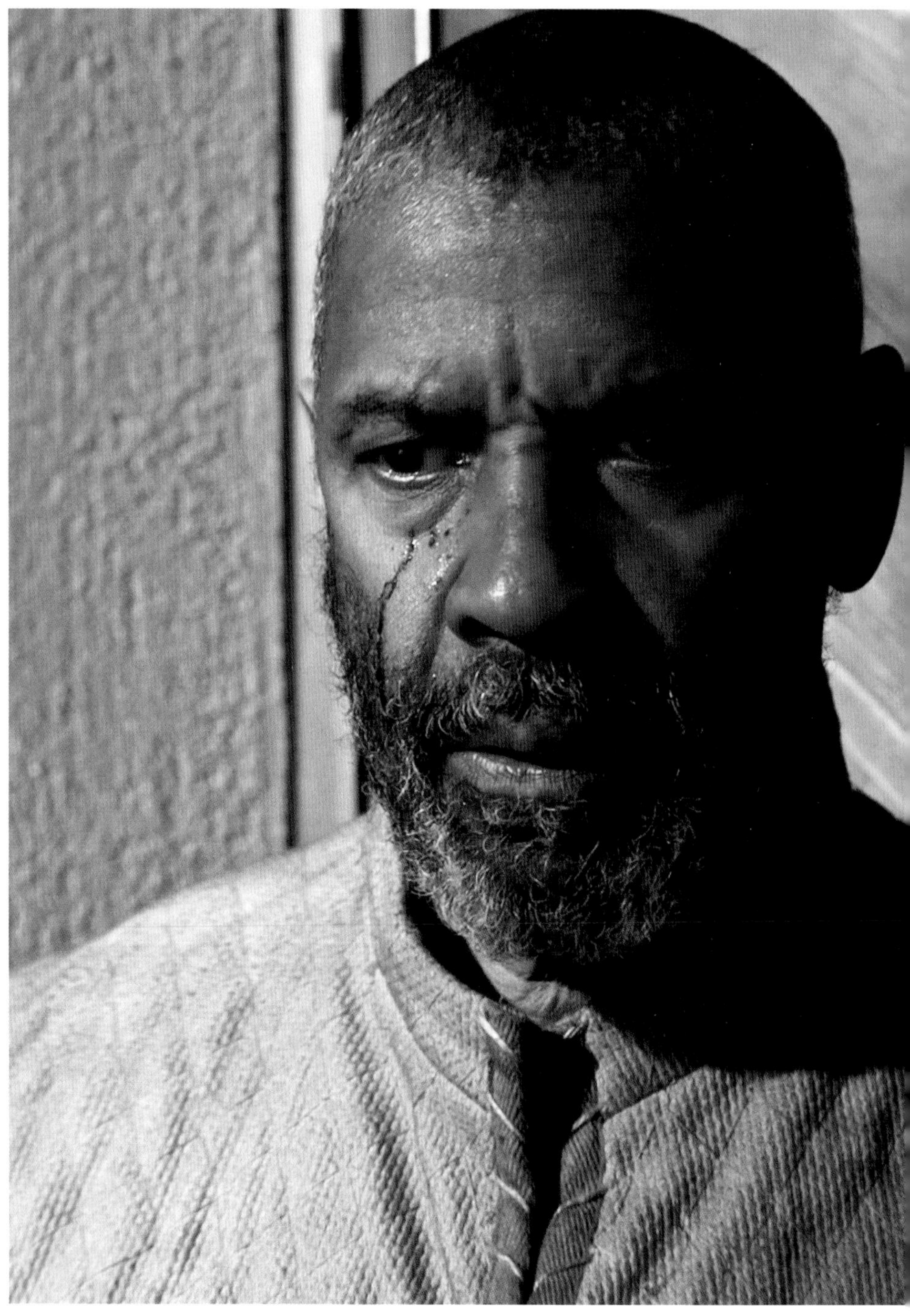

*'Our separated fortune
shall keep us both the safer'*

SOLO VENTURES

THE TRAGEDY OF MACBETH
2021

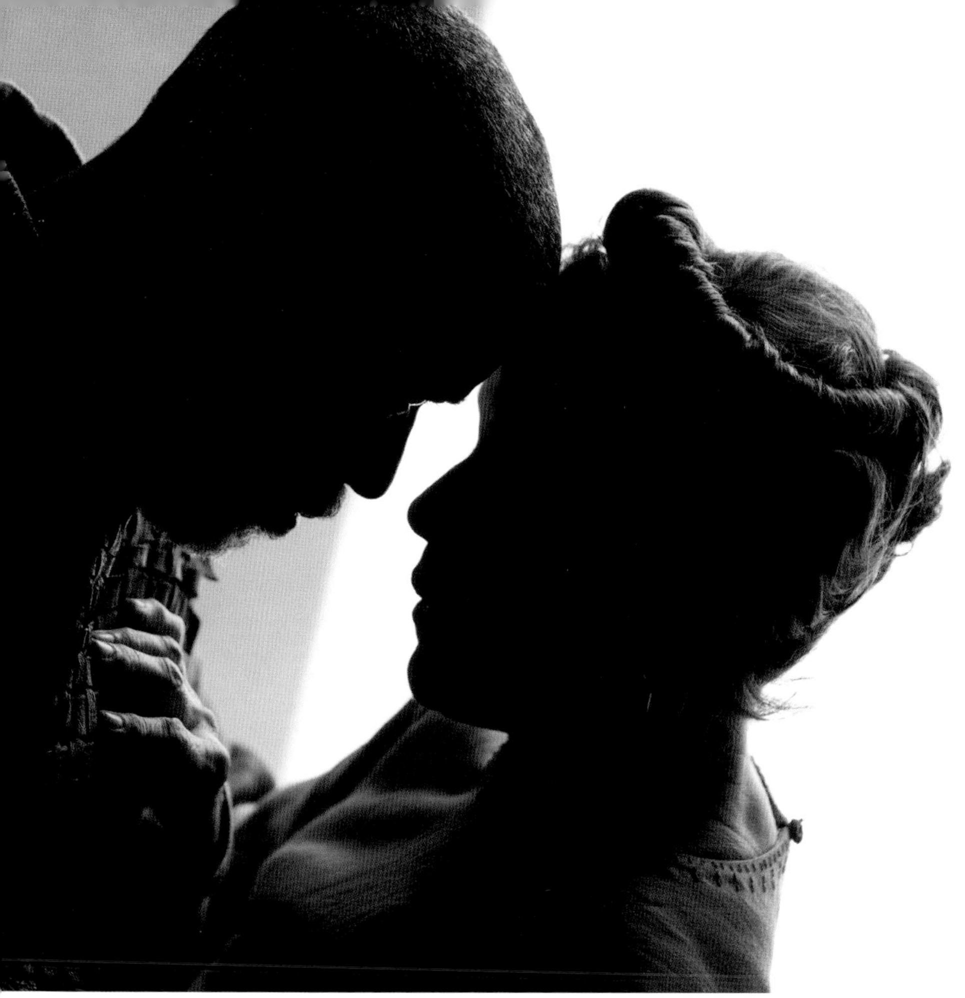

In early 2022, two weeks after the release of his stunningly monochromatic vision of one of Shakespeare's most revered and widely known plays, Joel Coen confessed that he was 'not a Shakespeare guy.' An avid theatregoer, he'd seen and read a lot of Shakespeare over the years, he explained, 'but it's not really my background.'

This was partly why, in 2016, he turned down a request from Frances McDormand to direct her as Lady Macbeth on stage.

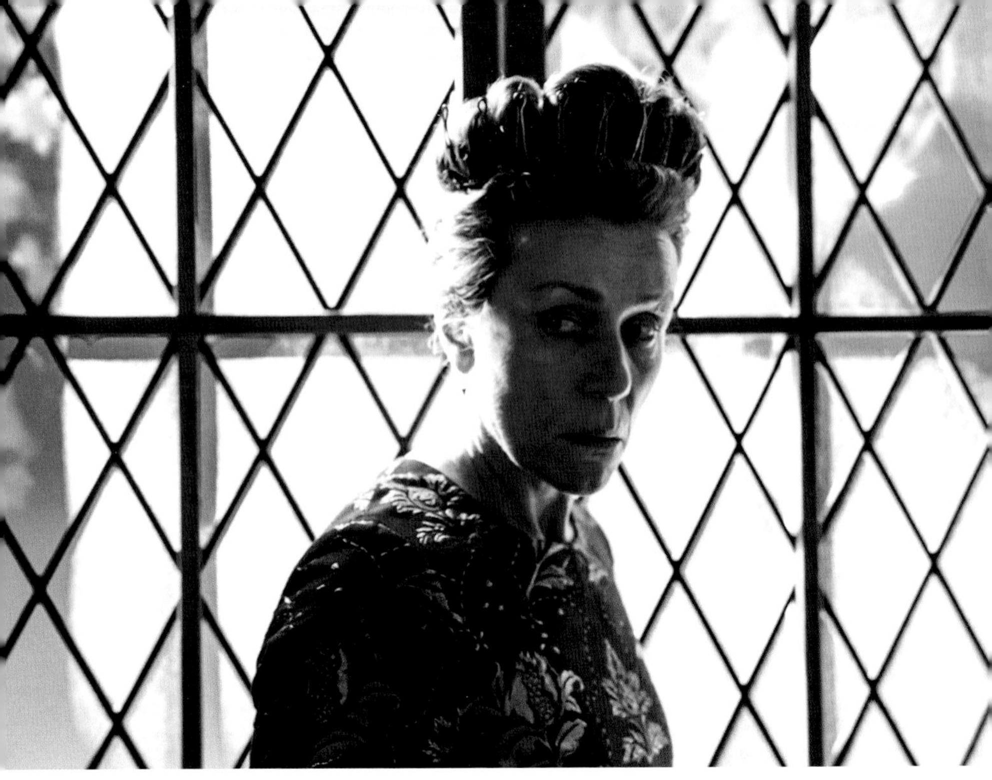

ABOVE: McDormand felt her and Washington's age gave Shakespeare's story more suspense and urgency.

Joel also, he admitted, didn't feel capable of directing theatre. So McDormand went ahead and did the play without him, with Daniel Sullivan directing and *Game of Thrones'* Conleth Hill in the title role. But while watching Sullivan's production, Joel got thinking: perhaps there was a way to do *Macbeth* with McDormand as a movie. One that could stay faithful to the play's theatrical roots, while also being excitingly cinematic. And as something like that would never appeal to Ethan, his brother's recent decision to take a break from movies made it ideal timing.

It also struck Joel that, even if he wasn't a Shakespeare guy, Shakespeare was, in a strange, anachronistic way, a Coen guy. 'It's amazing how this play prefigures 20th-century pulp-noir tropes,' he said. Tropes that had so inspired him and Ethan throughout their career. He even drew 'a direct line' from the Macbeths' regicidal murder plot to *Blood Simple*'s murderous antics, and related *Macbeth*'s horror to *Blood Simple*'s construction as 'a sort of horror movie/thriller hybrid'. From a genre perspective, at least, he knew he'd be on familiar ground.

Joel's version of *Macbeth* might extend the title of the play to its full length, but it hones the original text down to a leaner form, excising about 15 per cent. 'The ambition was to give it a rhythm and pace that was very, very relentless,' he said.

His script also reduced the three weird sisters into a single sinister figure (played by Kathryn Hunter), and upgraded the character of Ross (Alex Hassell) from mere messenger to an arch-manipulator who shifts allegiances, like Tom Reagan in *Miller's Crossing*. The film even hints that it is Ross who kills Lady Macbeth, rather than her taking her own life.

But the most distinctive aspect of Joel's take on The Scottish Play is the way it embraces the age of its two leads. McDormand (who also produced) was 62 at the time of shooting in early 2020, and Denzel Washington, working for the first time with Joel, was 64. During his 'deep dive' into the play, and many of its previous incarnations on film, Joel realized it is obsessed with time. 'The word "time" is used maybe 40 times in the text,' he observed. 'It starts with a "when"' – spelled out in white-on-black uppercase lettering at the very opening of the film – 'and time-marking things are in almost every speech and soliloquy.' This chimed well, he found, with having a 'post-menopausal' Lady Macbeth at its heart.

In McDormand's mind, this only enhanced the play's tragedy and earned its use of the full title. 'In Joel's adaptation we are exploring the age of the characters,' she explained. 'Both Denzel and I are older than what is often cast as the Macbeths. We're past childbearing age. So that puts a pressure on their ambition to have the crown. I think the most important distinction is that it is their last chance for glory. There's a real suspense and a real ticking clock. It propels the storytelling.' As Joel put it, 'Time, mortality and the future are vital themes.'

In truth, it is quite easy to miss this interesting thematic variation. This is not at all a fault of the movie, just the result of its strikingly abstract style and progressive casting, which could lead one to overlook the sexagenarianism of the leads, or treat it as irrelevant. Joel brought together actors from all over the world, allowing them to keep their accents, and cast the roles colour-blind, as Washington's impressive presence as the Thane of Cawdor (along with younger actors such as Corey Hawkins and Moses Ingram as Lord and Lady Macduff) makes clear.

Joel was not concerned with presenting the story's events as specifically happening in 11th-century Scotland, but rather abstracted them out to more of a 'generic past'. The film, he explained, 'wasn't about any real fidelity or defining the time period or the location.' Which was 'a strange exercise' for him, given how precisely he and Ethan located all their previous movies through very particular vernaculars and meticulous visual design.

Which isn't to suggest there was nothing meticulous about *The Tragedy of Macbeth*'s visual design. There is a strong case that it is the most elegantly, compellingly and inventively designed film of Joel's entire career. Motivated in part by the exhausting experience he had shooting *Buster Scruggs*, the entire production was shot indoors, on the soundstages of the Warner Bros lot in Burbank, California. But Joel mainly took this approach to emphasize the 'playness' of the material. 'I wasn't interested in a realistic, rent-a-castle version,' he said. 'I wanted people in the audience to always be aware that this was a theatrical experience.'

Any backdrops, for example, were painted and then enhanced with visual effects, to give the sense of incredibly upgraded theatrical scrims. The sets, designed by Stefan Marchant, a new collaborator for Joel, were created to be minimal and uncluttered, like the empty surrealist cityscapes of Giorgio di Chirico, who is most obviously referenced in the film's tall archways. Each location was reduced to its barest essentials. 'There's an idea of a castle, there's the atmosphere of a mountain,' said Joel. 'Don't put everything in there. Don't make it look like a Disney thing.'

Inspired by the films of German expressionists F W Murnau (especially 1927's *Sunrise*) and Carl Theodor Dreyer (1928's *The Passion of Joan of Arc* was the film's most prominent touchstone), Joel presented the film in high contrast black-and-white. Though shot in colour and converted in post-production, the sets and

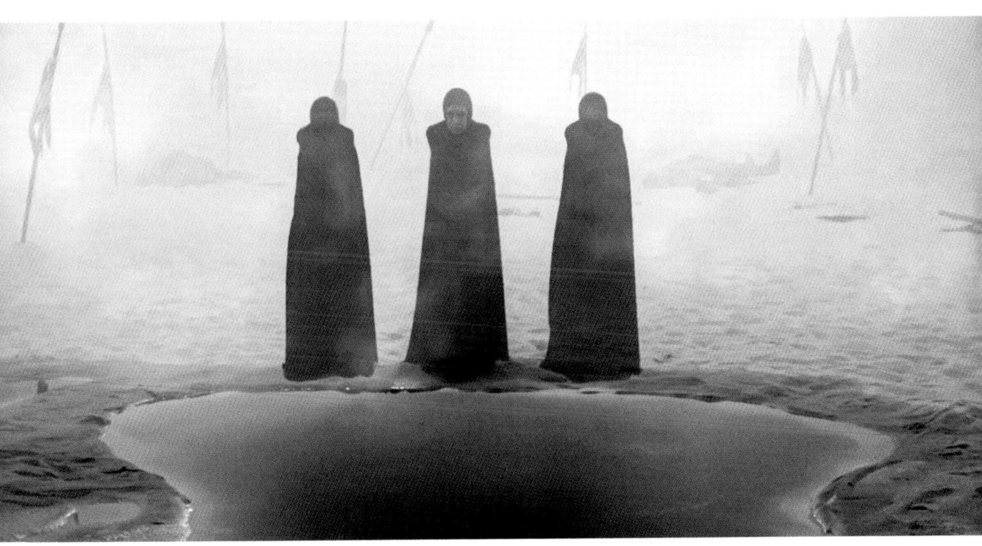

ABOVE: Renowned for her 'shapeshifting' talent, British stage actress Kathryn Hunter played all three Weird Sisters as a single witch.

costumes (by Coen regular Mary Zophres) were rendered in shades of grey. It was also portrait-framed in the Academy format rather than the common widescreen ratio, to give both its character closeups and the sheer verticality of its design greater impact.

The film's abstract quality, close to dreamlike at times, is also emphasized by its tricks of perspective and *trompe l'oeil* techniques. During its opening scene, we watch three ravens (representing the witches) circling in a foggy sky. At first, it appears we are looking up at them from the ground, as you'd expect. But as the fog clears, we realize we are looking directly *down* on them, and what we thought was white sky is in fact the pale sand of a beach. The effect is gloriously disorientating; up is down, down is up. It's a visual reflection of the witch's statement that 'fair is foul, and foul is fair', indicating that the kingdom is about to be upturned.

One of the film's most impressive illusions is the manifestation of the iconic dagger that Macbeth sees before him while approaching King Duncan's (Brendan Gleeson) bedchamber. Like the Thane, the audience can perceive the weapon glowing and floating at the far end of the corridor. Only as he moves close does it become clear it is merely the handle of the door catching the light in a certain way. This, Joel revealed, was inspired by a photograph of 19th-century banker J P Morgan by Edward J Steichen, in which a chair arm he's gripping looks oddly like a flashing knife. So, while revelling in the play's theatricality, the film is also deeply photographic and cinematic – even though, like *Buster Scruggs*, it was backed by a streamer rather than a film studio, this time Apple.

Though *The Tragedy of Macbeth* was undoubtedly a triumph that proved Joel could soar while flying solo (the film received three Oscar nominations: for production design, Bruno Delbonnel's cinematography and Washington's performance), there is a tinge of wistfulness in the interviews he gave while promoting it.

'I missed him,' Joel said of Ethan. 'That's the bottom line. I've worked with him for over 35 years, and if ever there was a problem on set we would look at each other first.' But, he emphasized, 'this isn't a movie that would have interested him.'

However, by the time the movie came out, it was clear Ethan wasn't actually done with filmmaking. He was soon to go into production on his own feature. One that was very different in style, tone and intent to Joel's, but did share a major similarity: it could never have been made, Ethan asserted, with his brother.

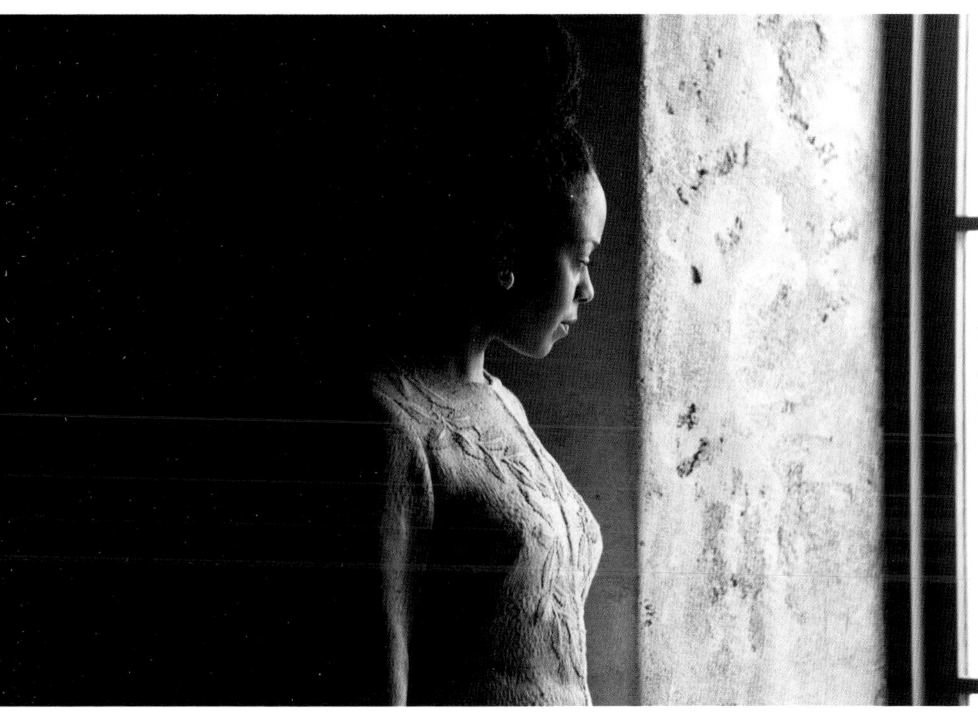

ABOVE: Moses Ingram (*The Queen's Gambit*) as the short-lived Lady Macduff.

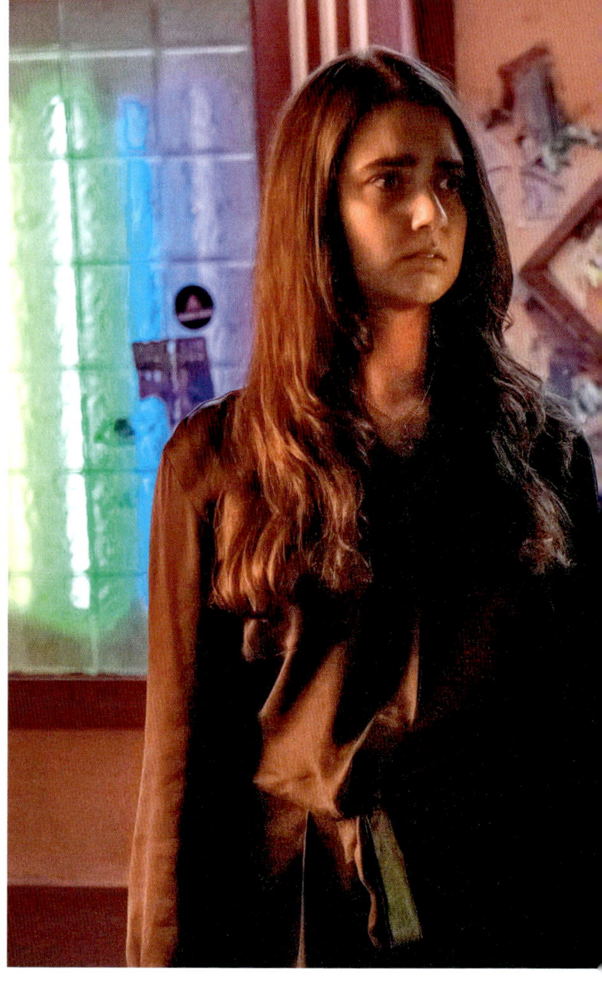

DRIVE-AWAY DOLLS
2024

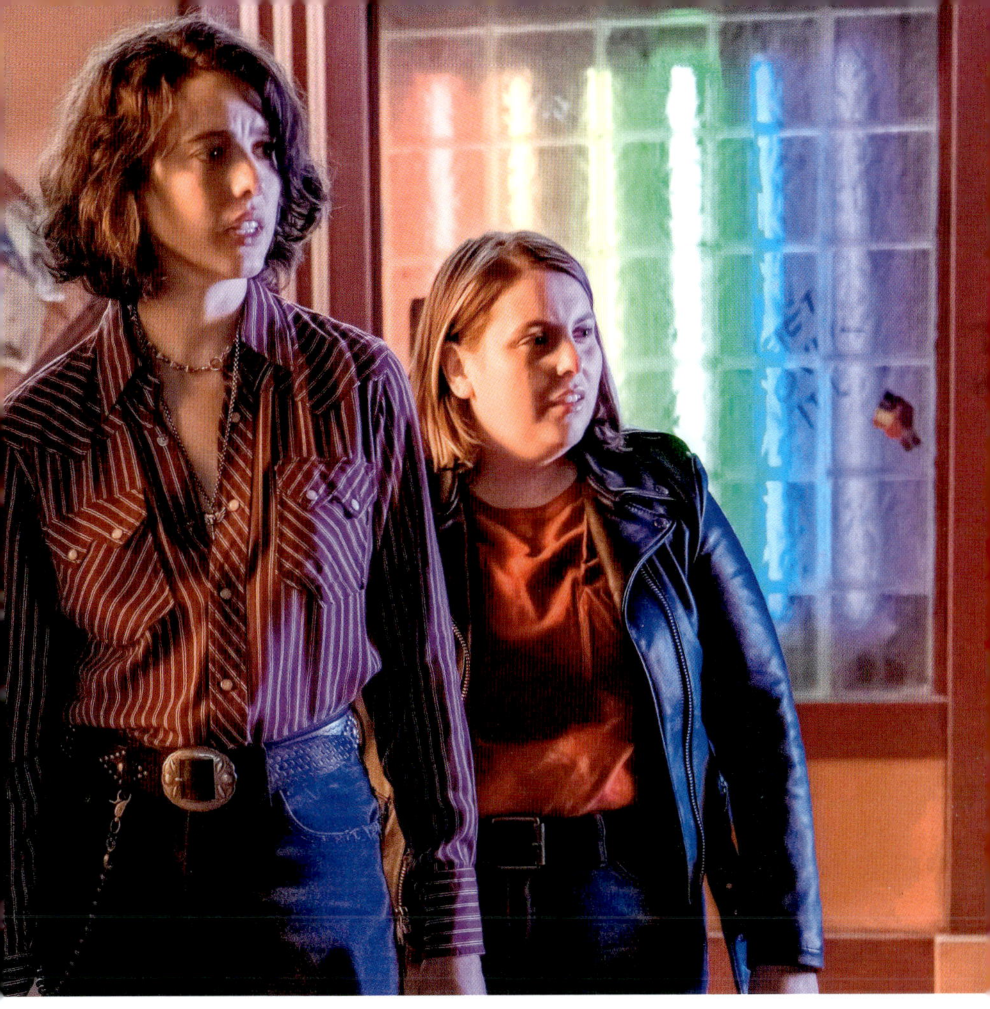

Ethan Coen was brought back to the movies by the very same event that kept most of the world away from them. Two weeks into the Covid lockdown, T Bone Burnett approached Ethan and his wife Tricia Cooke (who edited *O Brother, Where Art Thou?* and *The Man Who Wasn't There* with Roderick Jaynes) to make an archival documentary about Jerry Lee Lewis. Once that was done, the boredom and frustration of confinement further spurred the spouses to blow the dust off an old script they had co-written.

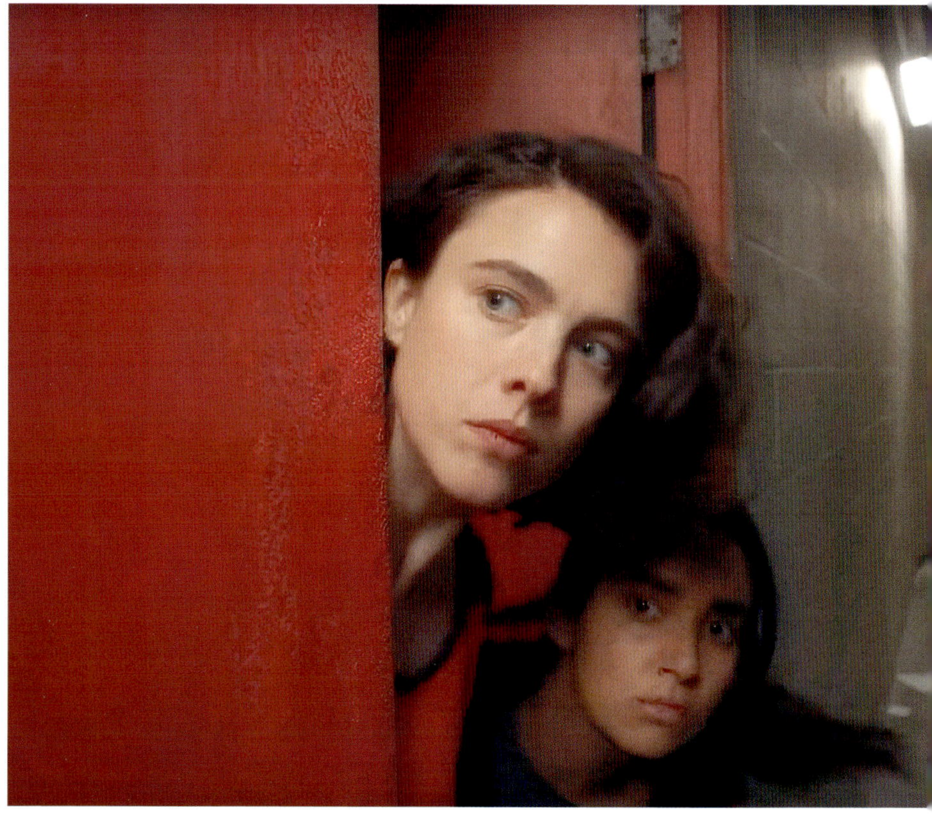

The script was *Drive-Away Dykes*, a road-trip romantic comedy, in which party girl Jamie (reeling from a recent break-up) and her uptight friend Marian (who has a secret crush on Jamie) drive to Tallahassee in a rented car, unaware they have a mysterious package in the trunk that a powerful Republican senator desperately wants to retrieve. The couple had written it almost 20 years earlier, when Cooke, who has identified as a lesbian since she was 15 ('it's a very unconventional relationship,' she's said of their marriage), came up with the title while out drinking with a friend. After sharing it with Ethan, they decided it was too good not to turn into a movie, which they originally wrote for their friend Allison Anders to direct.

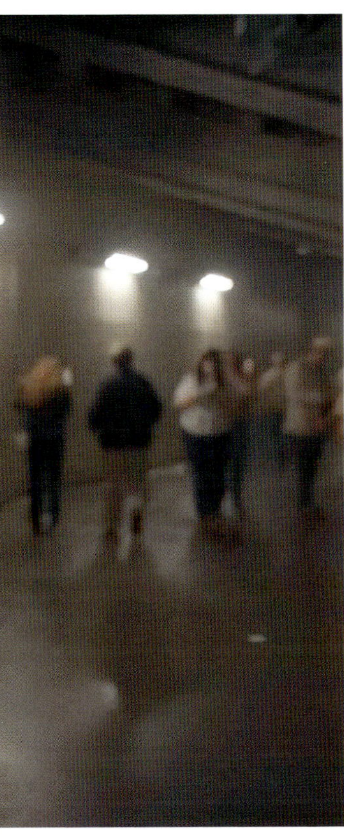

ABOVE: Jamie and Marian become embroiled in a misadventure no less entertainingly absurd than *O Brother, Where Art Thou?* or *The Big Lebowski.*

Anders, who had made her name on the indie scene in 1992 with trailer-park drama *Gas Food Lodging*, was immediately taken by the script. 'It's really a girl buddy movie, from a female point of view,' she said in 2007. 'But it's also very Russ Meyer-esque, with that same kind of innocence.' Anders' reference to sexploitation maestro Meyer (whose films include 1965's *Faster, Pussycat! Kill! Kill!* and 1970's *Beyond the Valley of the Dolls*) reflected a deliberate intention on the part of Cooke and Coen. 'We wanted to have a lot of sex in it, and to feel a little bit like a B-movie,' Cooke said. 'It's down and dirty.'

Various actors were considered for the lead roles, including Holly Hunter, Selma Blair, Christina Applegate and Chloë Sevigny. Unfortunately, the film proved too down and dirty for potential backers in the 2000s. The project collapsed, Anders exited, and the script went back in Coen and Cooke's drawer, destined, they thought, to become an artefact they'd one day pull out and show to their kids for a laugh.

The problem, Ethan reasoned, wasn't so much that it was a movie about lesbians, but that it was not an 'important lesbian movie'. Although it *was* important to Cooke, in the sense that she had always wanted to make 'a queer movie that didn't take itself too seriously'. This ambition is suggested by the short comedy film she directed with Carrie Schraeder (and co-wrote with Ethan) in 2008, titled *Don't Mess With Texas*, in which a pair of road-tripping lesbians have their preconceived notions about small-towners upended in a Texan diner. It was why Ethan could never have made the movie with his brother, he insisted, despite the DNA it obviously shared with their previous films, from Jamie's Hi McDunnough-style verbiage, to the *Fargo/Raising Arizona* crap-goon double act of Joey Slotnick and C J Wilson. This movie (eventually retitled *Drive-Away Dolls* to avoid a potential boycott by conservative theatre owners) required Cooke's involvement and perspective to bring it into being. 'It's whatever weird A/B combination of me and Trish,' said Ethan.

Drive-Away Dolls certainly stands out from his movies with Joel, featuring explicit sex scenes (mostly played for laughs) and focusing on female characters, with a warmth and sweetness underpinning the central relationship that contrasts the wry edginess of much of the Coens' oeuvre.

Ethan and Cooke's cast included only one previous collaborator, Matt Damon, who contributed what is essentially an extended cameo as the nefarious senator. For the most part it featured a fresh mix of excellent character actors (Bill Camp, Colman Domingo, Beanie Feldstein) and one recently risen star: Pedro Pascal, of *The Last of Us* and *The Mandalorian* fame, though he spends most of the film as a decapitated head in an ice bucket.

For the two lead roles, they decided to cast young, with twentysomethings Margaret Qualley (daughter of Andie MacDowell) and Geraldine Viswanathan playing Jamie and Marian, respectively. Their callowness was a requirement for the characters, much younger than typical Coen protagonists. It needed to be believable that they quit their jobs to take a road trip. Besides, Ethan pointed out, 'They go clubbing. One of them is

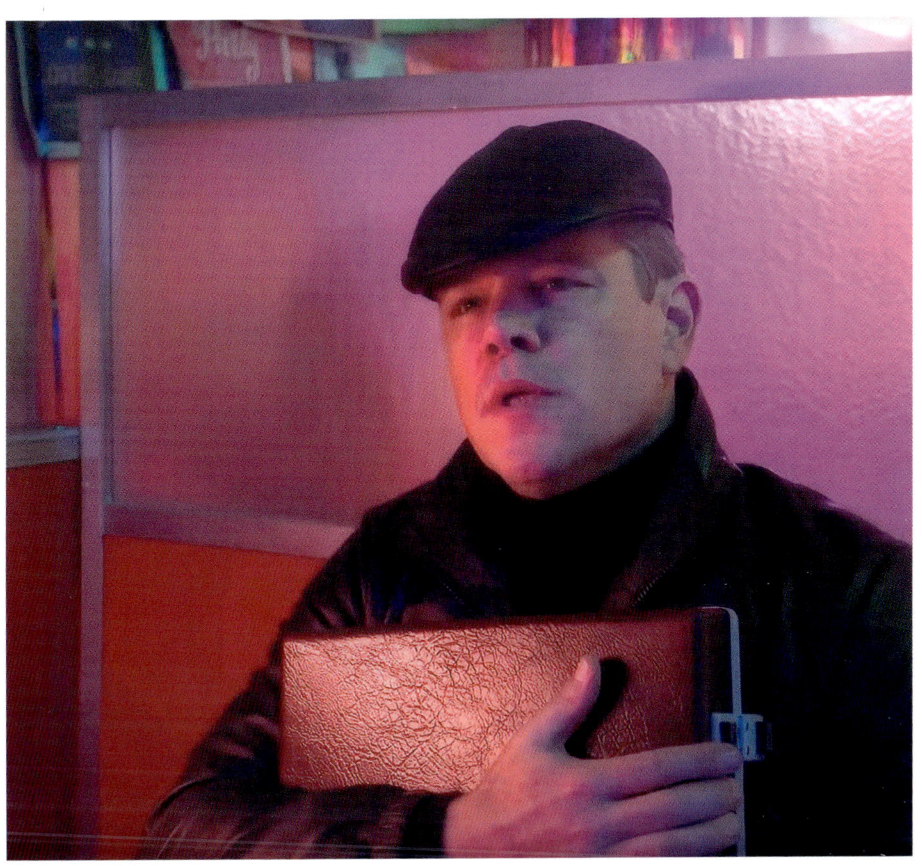

ABOVE: Matt Damon makes a brief appearance as a right-wing senator who'll do anything to protect his reputation.

a good-time party girl. They have characteristics that would be a little depressing in a 40-year-old.'

While the film's directorial credit is given only to Ethan, he has maintained that *Drive-Away Dolls* should not be seen as a solo venture. He and Cooke were co-writers, co-producers and co-directors, just as he and Joel had been on all the movies that were solely credited to his older brother. 'Much as it was with Joel, the

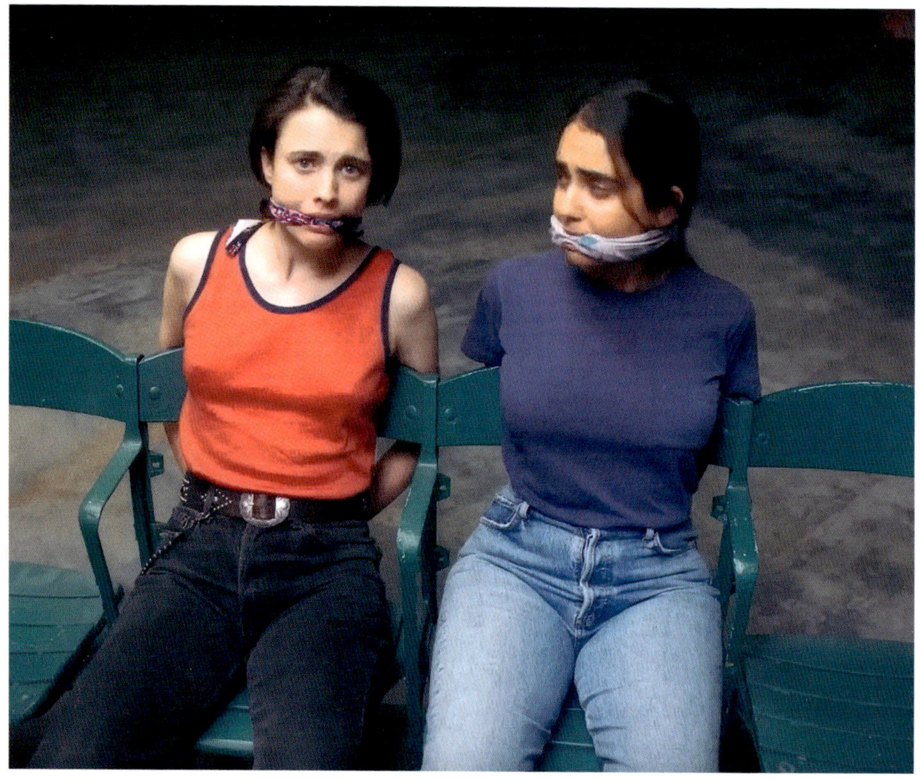

ABOVE: Jamie and Marian's road trip turns perilous after they find a severed head in the trunk of their hire car.

whole process is just the two of you doing it,' he said. 'It felt as natural in its way as it was working with Joel.'

You could almost feel sorry for the older Coen: missing his partner in crime while pressing on alone, and his brother, presumed retired, suddenly returning to filmmaking as part of a new partnership. One that looks set to continue. Cooke and Coen have another 'lesbian genre movie' titled *Honey Don't* in the works, and intend to complete a trashy B-movie 'trilogy' with a third entry, *Go Beavers*. However, Ethan has teased, this isn't necessarily the end for him and Joel. The Coen brothers may yet ride again.

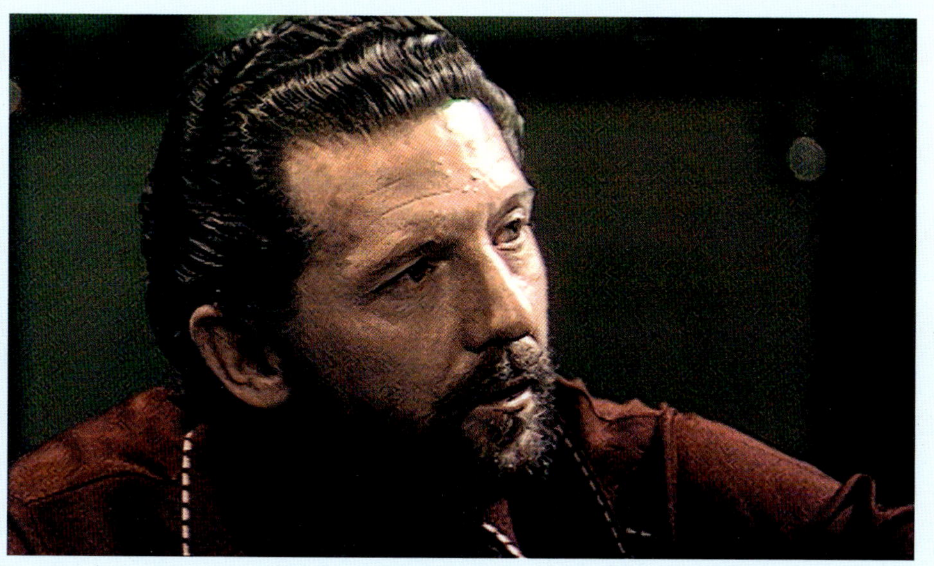

Ethan's doc: *Jerry Lee Lewis: Trouble in Mind* (2022)

In 2020, Jerry Lee Lewis was the last living rock 'n' roll legend, still performing well into his eighties. One of his final music projects was a gospel album he recorded with T Bone Burnett in 2019. Feeling this was an event worthy of commemoration, Burnett approached Ethan and Tricia Cooke to see if they were interested in making a documentary about it.

Cooke and Ethan (credited as editor and director respectively, though sharing both responsibilities) were less interested in documenting the album than they were in telling the story of Lewis' entire career. Combining footage of TV interviews and live performances (presented sometimes in their entirety, and at other times as elegantly constructed montages), the film is ostensibly unjudgmental of a controversial figure. Though it doesn't shy away from his darker side, including references to Lewis shooting his bass player and marrying his 13-year-old cousin (the second of his seven wives), the film simply presents the man as he chose to present himself, and leaves it up to us to decide whether or not he's irredeemably arrogant or forgivably unrepentant. Either way, across 70 fascinating minutes, Ethan and Cooke present irrefutable evidence of his musical talent.

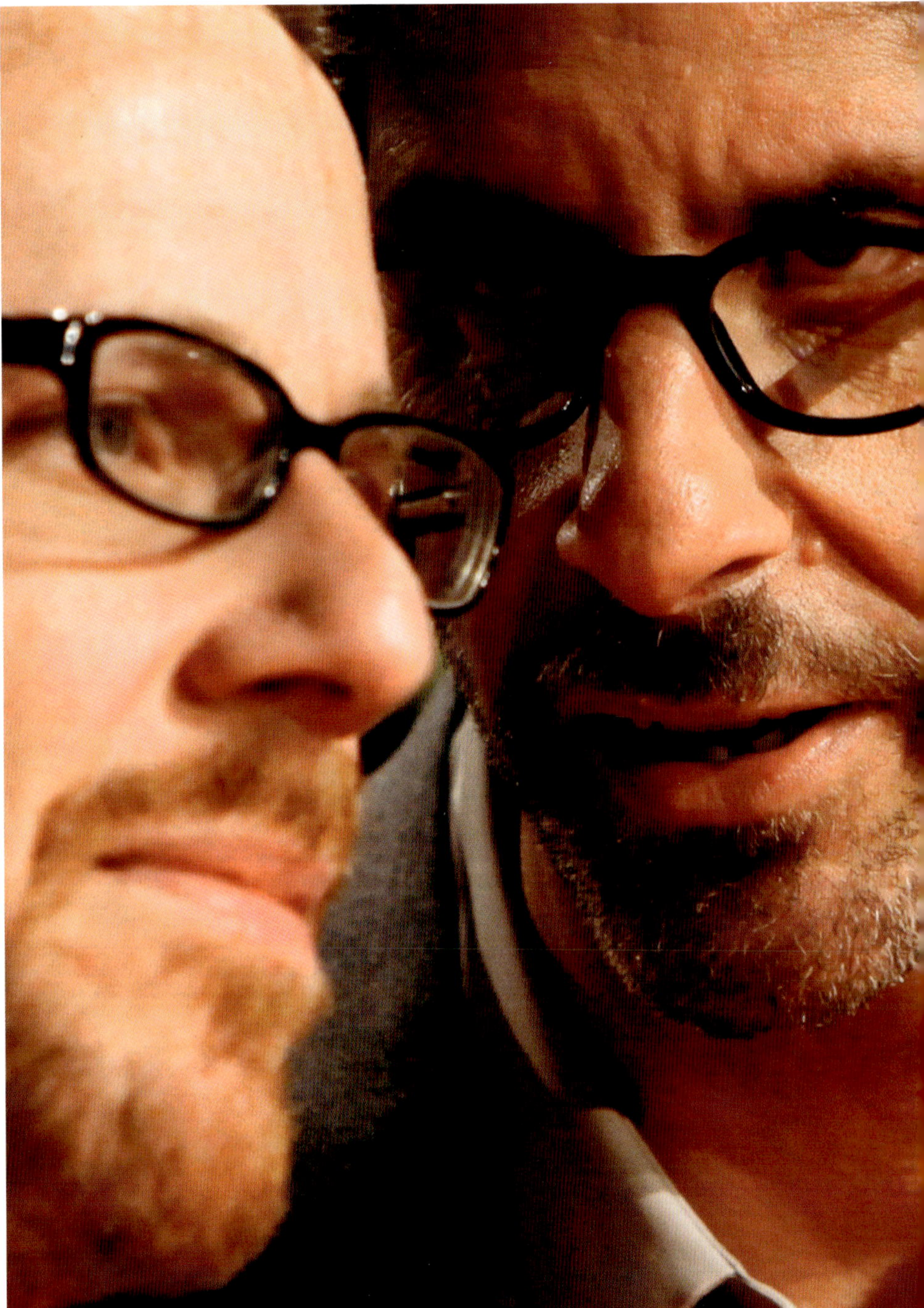

Brothers beyond

THE COMING YEARS

In June 2023, with just seven words, Ethan put an end to Coen aficionados' fears that the brothers would never again collaborate as filmmakers: 'I'm working on something with Joel now,' he confirmed. Without, of course, confirming what that 'something' was.

It had been recently reported that Joel and Ethan's next film could be *The Zebra-Striped Hearse*, an adaptation of Ross Macdonald's 1962 detective novel, and the author's tenth mystery to feature Marlowe-esque private eye Lew Archer. With its retro setting, road-trip spine and pile-up of dead bodies, it's easy to discern the book's appeal to the Coens, who'd written a draft years earlier for their *Hudsucker* producer Joel Silver.

However, there were many other possibilities for the brothers' 19th feature together. It could have been any of the unmade films stashed in the drawers of Mike Zoss Productions. Their Cold War comedy *62 Skidoo*, perhaps. Or their once-mooted adaptation of Michael Chabon's counter-factual historical crime novel *The Yiddish Policeman's Union*, set in an Alaskan Jewish settlement. Or *Dark Web*, a Dennis Lehane thriller script they reworked in 2016, based on the life of Ross William Ulbricht, aka Dread Pirate Roberts, who founded online illegal-drug market The Silk Road.

Then, in January 2024, while participating with Tricia Cooke in a masterclass at Tromsø International Film Festival, Ethan let it slip: he and Joel had co-written and would direct 'a pure horror film' together. 'It gets very bloody,' he grinned, before drawing a line all the way back to his and Joel's debut. 'If you like *Blood Simple*, I think you'll enjoy it.' Judging by their dalliances with the genre in *Blood Simple*, *Barton Fink* and *No Country For Old Men* (as well as, for Joel, *The Tragedy of Macbeth*), the idea of a full-on horror certainly holds much appeal for Coen fans. Though we can't be sure how 'pure' it will actually be; it is also, Cooke said, 'horribly funny.'

Where Joel and Ethan go after that is impossible to predict. Though it can be said with some certainty what they *won't* do, having definitively ruled out two destinations from their shared creative future. The first is space. 'I think outer space is maybe a little too sterilized, even for us,' said Ethan in 1998. 'I don't think we could get our minds around the whole spacesuit thing,' added Joel in 2007.

The second is television. Where other directors have felt the lure of long-form narrative TV, it appears to hold no attraction for

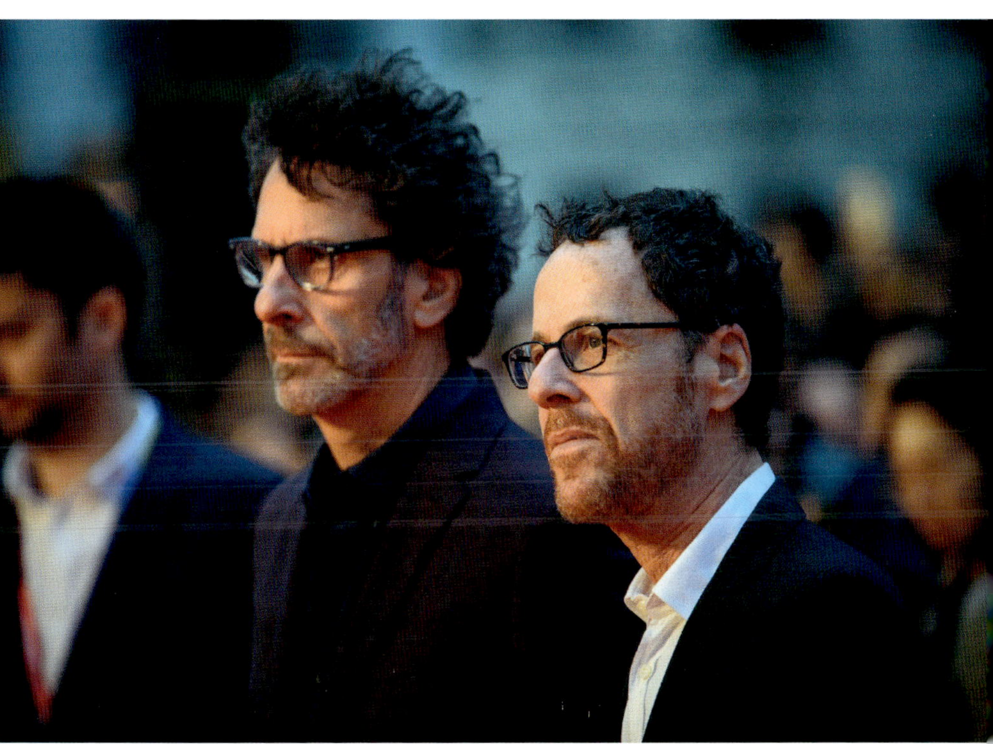

ABOVE: The Coens attend the London premiere of *The Ballad of Buster Scruggs*, the last film they made together.

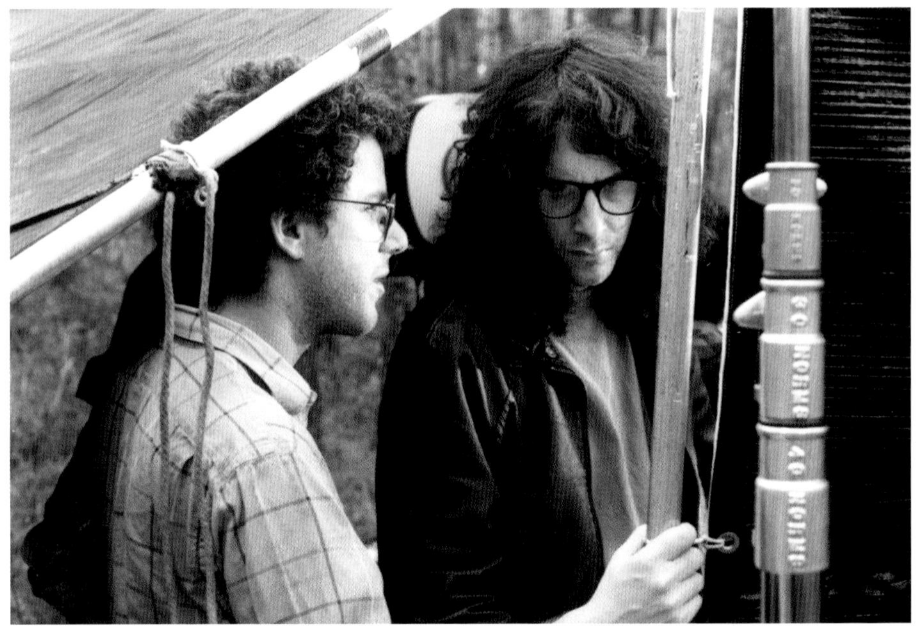

ABOVE: Ethan and Joel putting their heads together on the set of *Miller's Crossing* in 1990.

Joel and Ethan. 'Television is a different paradigm,' said Joel. 'Not to be shitty about it, I look at stories as having a beginning, a middle and an end. But so much of television is it's got a beginning, a middle, a middle, a middle, a middle, until the whole thing dies of exhaustion.' In the same interview, Joel also suggested that the brothers were finished with the Western. *The Ballad of Buster Scruggs* seems to have been their final word on that genre.

Looking back at four decades of Coen films does not help us determine what their remaining years will look like. 'There's never been any real design or architecture to what we've done,' said Joel while promoting *The Tragedy of Macbeth*. It would be 'a mistake to think that any of it is planned.'

As this journey through their movies has shown, Joel and Ethan are, above all else, instinctive filmmakers, basing their decisions on what feels right at a given moment, rather than strategizing to meet a perceived demand. There have been moments of calculation, such as pitching *Blood Simple* towards horror, to better attract small-time investors and replicate what Sam Raimi achieved with *The Evil Dead*. And there have also been times when reaching a certain (or bigger) audience has been in their minds, such as with *Intolerable Cruelty*, *True Grit* and *The Tragedy of Macbeth*, which Joel wanted to make accessible to those who had never seen or read any Shakespeare. But their shared career has, above all, always involved forging their own cinematic path.

Even this wasn't conscious. Because they financed *Blood Simple* themselves, the brothers had the freedom to make it exactly how they wanted, establishing a precedent they've taken forward into every film since, whether or not a big studio was involved. 'I've never had a studio note I had to listen to,' said Joel. 'And I've had very few studio notes in my life.' Yet, the brothers have claimed, if a studio had offered to finance their first film, they would have said 'sure, yeah, let's do that,' and relinquished some creative control.

That is very hard to imagine. More likely, they would have found a studio-compromised job too frustrating, and fought for their vision. Although, conflict is notably absent from Joel and Ethan's history. Aside from some hazing by M Emmet Walsh on *Blood Simple*, and hints of dissatisfaction in their dealings with Nicolas Cage on *Raising Arizona*, their productions have largely been amicable. There is not a single report of the brothers falling out. Jeff Bridges could only remember one small instance of disagreement during the shoot for *The Big Lebowski*. While filming the Busby Berkeley dream sequence, Joel wanted Bridges to 'wince a bit' as The Dude flew towards the pins. Ethan wanted him to smile, figuring he'd enjoy being a bowling ball. After some measured back and forth, they said, 'Well, let's shoot it both ways.' The Coens' conviviality fosters an atmosphere of secure collaboration on their sets; *No Country*'s Kelly Macdonald said they weren't so much a two-headed monster as 'the two-headed friend. I felt really safe having both of them there. You're lucky if you get one good director on a film. This way we get two.'

Over the years, the Coen brothers have been repeatedly judged as condescending and cold-hearted towards their characters, while the siblings' resistance to discussing theme and subtext has led to a broad impression of them being spiky and aloof (encouraged, it must be said, by the fact that they have never enjoyed publicity). But their affection for their characters, and also for the films and genres they've channelled so effectively and accessibly, is as evident as their appeal to potential collaborators; so great that George Clooney agreed to make a film with them before even reading the script. And if the brothers themselves resist interpreting an oeuvre that shimmers with patterns and constantly invites us to test its depths, that's simply because they don't see it as their job. Leave that to the critics.

Or simply accept that finding meaning in their films is like trying to find it anywhere else in a meaningless universe, as Larry Gopnik failed to in *A Serious Man*. Meaning is no easier to grasp than the money in *Fargo*, *No Country For Old Men* and *Hail, Caesar!* Or success in *Barton Fink* and *Inside Llewyn Davis*. Or the plot in *Miller's Crossing* and *The Big Lebowski*.

Every movie the Coens have made is an invitation to 'accept the mystery' and have the best possible time while doing so. Films are there to be enjoyed above all else, just as Joel and Ethan learned from *Sullivan's Travels*. Art and entertainment are, to the brothers, indivisible. 'That's a distinction that I've never understood,' said Joel early on in their career. 'If somebody goes out to make a movie that isn't designed primarily to entertain people, then I don't know what they're doing.' Without a doubt, Joel and Ethan deliver both art and entertainment. In bloodstained spades.

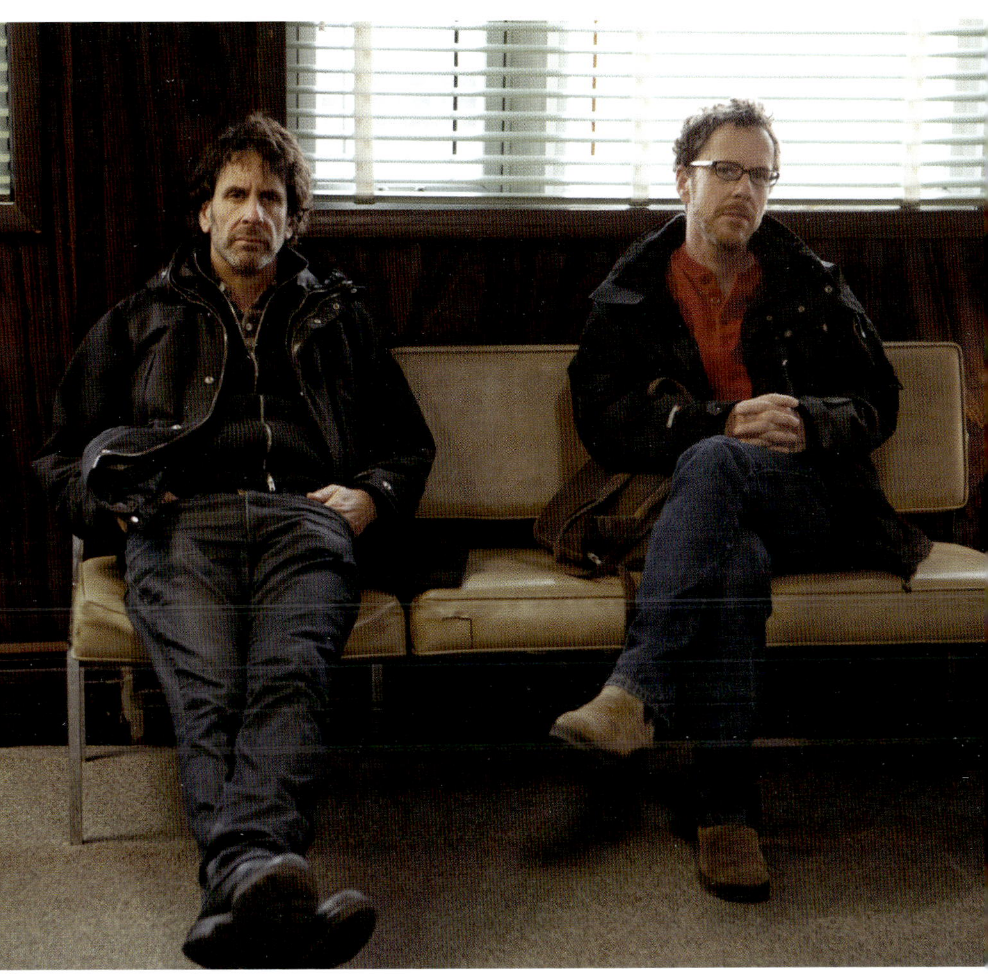

Resources

Chapter One

Ciment, Michel, and Hubert Niogret, 'Interview with Joel and Ethan Coen', *Positif*, July/August 1987

Edelstein, David, 'Invasion of the Baby Snatchers', *American Film*, April 1987

Hajari, Nisid, 'Talking with Rena Coen', *Entertainment Weekly*, 28 February 1992

Hinson, Hal, 'Bloodlines', *Film Comment*, March/April 1985

Hoad, Phil, 'How We Made Blood Simple', *The Guardian*, 6 November 2017

Klemesrud, Judy, 'The Brothers Coen Bow In With *Blood Simple*', *The New York Times*, 20 January 1985

Minnesota Nice, *Fargo* DVD

Pooley, Eric, 'Warped in America: The Dark Vision of Moviemakers Joel and Ethan Coen', *New York Magazine*, 23 March 1987

Chapter Two

Barth, Jack, 'Praising Arizona', *Film Comment*, April 1987

Bergan, Ronald, *The Coen Brothers*, Phoenix/Orion, 2001

Billson, Anne, 'Simply Bloody', *Time Out*, 31 January 1985

Breitbart, Eric, 'Joel and Ethan Coen', *American Film*, May 1985

Ciment, Michel, and Hubert Niogret, 'Interview with Joel and Ethan Coen', *Positif*, July/August 1987

Coursodon, Jean-Pierre, 'A Hat Blown By The Wind', *Positif*, February 1991

Edelstein, David, 'Invasion of the Baby Snatchers', *American Film*, April 1987

Harrington, Richard, 'Tales of the Brothers Coen', *The Washington Post*, 7 October 1990

Hinson, Hal, 'Bloodlines', *Film Comment*, March/April 1985

Hoad, Phil, 'How We Made Blood Simple', *The Guardian*, 6 November 2017

Klemsrud, Judy, 'The Brothers Coen Bow In With *Blood Simple*', *The New York Times*, 20 January 1985

Levy, Steven, 'Shot By Shot', *Premiere*, March 1990

Miller's Crossing Production Notes, 20th Century Fox

Rich, Katey, 'Watch Bruce Campbell in the Fake Trailer That Started the Coen Brothers' Careers', vanityfair.com, 24 June 2016

Team Deakins podcast, 2 August 2020

'The Coen Brothers – An In-Depth Look at Their Early Career', Death By Films

The Making of Miller's Crossing, *Miller's Crossing* DVD

Variety staff, 'Blood Simple', *Variety*, 23 May 1985

Wakeman, Gregory James, 'An Oral History of *Raising Arizona*', *Business Insider*, 16 March 2022

Yuan, Jada, 'Roderick Jaynes, Imaginary Oscar Nominee for "*No Country*"', vulture.com, 22 January 2008

Chapter Three

Aftab, Kaleem, 'I Just Like Doing My Job: DP Roger Deakins on Working with the Coens, Digital vs. Film and his Most Difficult Shots', *Filmmaker* magazine, 30 July 2015

Ciment, Michel, and Hubert Niogret, 'A Rock on the Beach', *Positif*, September 1991

Clark, John, 'Strange Bedfellows', *Premiere* US, April 1994

Deakins, Roger, 'Looking at Lighting', Rogerdeakins.com

Harkness, John, 'A Sphinx Without A Riddle', *Sight and Sound*, August 1994

Lipper, Hal, 'Another Fiery Tale from the Coen Brothers', *The Tampa Bay Times*, 14 March 1993

McCarthy, Todd, *Variety*, 31 January 1994

Naughton, John, 'Double Vision', *Premiere* UK, September 1994

Rosenberg, Adam, 'Coen Brothers Want John Turturro To Get Old For *Barton Fink* Sequel *Old Fink*', MTV Movies Blog, 21 September 2009

Sharkey, Betsy, 'Movies of their Very Own', *The New York Times*, 8 July 1990

Chapter Four

Biskind, Peter, 'Joel and Ethan Coen', *Premiere* US, March 1996

Ciment, Michel, and Hubert Niogret, 'Closer to Life Than the Conventions of Cinema', *Positif*, September 1996

Ciment, Michel, and Hubert Niogret, 'The Logic of Soft Drugs', *Positif*, May 1998

Ehrlich, Richard S, 'The Man Who Founded a Religion Based on *The Big Lebowski*', CNN, 20 March 2013

Gross, Terry, 'The Coen Bros On Writing "Lebowski" and Literally Herding Cats', *Fresh Air*, NPR, 17 December 2013

Hochman, Steve, 'An Offer Clooney Didn't Even Consider Turning Down', *Los Angeles Times*, 22 December 2000

Jolin, Dan, interview with Jeff Bridges conducted for *Empire* in October 2010

Kyriazis, Stefan, 'George Clooney: why am I always cast as imbeciles or idiots with sex toys? *Daily Express,* 13 July 2016

Lowe, Andy, 'The Brothers Grim', *Total Film,* May 1998

Minnesota Nice, Fargo DVD

'O Brother, why art thou so popular?' *BBC News*, 28 February 2002

'Production' featurette, *O Brother, Where Art Thou?* DVD

Romney, Jonathan, 'Double Vision', *The Guardian* 19 May 2000

Rose, Charlie, '*Fargo*', 10 March 1997

Scott, A O, 'Film Review; A Feel-Good Ode To Ol'-Time Music', *The New York Times*, 15 June 2001

Sharf, Zack, 'The Coen Brothers and George Clooney Uncover the Magic of *O Brother, Where Art Thou?*' at 15th Anniversary Reunion', *IndieWire*, 30 September 2015

Stone, Doug, 'The Coens Speak (Reluctantly)', *IndieWire,* 9 March 1998

Willman, Chris, 'The Music Behind *The Big Lebowski*', *Entertainment Weekly,* 3 April 1998

Chapter Five

Bradshaw, Peter, 'Review: *The Man Who Wasn't There*', *The Guardian*, 26 October 2001

Ebert, Roger, '*Intolerable Cruelty*', RogerEbert.com, 10 October 2003

Einav, Dan, 'Is this the Coen brothers' most underrated movie?', *Little White Lies*, 18 February 2017

Elias, Debbie Lynn, '*Intolerable Cruelty*', Behind The Lens, 2003

Higgins, Charlotte, 'Hanks says his *Ladykillers* sidesteps the Ealing art', *The Guardian*, 19 May 2004

Kelly, Kevin, 'The Coen Brothers, *Burn After Reading*, Toronto 2008', SpoutBlog

Michael, David, 'Catherine Zeta-Jones Interview: *Intolerable Cruelty*', BBC Movies, 2003

Mottram, James, 'Joel and Ethan Coen', bbc.co.uk, 2001

Mundhra, Smirti, 'Interview with Joel Coen', IGN, 2 November 2001

Rose, Charlie '*Intolerable Cruelty*', 10 June 2003

Team Deakins podcast, 2 August 2020

'*The Ladykillers*, Q&A with Tom Hanks', Phase9 Entertainment

Wise, Damon, '*Intolerable Cruelty* Review' *Empire*, November 2003

Chapter Six

A County Sheriff's Diary, No Country For Old Men DVD

Barlow, Helen, 'In For The Kill', *The Sydney Morning Herald*, 21 December 2007

Finding The Burn, Burn After Reading DVD

Gilchrist, Todd, 'Interview: Joel and Ethan Coen', IGN, 9 November 2007

Grossman, Lev, 'What Happened When a Very Private Writer. . .: A Conversation Between Cormac McCarthy and Joel and Ethan Coen', *Time*, 18 October 2007

Insiders Run Amuck, Burn After Reading DVD

Kelly, Kevin, 'The Coen Brothers, *Burn After Reading*, Toronto 2008', SpoutBlog

Rose, Charlie, '*No Country For Old Men*', 16 November 2007

Team Deakins podcast, 2 August 2020

Team Deakins podcast, 14 April 2021

The Making of No Country For Old Men, No Country For Old Men DVD

Welcome Back George, Burn After Reading DVD

Wise, Damon, 'Joel and Ethan Coen', *Uncut*, 10 October 2008

Chapter Seven

A Serious Man Production Notes, Focus Features

Carr, David, 'The Coen Brothers Shooting Straight', *The New York Times*, 10 December 2010

Dargis, Manohla, and A O Scott, 'We Are The Establishment Now', *The New York Times*, 4 September 2013

Ebert, Roger, 'Coens retell Book of Job in a quiet Minneapolis suburb', RogerEbert.com, 10 October, 2009

Gross, Terry, 'Coen Bros On Wet Horses, Kid Stars: It's A Wild West,' *Fresh Air*, NPR, 12 January 2011

Gross, Terry, 'The Coen Bros On Writing "*Lebowski*" and Literally Herding Cats', Fresh Air, NPR, 17 December 2013

Gross, Terry, 'The Coen Bros Reflect on Making a "Gritty" Western', *Fresh Air*, NPR, 11 February 2011

Hebblethwaite, Phil, 'T Bone Burnett: the art of matching music with movies', *The Guardian*, 27 December 2013

Jolin, Dan, interview with Jeff Bridges, conducted for *Empire* on 27 October 2010

Jolin, Dan, interview with Matt Damon, conducted for *Empire* on 28 October 2010

Jolin, Dan, interview with Hailee Steinfeld, conducted for *Empire* on 5 November 2010

Kelly, Kevin, 'The Coen Brothers, *Burn After Reading*, Toronto 2008', SpoutBlog

Lidz, Franz, 'Biblical Adversity in a 60s Suburb', *The New York Times*, 23 September 2009

Romney, Jonathan, 'Double Vision', *The Guardian*, 19 May 2000

Team Deakins podcast, 2 August 2020

Thompson, Anne, '*Inside Llewyn Davis* Secrets and a New Coens Movie Revealed', *IndieWire*, 11 December 2013

Tilly, Chris, '*True Grit* exclusive', IGN, 27 October 2009

Chapter Eight

Coen, Joel, New York Film Festival press conference, 9 October 2018

Coyle, Jake, 'Ethan Coen on his Jerry Lee Lewis doc and filmmaking return', Associated Press, 23 May 2022

Gross, Terry, 'Filmmakers Joel and Ethan Coen on Singing Cowboys and Working With Oxen, *Fresh Air*, NPR, 19 November 2018

Hail Caesar! Production Notes, Universal Pictures

Ordona, Michael, 'The road less travelled leads to *No Country*', *Los Angeles Times*, 10 February 2008

Rottenberg, Josh, 'The Coen brothers on their Western anthology film *The Ballad of Buster Scruggs*, Netflix and the future of moviegoing', *Los Angeles Times*, 14 November 2018

Team Deakins podcast, 2 August 2020

Turan, Kenneth, 'Joel Coen wouldn't have made *Macbeth* with his brother Ethan. Here's why', *Los Angeles Times*, 7 January 2022

Chapter Nine

Bradshaw, Peter, 'A post-menopausal Macbeth': Joel Coen on tackling Shakespeare with Frances McDormand, *The Guardian*, 3 December 2021

Coen, Joel, interviewed by Guillermo Del Toro for DGA podcast The Director's Cut, 4 February 2022

Fernandez, Jay A, 'A mischievous Road', *Los Angeles Times*, 10 January 2007

Jolin, Dan, 'A new kind of Coen collaboration', *Empire*, August 2023

Jolin, Dan, interview with Ethan Coen and Tricia Cooke conducted for *Empire* on 15 June 2023

Michieletto, Damiano, interview with Frances McDormand on Instagram for *FilmStage*, 13 April 2020

Weintraub, Steve, 'Ethan Coen says *Drive-Away Dolls* Has Something a Coen Brothers Movie Never Had', *Collider*, 23 June 2023

Woodward, Adam, 'Joel Coen: How We Made *The Tragedy of Macbeth*', *Little White Lies*, 14 Jan 2022

Chapter Ten

Hinson, Hal, 'Bloodlines', *Film Comment*, March/April 1985

Itzkoff, Dave, 'Watch the Throne: How Joel Coen Came to Make *The Tragedy of Macbeth*', *New York Times*, 28 January 2022

Jolin, Dan, 'A new kind of Coen collaboration', *Empire*, August 2023

Kristiansen, Lars Ole, '"Joel and I are going to make a horror film" – Ethan Coen reveals new projects in our interview', reporting on Tromsø Film Festival masterclass hosted by Kaleem Aftab, *Montages*, 25 January 2024

Lowe, Andy, 'The Brothers Grim', *Total Film*, May 1998

Patterson, John, 'We've Killed a lot of Animals', *The Guardian*, 21 December 2007

Sharf, Zack, 'Jeff Bridges Saw The Coen Brothers Fight Only Once, and It Was During an Iconic Scene', *IndieWire*, 1 February 2019

Team Deakins podcast, 2 August 2020

Working With the Coens, No Country For Old Men DVD

Index

Bibliography

Bergan, Ronald, *The Coen Brothers*, Phoenix/Orion, 2001

McBride, Joseph, *The Whole Durn Human Comedy: Life According to the Coen Brothers*, Anthem Press, 2022

Nayman, Adam, *The Coen Brothers: This Book Really Ties the Films Together*, Abrams, New York, 2018

Robson, Eddie, *Coen Brothers*, Random House, 2007

Woods, Paul A, *Joel & Ethan Coen: Blood Siblings*, Plexus London, 2000

Picture credits

Acknowledgements

Huge thanks, first of all, to the editorial team at Quercus: Kerry Enzor, who kindly thought of me as the launch writer for this cool new series and trusted in my decades-long enthusiasm for the Coens; Anna Southgate, whose cuts were as painless as they were necessary; and Julia Shone at Greenfinch.

I'm deeply grateful to my other, better half, Lucy Jolin, who not only endured my diminished commitment to domestic duties and teenage-offspring-ferrying because I was too busy watching and writing about movies I love, but was also my first reader and super-ace copy-tidier. (She definitely would have told me to shorten that last sentence.)

I'd also like to thank Dorian Lynskey and Nick de Semlyen for their valuable advice and friendship; my *Senet* magazine co-founder James Hunter for putting up with all my book-related ramblings; and all the commissioning editors I was unable to help out while working on this book. Namely: James Dyer, Alex Godfrey, Chris Hewitt, John Nugent and Beth Webb of *Empire* magazine; Charles Gant and Matt Mueller of *Screen International*; Phil de Semlyen of *Time Out* London; and Matt McAllister of *Dungeons & Dragons Adventurer*.